Those Who Act Ruin It

SUNY series in Chinese Philosophy and Culture

Roger T. Ames, editor

Those Who Act Ruin It
A Daoist Account of Moral Attunement

Jacob Bender

Published by State University of New York Press, Albany

© 2024 State University of New York

All rights reserved

Printed in the United States of America

No part of this book may be used or reproduced in any manner whatsoever without written permission. No part of this book may be stored in a retrieval system or transmitted in any form or by any means including electronic, electrostatic, magnetic tape, mechanical, photocopying, recording, or otherwise without the prior permission in writing of the publisher.

Links to third-party websites are provided as a convenience and for informational purposes only. They do not constitute an endorsement or an approval of any of the products, services, or opinions of the organization, companies, or individuals. SUNY Press bears no responsibility for the accuracy, legality, or content of a URL, the external website, or for that of subsequent websites.

For information, contact State University of New York Press, Albany, NY
www.sunypress.edu

Library of Congress Cataloging-in-Publication Data

Name: Bender, Jacob, 1989– author.
Title: Those who act ruin it : a Daoist account of moral attunement / Jacob Bender.
Description: Albany : State University of New York Press, [2024] | Series: SUNY series in Chinese philosophy and culture | Includes bibliographical references.
Identifiers: LCCN 2023055107 | ISBN 9781438498584 (hardcover : alk. paper) | ISBN 9781438498591 (ebook) | ISBN 9781438498577 (pbk. : alk. paper)
Subjects: LCSH: Taoist ethics. | Taoism.
Classification: LCC BJ1290.8 .B46 2024 | DDC 170—dc23/eng/20240331
LC record available at https://lccn.loc.gov/2023055107

*To my father, David Bender,
and to the memory of my mother, Denise Bender*

Contents

Acknowledgments		ix
Introduction	Lao-Zhuang Daoism	1
Chapter One	An Embodied Account of Experience and Meaning in Daoist Philosophy	21
Chapter Two	"Without Action"	47
Chapter Three	On Being "Without Desire" in Lao-Zhuang Daoism	79
Chapter Four	The "Nonnaturalistic Fallacy" in Lao-Zhuang Daoism	105
Chapter Five	Alienation and Attunement in the *Zhuangzi*	141
Chapter Six	The Daoist Critique of Moral Bigotry	157
Conclusion	A Daoist Alternative to the "Sages"	175
Notes		183
Works Cited		207
Index		215

Acknowledgments

There are many people that must be given gratitude for the existence of this book. Some of these people are teachers and educators that I met earlier in my life at a time when I did not even believe that going to college was a practical life choice. If not for the people that put the thought into my mind that I might make a good teacher one day, I would have never considered going to college.

As an undergraduate, the many teachers that introduced me to Buddhism, Chinese philosophy, and the humanities have all helped to shape my foundations as a scholar. In particular, a special thanks goes to both Dr. Christopher Kirby and Dr. Kevin Decker (Eastern Washington University). Their classes helped lay the foundation for my graduate studies.

From the University of Hawaii at Manoa, I would especially like to thank Dr. Masato Ishida and Dr. Roger Ames for having supported my continuing work in academia and for the time I spent as a student working under both of them. Another special thanks must be given to Dr. Ames for taking me on as a postdoctorate fellow at Peking University (北京大学). I was able to complete all of the new additions to this book as well as start on the revisions for my next book project because of this opportunity.

From Nanyang Technological University, I must thank my dissertation committee, consisting of my supervisor, Dr. Li Chenyang; co-supervisor, Dr. Randy LaPolla; Dr. Winnie Sung; and Dr. Brook Ziporyn. I am especially grateful to Dr. Li for allowing me to pursue the research project of my choice. I am also grateful that I was able to study with Dr. Ziporyn while he was a visiting professor in Singapore for three years. His classes were instrumental to my growth as a scholar and to my understanding of Mahayana Buddhism. Dr. LaPolla and I spent many hours practicing classical Chinese together, and I am incredibly grateful for both his guidance in learning Chinese and for his insights into pragmatism and linguistics.

Finally, and most importantly, I must thank my family; both the family I was born into and the family I married into. My mother-in-law, Xueping Zuo, has been like a second mother to me. With all the pressures that come with life, she has continuously been there in support of my work in becoming an academic. My wife, Shuchen Xiang, is an exemplary scholar who has the courage to say exactly what needs to be said and has not sacrificed her scholarly integrity in spite of (Western, "white") academic chauvinism. Without her companionship and love, the challenges of academia would not have been as easy to traverse and perhaps not even worth tolerating. I look forward to many more years of growing with her as fellow scholars and comrades against the hegemonic ethnocentrism of Western academia.

Ultimately, I would not have been the person I am, with the predispositions that I have, without the care and support of my parents—David and Denise Bender. Both of my parents were open-minded, loving (former) hippies, and it is their openness that was most instrumental in shaping my views as a scholar. Although my father is still alive to see the person that I have become, my mother left the world far too soon to witness that I was finally able to achieve what I had set out to do many years ago. Although I am thankful to both my parents for what they have done for me, this book is especially dedicated to the memory of my mother.

An earlier version of sections of chapter 3 was originally published in the journal *Asian Philosophy* in an article called "On Being without Desire in Lao-Zhuang Daoism." An earlier version of parts of chapter 4 was originally published in the journal *Philosophy East and West* as "The 'Non-Naturalistic Fallacy' in Lao-Zhuang Daoism." Finally, an earlier draft of chapter 5 was originally published with the journal *Sophia: International Journal of Philosophy and Traditions* as "Alienation and Attunement in the *Zhuangzi*." I am thankful to each of the journals for giving me permission to republish the content of those papers as chapters of this book.

Introduction

Lao-Zhuang Daoism: An Introduction

This book presents an iconoclastic account of morality and moral discourse from the perspective of Daoist philosophy. Such a project needs to be iconoclastic because the Daoist texts likewise present an incredibly novel philosophical mode of thinking that is unique in how it critiques the political and philosophical discourses of its time. The texts are highly poetic and at times ambiguous with their meaning. Part of that ambiguity, as this book argues, has to do with the iconoclastic character of Daoist philosophy. For the typical moral philosopher, there are claims throughout the Daoist texts that will seem either dubious or inconsistent with other lessons presented. What the Daoist philosopher invites the reader to do more than anything else is to question the efficacy and validity of the moral discourses of their own cultures. What at first might sound like either mere moral skepticism or moral relativism is in fact a far more nuanced critique of how the moral discourses of their contemporaries (and of moral discourse generally) are guilty of the very same practices that these discourses condemn. The moral theorist is often merely helping to normalize and legitimize coercive and oppressive social practices. The Daoist alternative to the morality espoused by their counterparts does not lead to moral chaos. Instead, in radically breaking away from the misguided epistemology of their counterparts, the Daoist framework helps to provide solutions to the same social ills that the Confucians, Mohists, and other philosophers cannot address.

This monograph defends the Daoist understanding of social and political reality. From their perspective, there are no such things as "moral facts," morality does not need to appeal to "principles," and the world would be better off without the "question-begging" metaphysical framework of the moral philosopher. What the Daoist proposes is that we cultivate certain dispositions or sensitivities to act and react to situations. In becoming free of the epistemological framework that the Daoist critiques, people can be said to maintain a naturalness that enables them to spontaneously respond to situations in a noncoercive manner. They thereby achieve a greater level of freedom; a freedom that is nonetheless grounded and situated in the precarious natural world of conditioned and conditioning interrelationships. Such cultivated freedom takes them beyond the coercive ideals of the "sages" and "criminals" that the Daoist describes in their works. It is a position that is *beyond* the traditional distinction between objectivism and relativism that philosophers still insist on framing their ideas within. Properly understanding the Daoist texts will involve seeing how the moral philosopher and the "moral attitude" are, in fact, contributing to the very same coercive behaviors they have reason to critique. The Daoist's naturalism promises to bring about a more harmonious and desirable world than the philosopher who insists on clinging to nonnaturalistic metaphysical assumptions.

Philosophical Daoism is one of the three main philosophical and religious traditions in China along with Confucianism and Buddhism and is one of the main schools of philosophy that emerged in what was called the "Hundred Schools of Thought" (*zhuzi baijia*, 諸子百家) during both the Spring and Autumn and Warring States periods (6th century BC to 221 BC). There is a wealth of scholarship written on Daoism in both the West and China, and there are diverse interpretations of the tradition. With interpretations ranging from mysticism, skepticism, and relativism (and many more), anyone familiar with the scholarship on Daoist philosophy will be familiar with the difficulties that come with studying these texts. Although there are other philosophical and religious treatises that are rightfully labeled "Daoist," this book focuses on the *Daodejing*, the *Zhuangzi*, and the traditional commentaries on each of these texts. There are scholars who might take issue with grouping these two texts together as their respective content diverges from each other at times. With any reading of the *Daodejing* and the *Zhuangzi* that tries to make sense of how these texts present a single philosophical worldview, there will always be passages and chapters of these that are harder to present as consistent with the rest.[1] This book follows the traditional grouping in considering the *Daodejing* and the *Zhuangzi* to represent a particular strain of thinking that has been called "Lao-Zhuang Daoism."

In exploring the Daoist texts, this book also highlights the important commonalities between them.

Throughout both the *Daodejing* and the *Zhuangzi*, there are claims that sound like moral relativism and others that sound like "amorality" or the refusal to even use a moral vocabulary when discussing the human condition. There are also numerous passages that discuss how greed and having too many desires is antithetical to Dao or "the way." Recognizing these features of nature and human social life then leads to the capacity to care for and nurture things like a mother or in a way similar to how rainwater tends to nourish life equally and impartially. In other words, the moral relativity and amorality are viewed, by the Daoist, as compatible with frugality, altruism, and an impartial yet motherly care towards all things. These themes, among many others, are prevalent throughout both of these texts. Although it might seem like amorality, moral relativism, the absence of desires and motherly care should be considered distinct and even conflicting positions, there is a logic underlying these ideas that helps to explain their relationship. Ultimately, it is the Lao-Zhuang Daoist's understanding of nature, persons, and their relationship that unite these different positions. What is required is that scholars exhaustively understand the Daoist account of how all things of nature are, at the most fundamental level, interdependent, overlapping, and "indeterminate" or *wu* (無). For the remainder of this book, I refer to this position simply as "Daoism." Although there are other interpretations of both the *Daodejing* and the *Zhuangzi* (namely, the religious form of Daoism), the naturalistic account of these texts is the one that most adequately accommodates and explains each of these diverging aspects of the Daoist view on morality: its amorality, its recognition of the relativity of all perspectives, greed as being the root source of social ills, and the motherly care of the sage. We can make sense of the Daoist position in light of their naturalistic metaphysics.

The *Daodejing*: An Introduction to Its Complexity

Before moving forward, it will be useful to see exactly what aspects of Daoist philosophy can potentially be viewed as contradictory philosophical positions. What this book aims to do is show how they are all in fact one and the same philosophical position when viewed in light of an embodied account of experience and a processual metaphysics. For those unfamiliar with the *Daodejing*, readers might notice these (*seemingly*) diverging themes in the first ten passages. As *Daodejing* passage 2 suggests, the value judgments of the "good" and the "beautiful" are both relative and dependent on their opposites; the "bad" and the "ugly." "When all under heaven knows the 'beautiful' as being beautiful, thus there is already foulness. When all know the 'good' as being good, thus there is already the 'not good.' Thus, the 'determinate' (*you*, 有) and the 'indeterminate' (*wu*, 無) mutually generate each other [*xiang sheng*, 相生]."[2] In this passage, the Daoist suggests that when society can name and determine the "beautiful" and the "good," such a determination was necessarily done through the *exclusion* of that which is "undetermined." The process of determining what is of value, especially after everyone knows this particular way of determining value, can end up being highly coercive. If "all under heaven" knows to value certain features of nature, then they have already become habituated with negative attitudes towards that which is "not good." These attitudes have become ossified and reinforced by cultural institutions. What the Daoist is critical of here is a bivalent, either/or account of values. Because value is always a product of context and perspective, no aspect of experience should be understood as being of value or disvalue in a final or complete sense. That which is individuated out of a context, *you*, is inseparable from its opposite, *wu*. The point is not to simply relativize the distinction between that which is "good" and that which is "not good." The very attitude that clings to values as if they were "fixed" is itself highly problematic. When framed through such a strict dualism, conduct at the extremes reverts and reverses into the opposite extreme. What is implied here (and what will be clarified further in this book), is that conduct that was initially deemed to be of value tends to revert and function like that which was deemed to be "not good" when we become "fixed" on said values. For the Daoist, each distinction is made within the context of the indeterminate (*wu*). Consciousness does not experience a world that is already made of distinct and definite things. All forms of possible experience are contextualized by the indeterminate and immediate (unmediated) field of experience. The experience of any *you* or "being" is always a function of the background, *wu*. The determined (*you*) is *internally related to* and *constituted by* the indeterminate (*wu*). Chapter 4 of this book will cover both the metaphysics and epistemology underlying this naturalistic account of experience more.

What is perhaps most worrying for some philosophers is the idea that the "good" and the "not-good" mutually generate each other (*xiang sheng*, 相生). Similar claims can be found in *Daodejing* passage 5. "Heaven and Earth are not humane. They regard the ten thousand things as straw dogs. The sage is not humane (*ren*, 仁). He regards all the people as straw dogs. The space between heaven and earth—Does it not resemble a bellows? Empty, but not consumed, the more it is moved, the more comes out. Hearing a lot, investigating much—this is not as good as holding on to the center."[3] The picture of the universe that the Daoist is presenting does not sound like one hospitable to moral concerns. In light of Confucian philosophy, the passage suggests that the natural world or "heaven" (*tian*, 天) does not reward or punish behavior. Nature is impartial towards the affairs and activities of humans and is not "benevolent" (the central Confucian virtue). Following the claim that the cosmos does not necessarily involve a "moral order," the passage continues with a description of the natural world likened to an "empty bellows." The natural world as empty can continuously fill up and animate things. Although "heaven and earth are not humane," the passage ends with a prescription: safeguarding or "holding on to the center" (*zhong*, 中). The Daoist provides a description of nature and a prescription ("holding to the center") that, one can assume, is derived from their understanding of nature. As Hans-Georg Moeller describes it, from the "Daoist perspective, however, to 'hold to the center' is more effective. The sage has to stay calm at the center of society just as the hub stays unmoved at the center of the wheel."[4] Philosophers might view this as inconsistent; a natural world devoid of a "moral order" and yet the Daoist is still prescribing and evaluating different forms of human conduct.

It gets even stranger. *Daodejing* passage 7 suggests that the Daoist sage is altruistic. "Heaven is long lasting and earth is enduring. That which is why heaven and earth are capable of longevity and also enduring, it is by means of their not living for themselves, thus they are capable of long life. Therefore, the Sage puts their own body behind them [i.e., out of sight] yet their body is first; puts their own body outside them [i.e., out of mind] yet the body is sustained. Is it not by means of their being without 'self-interest' (無私)? Thus, they are capable of completing their 'self-interest' " (私).[5] Earlier, the *Daodejing* claimed that "Heaven and earth are not humane." Now, it suggests that the sage is "enduring and long-lasting" because they "do not live for themselves." The people that do not live for themselves, that is, "puts their own body behind them [i.e., out of sight] yet their body is first" end up as the people that can endure. The person that puts "their own body outside them [i.e., out of mind]" is the one that can "sustain their own body." As Wang Bi's comments describe it, "To be utterly free of self-interest [*wusi*] means to make no conscious effort for one's own sake. Such a person will always find himself in front and his person preserved."[6] The Daoist sounds like they are describing a kind of altruism, yet how can we arrive at a prescription such as altruism without anything like a "moral order"?

Related to this are claims in the *Daodejing* that condemn extravagant wealth and greed. As *Daodejing* 9 claims, "To pile it up and to fill it is not as good as ending it. By forging and sharpening it you cannot keep it for long. A room full of gold and jade—no one can guard it. To be esteemed, wealthy, and proud, is to draw misfortune to oneself. To withdraw oneself when the work proceeds—this is the Dao of Heaven."[7] If all things, good and bad, are relative and simultaneously generated, and if "heaven and earth are not humane," why does the *Daodejing* describe the "way of heaven" (天之道) as involving the capacity to know moderation? Like *Daodejing* passage 5, the Daoist sage is described as not having overextended. Moving far away from the "center" is one way that nonvirtuous behavior is understood. Other examples of Daoist virtue that also appeal to a "center" metaphor include the capacity to sit in the center hub of the "hinge of Dao" (*Daoshu*, 道樞) and to "reflect all things in an unadulterated way, like a mirror" (*Zhuangzi*, Chapter 7).

For some readers, it will not be obvious how the Daoist could be consistent when making these different claims. What *Daodejing* 9 suggests, as is also the case in *Daodejing* 7, is that to be "esteemed, wealthy, and proud" is antithetical to being a Daoist sage. Thus, like *Daodejing* 5 suggests, we can consider these to be antithetical to dwelling in the "empty center." In light of these passages, what the Daoist is describing is how different manifestations of egoism, although subtle in their moralist forms, become self-undermining and are susceptible to reverting to their opposite extreme. Far from being inconsistent positions, the Daoist's process metaphysics helps to elucidate how these distinct features of Daoist philosophy form a coherent position.

Although philosophers informed by Western metaphysical assumptions might not believe these different ideas are consistent with each other, there is a rather simple solution that unites these many different positions. The Daoist account of nature and experience is critical of what can be called a "substance ontology." Such a metaphysics assumes that each "thing" has an underlying essential or substantial core. A substance account of the individuation of things assumes that each particular thing is ultimately independent. A substance, like an essence, does not change regardless of the particular relationships that the "thing" possesses, and each "thing," as a substance, takes precedence to their relationships. As Franklin Perkins' essay, "What Is a Thing (wu 物)?," concludes, because the Daoist had a radically different understanding of how things are individuated, "what is perhaps most striking, though, is how individuation becomes an issue not just for metaphysics and epistemology but also for self-cultivation, for ethics in the broad sense. It is not just that the basic metaphysical assumptions in early China differed from those of most Europeans. This difference shifted the very boundary between metaphysics and ethics."[8] The usual divisions that Western philosophy draws between ethics, aesthetics, and epistemology also need to be re-evaluated in light of Daoist metaphysics. The Daoist account of the ethical life (practice and cultivation) is indebted to a processual understanding of nature that collapses the rigid distinction between metaphysics, epistemology, and axiology. As this book illustrates, the *seemingly* divergent ethical positions of the *Daodejing* and the *Zhuangzi* are in fact the same if we can see them as indebted to a critique of a substance individuation of things or what is called a "substance ontology."

Daoism as beyond Objectivism and Relativism

There is a tendency in contemporary moral philosophy to frame the problems of morality and human flourishing within a particular metaphysical framework. Making sense of the Daoist's account of morality will require we understand how Daoism diverges from Western notions of individualism and a substance ontology. As this book aims to clarify, the Daoist understanding of the self is a relational self. All things of nature are interdependent and conditioned by their world. With the Daoist's naturalism, there is no sui generis, "in-itself," capacity or power that people can tap into that allows them to transcend their conditioned and embodied existence. Philosophers operating within the usual metaphysical framework, after hearing such claims, generally find them to be problematic and even morally suspect. For the philosopher operating in such a question-begging framework, a relational self and an account of nature as involving "internal relationships" (that is, that the relationships between different aspects of nature are *internal* to each other and things *constitute* each other to various degrees[9]) spells nothing but "anything-goes relativism" and "moral subjectivism." With "anything-goes relativism," no "meta" value or unconditioned reality exists that persons can appeal to when deliberating about the nature or accuracy of the values that are held by different persons or communities. In "moral subjectivism," values are the mere choices of each individual, and any set of values is just as good as any other. Both of these positions imply that there is no real force or "reason" to act in ways that are usually considered moral or contrary to arbitrary force, selfish desire, or what we would generally call "unethical" behavior. The framework for both models assumes that persons are most fundamentally independent (i.e., they are "substances"). They are bodies filled with desires and perhaps other morally suspect features of a thing called "human nature." If there are not things like "moral facts," a transcendent god, or other unconditional realities that human beings can appeal to, these independent subjects are not bound to each other politically or morally. Humans have no obligations towards each other; therefore, all the worse crimes that humans have committed are not condemnable. This model presents us with an "either/or" situation. Either such realities exist, or "anything goes." The problem is that both sides of the "either/or" are grounded in question-begging assumptions that no critical human being should take seriously in the modern world. That this discipline of philosophy, a discipline that prides itself on being the most rigorous and "scientific" of the humanities, has continued to frame their problems along these lines, testifies to an intellectual laziness that serves to defend a backward status quo (or an example of *disciplinary decadence*).[10] With a relational understanding of the self, where selves are *internally related* to their world, where selves are both *constituted by* and *constituting* their environments, the independent self of the "anything goes" relativist and the "moral subjectivist" is literally made into an unreality. There is no such thing as "anything-goes relativism" because the kinds of *beings* that such a relativism relies on do not exist. Within a processual framework, like the one we find in Chinese philosophy, most forms of Buddhism, and in some Western philosophy (such as the American pragmatists), both sides of the "either/or" are shown to be illusory. Philosophers operating in the traditional objectivism versus relativism framework are operating in an inaccurate account of social and political reality.

The above situation in modern moral philosophy highlights another problem that scholars encounter when doing work on Daoist philosophy, another problem this book endeavors to address. This book illuminates how the Daoist position involves a transition *beyond objectivism and relativism*. Within a processual framework, neither of these positions (as they are traditionally understood) presents philosophers with an accurate framework for understanding their world. Comparative philosophers and American pragmatists have previously made similar arguments. For example, Ma Lin and Jaap Van der Braak have provided an account of the *Zhuangzi* that they believe helps us to get beyond the traditional framework outlined above. As they argue in *Beyond the Troubled Waters of Shi/Fei*, they critique the idea that there must be one single "ideal language" that all other languages can be translated into. "While arguing for these preconditions and constraints, we emphatically deny the need for the ideal language assumption, the requirement of a common language, or the presupposition of a large number of universals shared by all humanity. Dropping these assumptions allows us to dissolve the 'either universalism or relativism' issue, and to replace it by the family-resemblance-principle and the construction of quasi-universals."[11] In their study, they draw on philosophers like Ludwig Wittgenstein and Hilary Putnam to outline their own solution to this dilemma. Ma and Van der Braak's position beyond objectivism and relativism involves embodying certain dispositions or epistemological attitudes they refer to as "stances."[12] In *Natural Moralities*, David Wong likewise suggests that we need to reject the traditional, "either/or dualism" between moral objectivism and radical moral subjectivism. Wong states that "the entirely justifiable desire to refute radical subjectivism should not move us toward the traditional view [i.e., "objectivism"]. What we need are plausible alternatives to these equally untenable views."[13] What Wong suggests, an insight that is shared by the Daoists of the *Daodejing* and the *Zhuangzi*, is that the framework itself and the arguments shaped by such a framework might be undermining the aims and goals of the moral theorists. After suggesting that we do not need to ground "rights" with the traditional notion of *autonomy*, Wong states:

> It is presumptuous to assume that others can make moral progress only if they adopt Western liberal values. It also is mistaken from a strategic viewpoint if one is truly interested in promoting some of the same protections and opportunities for individuals that are required by those same Western values. A plurality of adequate moralities prohibits cruelty and self-interested domination. On the other side, many institutionalized rights-centered moralities rightly receive criticism for their lack

of community, but one need not be a Confucian to recognize the force of such criticism.[14]

As this project outlines, the Daoist provides reasons for prohibiting cruelty and self-interested domination. They just provide a further, more critical account of the cruelty that can be justified and normalized through a rarefied moral discourse, the "moral attitude," and nonnaturalistic metaphysical assumptions. Richard Bernstein, in *Beyond Objectivism and Relativism*, and Mark Johnson, in *Morality for Humans*, have also presented theoretical alternatives to the traditional framework of moral philosophers.[15] Building on how these philosophers have analyzed this key issue, there is another, more important way of stating their case. If a philosopher insists that they are providing a philosophical framework that can get us *beyond* objectivism and relativism, then they are also claiming that the framework can outline particular constraints on values, forms of life, and human conduct that are not desirable, valuable and/or based on ignorance. Within the framework beyond objectivism and relativism, we can outline how and why certain forms of life are either ignorant or of no real value or desirability. As this book aims to show, a processual framework both entails a radically different understanding of values and provides a new way of thinking about the constraints on values.

From the Daoist perspective, there is a difference between two distinct forms of life that, on the one hand, involve achieving and understanding value and the nature of value and, on the other hand, forms of life that we can call ignorant or of disvalue and are inherently undesirable. The forms of life that form greater coherence with the world are forms of life that can be said to involve a degree of *attunement* to situations.[16] As this book outlines, we should see attunement as a cultivated sensitivity towards the novelty and particularity of nature and change. It is an attunement to the concrete relationships that constitute human experience. The critical features of Daoism then come to the foreground when we try to understand why the Daoist is critical of the forms of experience that involve a lack of attunement. Whether it be the accumulation of "desires" (*yu*, 欲) or "knowledge" (*zhi*, 知), people maintain a form of ignorance when they cannot perceive nature as fundamentally indeterminate. This book refers to these forms of life as involving *alienation*. Due to how human society enculturates its population with problematic "desires" or "knowledge," the population learns to view the world through an epistemological framework that inhibits them from being attuned to their world where attunement would otherwise have been their naturally endowed spontaneity. The Daoists' critique of their philosophical and cultural contemporaries can be understood best as a critique of how particular cultural beliefs (like the reification of values and human relationships) inhibit the community from developing the ability to understand the reasons behind social ills. This further inhibits them from achieving and sustaining forms of life that are actually valuable and desirable. In other words, a substance metaphysics and the reification of "things" and "values" contributes to the formation of an epistemological framework that occludes aspects of experience important for understanding our world. The amorality of the Daoist can then be better understood as a critique of how the two extreme moral positions (moral objectivism and moral subjectivism) end up behaving like each other (as I clarify in chapters 5 and 6). Both moral philosophers and those they criticize are, from the Daoist perspective, equally alienated from nature and their fellow human beings. The Daoist critique of the "moral attitude" is indebted to their understanding of nature as being constituted by overlapping, interdependent processes. From a processual framework, we can outline why moral objectivism and morality indebted to nonnaturalistic metaphysics is as equally problematic as the egoist's attitude. To borrow the terminology from the *Zhuangzi*, chapter 8, both the sages (i.e., moral fundamentalist) and the thieves (i.e., moral subjectivist) are operating within a problematic epistemological framework. Their framework only helps to perpetuate the same coercive social and political practices. Both extreme positions suffer from alienation from nature and their fellow human beings because they both reduce complex systems of relationships to things like substances.

"Those Who Act Ruin It":
The Daoist Alternative to Moral Fundamentalism

The Daoist sage is frequently described in unconventional ways throughout the Daoist texts. These descriptions of the Daoist sage present philosophers with a radically different account of ethics and moral philosophy; so much so that, from the Daoist perspective, the typical practices of the moral philosopher should be viewed with suspicion. As this book further clarifies, the Daoist is highly critical of the idea that rule following or being purposive in one's conduct is a good idea. Karyn Lai's analysis of Daoism has previously argued this point as well. She states that the

"[Daoist] ethic is not presented in terms of norms, rules, or principles. It is an other-regarding attitude and in that sense we may say that it is *more fundamental* than these other manifestations of ethical commitment" (my italics).[17] The Daoist sage is frequently described as possessing the capacity to perceive the world with greater sensitivity and their capacity to do so is because they are cultivating habits that are *more fundamental* to human perception than those associated with thinking and the formation of concepts. Lai elaborates on this point elsewhere: "The application of predefined absolute norms, indiscriminately and without consideration for the numerous morally significant particulars in each situation is rejected in Daoist thought. [. . .] The methodology suggested here recommends a fundamental way of seeing things and understanding situations and individuals that is not primarily goal-, rule- or outcome-driven. It is an ethically sensitive response that focuses on the fragility and spontaneity of interdependent individuals."[18]

The fragility that Lai references is that of the Daoist's responsiveness to situations that the term *rouruo* (柔弱) denotes in the *Daodejing*. The Daoist, as embodying a kind of "fragility," presents us with an alternative to the rule- and goal-oriented moral philosophers and the core assumptions of their metaphysical framework. Building on Lai's arguments, this book argues that conduct that is primarily goal, rule, or outcome driven is morally and epistemologically suspect. Such ways of being predisposed to situations are contrary to the Daoist sage's ability to perceive the world with greater sensitivity and receptiveness. It is not just that goal- and rule-oriented conduct is problematic. What is really being critiqued is conduct where the habits of thinking and concept formation within experience function as obstructions to perception. This leads to the inability to respond to and understand situations.

This is not at all to suggest that rationality and "reason" are intrinsically bad, leading then to a further argument that other, alternative human capacities are *solely* what we need for human flourishing. This book outlines, from the Daoist perspective, how certain instrumentalities (i.e., "language" and "concepts") *can* end up inhibiting and obstructing attention. That is *not* a claim that we should no longer think, use concepts or language. Indeed, if a scholar wanted to make that argument, they would just call Daoism a kind of "mysticism" or "Gnosticism" (which this book's thesis explicitly rejects). As instrumentalities, concepts can potentially be used poorly. When we lack the proper cultivation of *other* human potentials, being led merely by "reason" becomes highly coercive and alienating.

The human capacities to reason, perceive, and feel emotion all form a continuum where none can be said to inherently stand opposed to the others. It is only because of our *miseducation* and lack of cultivation that the different human capacities no longer function together in a harmonious way. In this sense, "reason" is suspect when it is no longer grounded in the somatic, perceptual, and emotional aspects of experience. When we look at the cultivation practices of Daoism, this is precisely the issue Daoists are trying to address; how and why is perception of situations obstructed and *what* is obstructing it? When persons interpret their world through problematic metaphysical assumptions, we can consider them to be operating within an epistemological framework that inhibits their sensitivity to situations. This is the logic underlying who and what the Daoist critiques. From the Daoist perspective, certain cultural and political institutions help to reproduce the same ignorant dispositions in people. As chapter 5 of this monograph further elaborates, we can consider this ignorance to be a form of *perceptual alienation* as it involves an inability to perceive that nature forms a continuous whole. Alienation involves an inability to recognize our interdependence and continuity with nature and the wider human community.

From the Daoist perspective, their philosophical counterparts are operating within a misguided epistemological framework. They are thus ignorantly perpetuating the same patterns of behavior they had hoped to ameliorate. Another way of putting this, as the *Daodejing* states perfectly, is that "those who act ruin it" (*wei zhe bai zhi*, 為者敗之). If scholars were tasked with presenting one single line of text that encapsulated the Daoist account of moral life and their critique of their philosophical contemporaries, this should be it. The Daoist ideal of *wuwei* or of being "without action" is not the literal absence of *all* action by the Daoist sage. In the Daoist texts, *wei* (為), or being "with purposive conduct," is used to specifically denote *coercive* forms of conduct. Conduct becomes coercive because persons embody dispositions that are indebted to an epistemological framework that reduces complex systems of interdependence to substances or independent things. Such a perspective fails to be sensitive to experience in all of its other qualities. Alternatively, we could say that "those who act" (為者) or those persons who act with "conduct" (為) are "imposing" in their conduct because they possess self-referential "standards" or "principles" that function like substances. For example, they may believe themselves to be like an entity that has the privilege of exerting a one-way causal influence on the natural world (i.e., a metaphysical way of describing egoism). Consciousness then can be understood as projecting a metaphysical framework onto experience that inhibits the perception of situations. Contrary to the Daoist sage, who can respond to situations with insight and understanding, the moralists of society are in fact behaving in ways that are contrary to their own intentions and desires. The moralist as "imposing" is in reality only justifying and normalizing oppression. Their interpretation of situations is self-undermining and thus leads to hypocrisy. *Their action ruins it*. Daoist exemplars, in being "nonpurposive" in their conduct, thus do not "ruin things."

Daoism as a Solution to Moral Fundamentalism

From the Daoist perspective, human culture can develop such that ideals and beliefs that were once held for pragmatic and naturalistic reasons become disjoined and disconnected from the concrete lives and needs of human beings. As chapter 4 aims to illustrate, values emerge from the immediate ways human beings make sense of their world and fulfill their basic needs. The Daoist exemplar is perceptually sensitive to the immediate way valuing occurs; that is, values are not an "order" external to nature and change but are constantly emerging from our embodied interaction with the natural world. Any moral ideology that departs from its naturalistic roots simply helps to perpetuate the same social ills such a discourse was meant to remedy. In other words, the belief that there is a kind of judgment that is sui generis "moral" or the belief that there exist "moral facts" that are independent of the human existence are likewise beliefs that are indebted to an ignorant and misguided epistemological framework (*those who* "act" *ruin it*). This question-begging epistemology, espoused by many modern philosophers, only obfuscates the ability to live morally and alleviate the ills of human life. Another way of expressing this is that the possession of a fixed or thick "final vocabulary" of moral terms obstructs one's ability to understand social ills. It is for this reason that the practices prescribed in the Daoist texts involve the cultivation of habits such that we no longer cling to an understanding of things as independent or what the Daoist ironically names as "knowledge" (*zhi*, 知). "Knowledge" obstructs the ability to perceive situations because such habits involve the failure to perceive the larger context of experience (i.e., the context that "knowledge" is related to and situated in). Becoming a perceptually sensitive and responsive human being requires that we maintain a wider "horizon of relevance" where no single "final vocabulary" can dominate human conduct. The Daoist solution to social problems is that we need a proper understanding of the nature of things and that involves adjusting how we perceive and understand the world. The solution is not merely "moral" but is, instead, a blending of morality, metaphysics, and epistemology.

Strictly speaking, Daoism espouses a form of amorality or the rejection that there exist sui generis moral judgments or "moral facts" about the world. Some philosophers believe that there are propositional statements or *truths* about morality that exist independent of the human mind. A (modern) Daoist would deem such ideas to be highly intellectually and scientifically dubious. From the Daoist understanding, such reified, metaphysical beliefs are inherently self-undermining and corrupting. Such things do not exist, and they are promoting the opposite of their intended effects (that is, they are legitimizing oppression). Following Mark Johnson's *Morality for Humans*, we can consider most nonnaturalistic accounts of values to be espousing "moral fundamentalism," that is, "the positing of absolute moral values, principles, or facts—[and it] is cognitively indefensible, because it is dramatically out of touch with contemporary mind science."[19] Not only is the philosopher that preaches that there are sui generis "moral facts" doing work that is highly intellectually and scientifically suspect, from the Daoist perspective, we never needed these question-begging beliefs to begin with. The Daoist understood that the source of social ills is the tendency of human consciousness to reify conceptual distinctions in experience to the point where such abstractions (which where only ever *instrumentalities* used to guide conduct and the process of growth) become ossified and are no longer grounded in the context of empirical experience.

The Daoist understanding of both nature and human perception shares much with different schools of Western philosophy. In light of philosophers like John Dewey and the processual metaphysics I outline in this book, Daoist philosophy can be understood as presenting a unique form of "ethical naturalism." As opposed to nonnaturalistic theories, "Naturalistic theories [in ethics], in contrast, see moral values and standards as arising out of our experience in the natural world, which involves biological, interpersonal (social), and cultural dimensions. There is no 'pure' a priori grounding for moral norms, so they have to emerge from our fundamental needs for survival, individual and group harmony, personal and communal flourishing, and consummation of human meaning and purpose."[20] The Daoist account of moral life, although naturalistic, is unique because it presents a critical account of the *source* of social ills. Because of particular habits of reflection and abstraction (that is, the reification of the process that individuates "things" in experience), humans ignore the qualitative particularity of nature. For the Daoist, nature is described using a multitude of terms and phrases. In the *Daodejing*, events and "things" are described as both "self-so" (*ziran*, 自然) and as being like an "uncarved block of wood" (*pu*, 樸), which is meant to signify their indeterminate, interdependent, and fluctuating character. As Robin Wang states, *ziran* "can be translated [as] 'spontaneity' or 'naturalness.' It refers to what is so of itself, without any external force or coercion."[21] In the *Zhuangzi*, it is that which is "genuine" (*zhen*, 真) or the "true person" (*zhenren*, 真人) that best expresses the natural world in its simplicity and the person that is capable of perceiving it as such. Because humans possess ossified habits of conceptualization (*zhi*,) and ungrounded, nonnaturalistic desires (*yu*, 欲), we are unable to recognize the novelty of things (*ziran*) and spontaneously respond to situations with greater levels of sensitivity and attunement (*wuwei*, 無為). When persons operate within such a problematic epistemological framework, this predisposes them such that they create extraneous suffering in the world and do not understand the nature or source of that suffering. As Wang continues, "*Ziran* is not only an element of the world but also the most potent mode of action for human beings. [. . .] This is the highest stage of human action, where there are no external forces or power compelling things to happen. [. . .] *Ziran* lets things be, in their own natural or raw state, just as heaven and earth have their own state (that is, *ziran*)."[22] This capacity to enable things to exist through noncoercion is, first and foremost, epistemological as it involves the absence of particular metaphysical beliefs that obstruct perception. To address these problems of perception, the Daoist prescribes the cultivation of habits that are more fundamental to perception. Such cultivation enables people to become more sensitive to situations because they no longer ignore the qualitative dimensions of experience underlying cognitive habits. Although "knowledge" (*zhi*) inhibits how experience of the world is disclosed, dealing with this requires us to cultivate habits such that we *ground* abstract "knowledge" and properly recognize it as a provisional and secondary aspect of experience. By no means does this book argue that persons should completely abandon all conceptualization and language. The goal of Daoist cultivation practices is to ground cognitive habits in noncognitive and embodied experience. When this happens then language, "names," and "knowledge" no longer play an obfuscating role in shaping how persons perceive situations.

The Daoist account of nature and of social and political relationships is rather different than what one typically finds in Western philosophy. They not only depart from the metaphysical assumptions of many Western philosophers, but they can also be understood as critiquing these assumptions as highly problematic. What the Daoist offers is a *metaethical* critique of the idea that the usual moral philosopher is providing us with an accurate interpretive framework. From the Daoist perspective, the "moral" philosopher is often helping to create and legitimize more suffering than they had promised to alleviate. The Daoist alternative to "moral fundamentalism" is that we must cultivate the capacity to properly perceive and understand nature. The cultivation of certain dispositions, as described by the Daoist, are the dispositions best capable of dealing with life in all of its change and indeterminacy. These dispositions are such that "knowledge" and the "names" (*ming*) of things no longer obstruct attention to situations. "Ethics," when informed by a substance metaphysics, is an endeavor that relies on an inaccurate account of reality, the nature of human experience, and the motivations of human conduct. As Jean Grondin claims, "all ethics presupposes metaphysics or ontology—that is, some understanding of who we are."[23] Part of the problem is that modern philosophy suffers from an ethnocentrism and provincialism that enables an ignorance of its metaphysical assumptions to exist unchallenged. Western philosophy has claimed universality for a long time while simultaneously maintaining an ignorance of other cultures and worldviews. Comparative philosophers are not helping themselves by insisting on the same narrow subdivisions in their field of study that Anglophone philosophers have set up.[24] Western ethicists make metaphysical assumptions. Their metaphysical assumptions further help to produce and sustain a highly dubious epistemological framework. What is problematic is the belief that things exist as ontologically distinct and independent, whether they be "persons" or "things." In Daoist metaphysics, the belief that things exist as distinct or self-contained, that is, as substances,[25] is just another instance of "reason" and the "will" imposing an external "form" on the particularity of nature and change. If philosophical traditions diverge with respect to their most fundamental assumptions, then we should not expect that all the theory and practice built on those foundations will end up looking the same. The Daoist provides an alternative account of human experience and action that is based on a processual metaphysics. An accurate understanding of nature and experience is what is most needed for mitigating human suffering. Perkins is correct when he argues that the Daoist understanding of things "shifted the very boundary between metaphysics and ethics." The Daoist exemplar does not need ethical principles or a sui generis "moral order" because Daoists provide a different understanding of the relationship between theory (*zhi*) and practice. They provide a radically different understanding of nature that functionally does the same job that the moral philosopher was supposed to do. There is no reason to believe that the possession of "moral facts" directly and immediately adjusts human conduct. What is most important is to abandon the "metaphysics" of the "sages" and moral philosophers.

Those Who Act Ruin It: Chapter Summary

Chapter 1 introduces the Lao-Zhuang Daoist's naturalistic account of embodied experience and noncognitive meaning. It is important to understand what noncognitive meaning is because some scholars will not accept that conduct can be guided "intelligently" and "reasonably" without rational principles and propositional statements. For the Daoist, humans are meaningfully related to their world prior to the meaning we attribute to the world through language and intentional conduct. We fail to recognize this because the concepts we form in experience, by their very nature, are projected on to the field of experience and can end up obscuring experience of situations. Furthermore, the Daoist account of experience involves seeing how the cognitive/noncognitive, rational/irrational ontological dualisms mischaracterize the nature of human experience.

Chapter 2 begins with a clarification of what "nonegoistic conduct" (*wuwei*, 無為) would look like for the Daoist. If certain habits of thinking and cultural beliefs (*zhi*, 知) dominate experience, then this obstructs how we perceive the meaning of situations. I then briefly juxtapose Richard Rorty's "ironist" with Daoism. Although some scholars find similarities between the two works, it is important to recognize that Rorty abandons many of Dewey's major insights. Rorty, in this sense, is more similar to Quine. Rorty's project does not work, I argue, because he abandons the pragmatist's account of noncognitive meaning.

Chapter 3 clarifies how and why Daoist philosophers critique desires. For the Daoists, desires obstruct the capacity for persons to understand and interpret situations. In particular, desires also obstruct the ability to understand that all things, including the self, are interdependent and relational. As Daoists argue, to be "without self-interest" (*wusi*, 無私) is (ironically) the form of life that promotes communal (and individual) well-being.

Chapter 4 then provides a naturalistic account of values. Values are always immediately felt and not actually abstract or conceptual objects. Rationality is also not the only faculty that can intelligently guide conduct. If we properly understand the nature of values, this simultaneously helps to guide human behavior. The Daoist account of nature also provides what can be called (anachronistically) the "nonnaturalistic fallacy." "Qualities" are the product of interaction. No such thing as a "value/good-in-itself" exists. This account of the nonnaturalistic fallacy will help to introduce the idea that, for the Daoist, committing the nonnaturalistic fallacy helps to legitimize coercive and oppressive hierarchical relationships.

Chapter 5 clarifies and defends the critique of the "sages" and "robbers" that is found in the *Zhuangzi*. As detailed in chapter 8 of the *Zhuangzi*, both the (non-Daoist) sages and robbers are equally responsible for society's ills. This is because both the sages and robbers are perceptually alienated from nature. This perceptual alienation involves the inability to perceive nature as fundamentally indeterminate (*wu*, 無). The Daoist alternative to the sages and robbers is to cultivate awareness of our interdependence with nature. This book calls this process an "attunement to nature" or, as chapter 8 describes it, to not depart from "the actuality of their endowed circumstances" (其性命之情) and to "see oneself when you see others/things" (自見而見彼). Attunement involves an awareness of how nature primordially forms an indeterminate continuum (*wu*).

Chapter 6 provides an account of impartial, compassionate, and nurturing behavior from the Daoist perspective. As *Daodejing* 49 states, the Daoist sage cultivates a capacity to see the world as one "chaotic muddle" through being "without heart/mind" (*wuxin*, 無心). When we are "with a constant heart/mind" and perceive the world through "knowledge," persons interpret situations through a "Moral Manicheanism." It is this Moral Manicheanism that the Daoist criticizes as sage behavior.

In abandoning the assumptions of a substance metaphysics, the Daoist sage can see all things of nature as parts of the same, underlying continuum. It is specifically this capacity to become empty of an independent sense of self that serves as the Daoist's alternative to the moralist philosopher's dogma. In emptying one's experience of the belief in independent things, persons become oriented in such a way that, not only can they behave in ways that help to mitigate suffering and social disharmony, but they can also do this in such a way where their attitudes do not become self-corrupting. It is specifically being "without egoistic conduct" (*wuwei*), "without self-interest" (*wusi*), and "without heart/mind" (*wuxin*) that the Daoist is capable of realizing everything the philosophical moralists were not able to achieve. The Daoist is thus *wuwei* and does not "ruin things."

Chapter One

An Embodied Account of Experience and Meaning in Daoist Philosophy

Daoism and Embodied Experience

When encountering philosophical Daoism, there are a few key features that should strike the Western audience as being at odds with Western common sense. Aside from the features and themes already highlighted earlier in the introduction, the relationship between "naming" (*ming*, 名), "desire" (*yu*, 欲), the capacity to observe (*guan*, 觀) the things of nature, and how the Daoist sage is "without knowledge" (*wuzhi*, 無知) all present an alternative view of human experience and of the human relationship to nature. The Daoist critique of society and their understanding of societal ills is grounded in their philosophy of mind and metaphysics. It is through the Daoists' antirepresentational account of experience that we can best make sense of how they provide an alternative framework to their contemporaries. For scholars unfamiliar with Daoist philosophy, the relationship between "naming," "desire," and "knowledge" is fundamental to understanding the Daoist account of experience. It should come as no surprise that, seeing how these ideas are so central to Daoist philosophy, the first passage of the *Daodejing* begins by associating these key features.

> The Way that is capable of becoming a way is not the constant way. The name that is capable of becoming its name is not its constant name. The nameless is the beginning of heaven and earth; the named is the mother of the ten thousand things.

> Thus, to be constantly without desire is how one observes the subtleties (*miao*, 妙) of things; To constantly have desire is how one observes their boundaries (*jiao*, 徼).
>
> These two features emerge together [同出] but are of different names [而異名]. Together they are called the "obscure." The obscure of the [again] obscure, the gateway of the manifold subtleties.[1]

With this opening passage of the *Daodejing*, parallel distinctions are set up: the named and the nameless, desire and being "without desire," the capacity to observe the boundaries and limits of things versus the capacity to observe the subtle and incipient. The "named," "desire," and the "boundaries" (*jiao*, 徼) correspond to one half of the dualism (the "determinate," *you*, 有), while the "nameless," being "without desire," and observing the subtleties of things (*miao*, 妙) correspond to the other half (the "indeterminate," *wu*, 無).[2] This passage presents an account of the natural world where the most fundamental aspects of reality are not entities with discreet boundaries. Even for those that tend to read mysticism into the *Daodejing*, this passage does not lend itself to a "two-tiered" or ontologically bifurcated account of nature. Both halves of the dualism emerge together (同出) but have different names (而異名) and this suggests continuity. A religious or mystical reading of the text still needs to take this into consideration. Passage 37 of the *Daodejing* highlights how the capacity to properly observe situations involves seeing nature as likened to a "nameless scrap of unworked wood" (無名之樸) and the absence of desires.

> *Dao* is really nameless (*wuming*), were nobles and kings able to respect this, all things (*wanwu*) would be able to develop along their own lines. Having developed along their own lines, were they to [create desires, *yu zuo*, 欲作], I would realign them with a nameless scrap of unworked wood. Realigned with the nameless scrap of unworked wood [無名之樸], they would leave off desiring. In not desiring [*buyu*, 不欲] they would achieve equilibrium [*jing*, 靜], and all the world would be properly ordered of its own accord [*ziding*, 自定] (with minor changes).[3]

Dao, the "path" or "way," is in a sense related to order and the processes of ordering reality. The Daoist understanding of order is self-determining (*ziding*, 自定) or an order that is *not externally imposed* onto nature. As Robin Wang describes Dao, "*Dao* ties together heaven, earth, and human beings, all of which are generated from the *Dao* and model its spontaneous and generative capabilities. *Dao* animates the whole world and leaves nothing out, giving this world unity and coherence. The world is not constructed from individual pieces, but rather is an indivisible whole taking patterns and processes of interrelatedness as its fundamental structure."[4] The Daoist view of order is one that is not hierarchical in the sense that it emerges from the unique particularity of each aspect of nature or as a function of the interrelationships between particulars. In following Dao, things are permitted to transform on their own accord (*zihua*, 自化). If "desires are created" (*yu zuo*, 欲作), this is to depart from the natural dispositions of things. Following Dao and being aligned with nature involves both not desiring (*buyu*, 不欲) and the capacity to perceive the world with pliant and accommodating tranquility (*jing*, 靜). In the *Daodejing*, persons are viewed as fundamentally "without desire," which is to be in accord with nature as "nameless." Through being "without desires," the Daoist believes we are of the dispositions that both perceive and navigate the world with greater sensitivity. As chapter 3 of this book explores in more detail, the Daoist is not at all interested in completely doing away with desires. It is the "creation of desires" that is problematic. Being "without desire" is not mere asceticism. From the Daoist perspective, desires are learned through cultural forms, whereas the basic needs for sustenance are considered more fundamental and unproblematic. The "creation of desires" inhibits our ability to understand and respond to situations.

Daoist cultivation practices result in the transformation of perception. The Daoist wants to be in accord with Dao or free of all those features of experience that play a role in inhibiting perception of situations. The features associated with inhibiting perception include the "named" and "desired" aspects of experience. Properly understanding Daoist cultivation practices requires that we understand how the above features of Daoist philosophy fit together. In particular, it is important to understand how the "named" and "desired" aspects of experience can inhibit one's capacity to observe nature as fundamentally "nameless," the subtleties of things (*miao*), and how nature is "self-ordering" (*ziding*). What we will find is that the Daoist account of experience is what we can call "antirepresentational." Reality is not made up of distinct "things" that the mind needs to accurately cognize. It is this antirepresentationalism that will help to explain how and why the Daoist is critical of both "knowledge" and "desires" and how each of these features of experience can inhibit perception. In order to help explain and distinguish this book's account of Daoist philosophy from previous scholarship, this chapter also presents Chad Hansen's account of Daoism from *A Daoist Theory of Chinese Thought*. As I will highlight below, one important feature of Daoism that Hansen misses is that different kinds of interaction with the environment should be understood as meaningfully and intelligibly felt in experience and in a way that is not necessarily reducible to the meaning created with language. Ultimately, the Daoist does not want to completely extinguish the "named," "desired," and "known" aspects of experience. Instead, the goal is to contextualize those aspects of experience within the larger context of experience as fundamentally "indeterminate" (*wu*). The goal of cultivation is to see the "named" within the context of the "nameless" or the foregrounded aspects of experience within the background continuity of experience. Through such a transformation of perception, people are then capable of responding to situations with greater sensitivity or as *wuwei*; with "nonegoistic action." Below, I outline the Daoist account of embodied experience in order to elucidate how perception of the world is transformed through cultivation.

Hansen on *Zhuangzi* and Language

In one major respect, the purpose of this book is similar to Hansen's account of Daoism in *A Daoist Theory of Chinese Thought*. On my reading, Hansen draws on Wittgenstein, Quine, and Putnam when providing an account of classical Chinese philosophy of mind and language that is antirepresentational. He argues that "all the ancient [Chinese] thinkers viewed languages as a way to coordinate and regulate behavior. No one in this tradition developed a theory that the central function of language was representing or picturing facts or reality."[5] Where I depart from Hansen, apart from his unfair prejudice against Confucianism,[6] is how best to understand the antirepresentational account of experience in the *Daodejing* and the *Zhuangzi* and of the ethical implications of such a position.[7] As Hansen suggests, the *Zhuangzi* involves an account of human life that would reject the Platonic myth of transcending nature. "Ancient Greek humanism [. . .] contrasted the reasoning faculty (the mind) with the irrational, base, physical desires and passions (the heart). Our beliefs, our ideas, come from the mind—the reasoning faculty. Our bodies supply us with our desires. We tied our conception of dignity to our possible independence from natural desires."[8]

In many respects, the discipline of philosophy still insists on clinging to the belief that humans maintain a place over and above nature and change. This dualism between the intelligible realm and bodily existence, the assumption that reality is bifurcated, is not a belief that all cultural traditions share, and unfortunately it has been a fundamental assumption for much of Western philosophy and religion. Hansen is right to suggest that the Daoist understanding of mind is antirepresentational[9] yet arguing that a philosopher holds an antirepresentational understanding of mind does not, by itself, describe only one alternative philosophical position. In the west, several antirepresentational accounts of experience have emerged, and they differ from each other in important ways.[10] As I highlight below, with Hansen's attempt to make Zhuangzi an analytic philosopher, he unwittingly smuggles back in assumptions he was hoping to abandon. In short, Hansen is not able to fully abandon representationalism due to how he reduces all meaning to the use of language (i.e., a monistic understanding of communication that I detail more below).[11] The difference between Hansen's reading of Daoism and the one I outline in this book is similar to the difference between Rorty and Quine on the one hand and Dewey on the other. When compared to the representational understanding of mind that still dominates much of Western philosophy, the Daoist philosophers have a much broader understanding of how an aspect of experience is knowable and recognizable as meaningful. Desire, perception, and emotions are all intelligible and meaningful *in their own way* and in a way that is not reducible to propositional statements.

Although Hansen might insist that he provides a pluralistic account of human experience, it is still guilty of a monistic understanding of meaning. What Hansen's account of the *Zhuangzi* misses is that all forms of interaction with the environment need to be understood as functioning differently. If we follow Quine (and Hansen) in believing that meaning was merely the property of languages (which includes "body language"), we still ignore how all experience is *already* expressing meaning. If we follow Quine's naturalism, we ignore other important aspects of Dewey's philosophy (the second half of *Experience and Nature*). For Dewey, we perceive both cognitive and noncognitive meanings in experience.[12] The way each kind of habit discloses the world is qualitatively different. This is, I take it, likewise an important dimension of both the *Daodejing* and the *Zhuangzi* and is one overlooked by Hansen.

Hansen's own project starts with a summary of what he takes to be a major problematic assumption in Western philosophy, that of assuming a representational account of knowledge.[13] Hansen claims: "The common Indo-European theory of mind centered on the cognitive faculty. The model of knowing was representing accurately through mental contents—true beliefs. The mental items arrange themselves into beliefs—mental compositions or sentences of mentalese. [. . .] Beliefs are true if the pictures are accurate, false if they are not. This model breeds skepticism of belief through doubt of the senses as causes of (evidence for) our beliefs."[14] For those that find the philosophy of the *Zhuangzi* morally suspect, perhaps much of what is found to be suspect has to do with the pervasive assumption in much of Western philosophy that nature is bifurcated and that there exists an ontological divide between the world of desire and the intelligible realm. The absence of skepticism directed towards sense data and empirical experience in the *Daodejing* and the *Zhuangzi* is not an accident. As Hansen points out, there is no need to be anxious about whether "representations" (mentalese) accurately correspond to the world if our understanding of experience is antirepresentational. In Hansen's functional account of language, he describes ontology as emerging from our basic, purposive way of managing our world. The ontological distinctions formed in experience are then provisional and grounded in practical considerations. "Carving up" reality and making distinctions is relative to our language and culture. This position is what is called the "ontological relativity" thesis. For Hansen,

> Stuffs can be numbered and counted from a plurality of perspectives and for different purposes. We can discuss individuals of human-stuff, families of human-stuff, and cities or states of human-stuff. Objecthood is derivative in this conceptual scheme. [. . .] They do not regard those unit clusters [i.e., objects carved out in experience,] as the ultimately *real* building blocks of the wholes out of which they are carved up. The part-whole structure marked by language is pragmatically relative.[15]

With this functional understanding of language, conceptual distinctions are made with respect to how certain aspects of experience relate to certain purposes we have. Producing different and new conceptual distinctions is useful and can help us refine our practices. The core problem emerges when we believe that the conceptual individuation of things in experience accurately represents the way reality exists "in-itself." Although Dewey would generally agree with the "ontological relativism" thesis, to believe that this exhaustively characterizes the nature of experience is misguided. Hansen's attempt to resolve the separation between the mind and body reduces all knowable objects and desires to *that same kind of intelligibility* that was supposed to, at least traditionally, transcend empirical existence. Instead of insisting that knowledge is about a reality behind the appearances of things, now it is simply assumed that the faculties of reasoning are pragmatic and immanent processes. This account of language and experience comes from the neopragmatism of Quine and is one that argues for "ontological relativism." Lakoff and Johnson describe Quine's account of language as giving "up on the possibility of constructing a single universally applicable logical language into which all natural languages can be translated adequately. It claims instead that each natural language carves up what is in the world in different ways—always picking out objects that are really there and properties and relations that are really there."[16] Lakoff and Johnson are correct to point out that Quine's work still tries to maintain a form of "realism."[17] Meaning for Quine is objective in the sense that it involves the correspondence of propositions in a language to objects in the world and to their relationship to other propositions in the same language. Ontologies are built into each language. Quine's work departs from, *and even misreads*, some of Dewey's most important insights when Quine puts forth his "ontological relativity" thesis. Quine's account of meaning still insists that it is only the property of language (although it includes forms of communication that are not necessarily "formal languages"). The best way to explain this is to see how Quine misquotes Dewey's *Experience and Nature*. Quine's misquote happens in *Ontological Relativity*: "Meanings are, first and foremost, meanings of language. Language is a social art which we all acquire on the evidence solely of other people's overt behavior under publicly recognizable circumstance. Meanings, therefore, those very models of mental entities, end up a grist for the behaviorist's mill. Dewey was explicit on the point: 'Meaning . . . is not a psychic existence; it is primarily a property of behavior.' "[18] This quote from Dewey's work *does not* exhaustibly represent how he understood "meaning" and meaningful experience. Quine only quotes half of Dewey's view in this particular instance. In its totality, Dewey claims that "meaning is not indeed a psychic existence; it is primarily a property of behavior, and secondarily a property of objects."[19] What is meant by "meaning" being "a property of behavior" covers a broader domain of experiences than Quine would have us believe. When Dewey's whole quote is taken into consideration, we can see how Dewey stresses that there is a more fundamental kind of meaning than that which is *attributed* to objects. The meaning attributed to objects is a secondary aspect of experience. Behavior and the meaning of that behavior is, for Dewey, 1) more fundamental than the meaning attributed to objects and 2) of significant enough a difference to warrant Dewey drawing this distinction between the two. Quine is neglecting an important distinction being drawn by Dewey in leaving off the remainder of the quote. In particular, "meaning" is not only attributed to objects. The meaning that is a property of behavior is a broader, more fundamental form of meaning than that which is attributed to the (conceptually individuated) objects of experience.

Human experience is constituted by its constant interactions with the environment and is thus qualitatively and continuously communicative. Regardless of any desire to communicate intention, humans are continuously and meaningfully *affected* by their environment. This does not mean that we are passively absorbing information about meaning from the environment. In *Experience and Nature*, Dewey stresses that experience is not "ready-made" and intrinsically meaningful.

> When inquiry reveals that an object external to the organism is now operative and affecting the organism, the pertinency of overt action is established and the kind of overt adjustment that should be made is in evidence. Perceptual meanings (sensory-perceptual) contrast with other meanings in that either (a) the latter cannot be overtly acted upon *now* or immediately, but only at a deferred time, when specified conditions now absent have been brought into being—conceptual meanings—; or (b) that the latter are such that action upon them at any time must be of a dramatic or literary or playful sort—non-cognitive meanings.[20]

There are three things being juxtaposed here: perceptual meanings, conceptual (i.e., cognitive) meanings, and noncognitive meanings. What Dewey is trying to do in this densely written passage is clarify how there is no such capacity to experience the "intrinsic meanings" of things (*because meaning is the relationship between things*). Sensory-perception meanings "are specifically discriminated objects of awareness; the discrimination takes place in the course of inquiry into causative conditions and consequences."[21] The things and objects discriminated in experience are the products of ongoing interaction with the environment. Empirically, sentient beings do not passively receive sense data of determinate objects. The ontological distinctions we form in experience are secondary and derivative aspects of experience (i.e., "ontologically relative"). The process of isolating the objects of inquiry from their contexts is not arbitrary. The process itself is grounded in human desires or (as Dewey puts it) the desire for "values" to be *consummated*. It means that the experience and *individuation* of objects is always *value laden*. "Perceptual meanings" are never experienced without being in a relationship to other meanings (i.e., there are two kinds of meanings, for Dewey, that help constitute the objects of awareness: cognitive and noncognitive). Conceptual meanings are juxtaposed with the noncognitive (what is emotional, psychological, aesthetic, and/or somatic in quality).[22] The distinction between noncognitive and conceptual meaning is likewise a distinction between the reflexive and affective interactions human beings undergo with the environment and the reflective and "intent-bearing" intersubjective communication between animals with the capacity to communicate intention. The best and clearest example of noncognitive meaning comes from taking Dewey's description literally. The "meanings" that are of a "dramatic" and "playful" sort come from *play*. Communication between humans and dogs, humans and toddlers, or even toddlers and dogs, can be understood as meaningful yet in a way that is not reducible to propositional statements (seeing how, to my knowledge, both toddlers and dogs are not forming propositional statements when they play). Play, as simple as it might sound, is communication that does not necessarily need to resort to abstract thinking and the formation of concepts. This brute, immediate form of communication is meaningful, just in a more primordial form.

Dewey's work on the difference between noncognitive and cognitive meaning is by no means straightforward. What is clear is that cognitive meanings emerge from the noncognitive context of qualitative experience. When we come to a problematic situation, for example, Dewey claims that "there is nothing intellectual or cognitive in the existence of such situations, although they are the necessary condition of cognitive operations or inquiry. In themselves they are precognitive."[23] What the exact relationship is between these two kinds of meaning is arguably unclear.[24] What can be said is that meaning is not *merely* a property of communicating intention because experience is already communicative and *value laden*. In other words, regardless of intention, *all experience is experience of value, and since each experience takes place in the context of multiple experiences, each experience of value is fundamentally entangled with other alternate experiences of value. Isolating one manifestation of value always takes place in the context of (plural) values being perceived.*[25] Interaction with the environment, regardless of whether it is with objects in the environment or with other sentient beings, will always involve noncognitive meanings. When cognitive meanings are present in the field of experience, they are nonetheless secondary and emergent aspects of experience.

Daoism and the Nature of Experience

Understanding the philosophy of the *Daodejing* and the *Zhuangzi* will require seeing these works as holding an embodied and naturalistic account of meaning. This will require a broader understanding of "meaning," knowledge, and intelligence than Western philosophers might be accustomed to. When describing this broader understanding of "meaning," this book uses the terms "intelligible" and "intelligibility" to express how consciousness can recognize the meaning of experience in broader and more diverse forms. An experience can be understood as "intelligible" in so far as it is expressive of significance. We can perceive and recognize the meaning of a given experience in at least two distinct senses; meaning is *attributed* to features of experience or it is already *inherent* in the perception of nature. For example, the quality of any experience is *meaningfully experienced* simply *as that quality*. The experience of sound provides the easiest example for this. As Don Idhe points out in *Listening and Voice*,[26] the sounds we experience are all immediately (un-*mediated*-ly) and meaningfully experienced when they occur. Sound is always perceived as having an immediate *directionality* and *intensity*. If a person is speaking behind me, the *directionality* of the "behind me" is immediately felt and the felt *sense* of the "behind me" is not mediated through language (sound is immediately perceived *as from* a direction with respect to the perceiver). Because sound has an immediate "sense" to it, it situates the perceiver in relation to their world. This capacity to feel how one is meaningfully situated can be considered a more fundamental form of meaning. The experience of sound is also present in any given context (i.e., literally a meaningful part of any possible context). As Dewey's later works also highlight, the *aesthetic* dimensions of experience or the basic ways human organisms are related to their environment are meaningfully felt and in a way that is not reducible to the meaning we create using language and concepts. There are then two forms of meaning; what can be considered 1) noncognitive and nonpropositional on the one hand and 2) cognitive and propositional on the other. Mark Johnson has described this Deweyan position as an "embodied theory of meaning." As Johnson states, "The meaning of a specific aspect or dimension of some ongoing experience is that aspect's connection to other parts of past, present, or future (possible) experiences. Meaning is relational. It is about how one thing relates to or connects with other things."[27] With a broader understanding of meaning as relational where the felt relationships between things can be understood as meaningfully situating persons, "intelligibility" denotes the way experience is meaningful in both propositional/cognitive and nonpropositional/noncognitive forms. With an embodied account of meaning and value, propositional meaning is grounded in the *meaning laden/sense giving context* (i.e., nonpropositional meaning). For Dewey, "to be aware of the meaning or value of something is to see it as a *functioning part within a larger whole*."[28] Propositional meaning is different from nonpropositional meaning only by degree of complexity and not because it constitutes a different kind of meaning. What this also means is that, with respect to navigating the world intelligently, we can be said to make both cognitive and noncognitive distinctions. By no means does this antirepresentational account of experience reject that people make cognitive distinctions, nor do I intend to deny the reality of these habits and their importance. By widening the scope of intelligent experience, this helps to explain how noncognitive experience can be understood as meaningful and how the meaning of cognitive experience is always tied to a natural, noncognitive context. In relation to Daoist philosophy, we can then say that perceiving and interacting with both the "named" and "nameless" aspects of existence is "intelligible" yet in such a way that each is qualitatively distinct.

Johnson, drawing on Dewey, calls the traditional account of meaning the "conceptual-propositional theory of meaning," which assumes that "sentences or utterances (and words we use in making them) alone are what have meaning. Sentences get their meaning by expressing propositions, which are the basic units of meaning and thought."[29] Johnson does "not mean to deny the existence of propositional thinking, but [he sees it] as dependent on the nature of our embodied, immanent meaning."[30] From a Deweyan perspective, Hansen ends up reducing the vastly different yet still meaningful ways humans are related to the natural world to a linguistic monism, albeit one that recognizes the potential of forming any number of different natural languages. This is apparent in Hansen's classification of the *Daodejing* as an "antilanguage" philosophy.[31] Even if the Daoist philosopher were to accept the label, being "antilanguage" does not mean that the Daoist is then left with only mysticism or irrationalism. "Ontological relativism" is only one part of the Daoist account of experience. The ability to even recognize that the ontological distinctions we draw are relative and functional itself depends on the ability to perceive how all immediately felt and knowable values and qualities are context dependent and are immediately intelligible only as aspects of the contexts they emerge from. If the only meaningful and intelligible ways humans interact with their world was through formal language, one unwittingly smuggles in the old assumption that the world is inherently meaningless (which is a dominant claim in the history of Western philosophy that Hansen was hoping to counter). Meaning is not mysterious but is instead simply a product of how embodied beings interact with and are related to their environment. Hansen's account of the *Zhuangzi* still assumes a monistic account of meaning that insists that meaning is merely the property of language and person-to-person communication. If meaning also occurs in a nonpropositional form, then intuitive knowledge does not necessarily imply mysticism or irrationalism. Intuitive knowledge could simply be somatic and aesthetic in character.

Adopting an embodied account of meaning is not at all to suggest that the world has a fixed meaning as this too would involve making assumptions fundamental to a representational account of mind and experience.[32] If the meaning and "sense" of a particular experience was not always reducible to the language we could form about it, this does not mean that reality has some innate meaning, "in-itself." What it does suggest is that the noncognitive *relationships* humans have with the natural world are equally *creating* meaning, that is, that the noncognitive *interactions produce meaningful experience*. The noncognitive dimensions of experience, the perceptual, emotional (*moods*), and somatic (desires), are also "sense giving" and intelligible. Human experience can then be said to involve meaningful distinction making with each of the noncognitive faculties. We should also not consider these faculties to be fundamentally contrary to each other. Each of these qualitatively different features of experience are interrelated parts of experience as a whole. These aspects of experience are always novel and qualitatively particular because "meaning" is a natural and cocreative process that is not simply a subjective reality. In light of the larger project of this book, we can make greater sense of what Daoist meditation practices involve and what they hope to achieve by rejecting the traditional, merely propositional account of meaning. Being "without knowledge" and "without desire," as the Daoist aspires to realize, involves the cultivation of attention such that people no longer ignore these noncognitive, nonproposition meanings in experience. The label of "irrationalism" simply misses the most important insights of Daoist philosophy.

Disclosing experience with a limited set of habits inhibits important features of situations from being brought to the foreground of consciousness. The Daoist project is one of cultivation, one that practices the quieting of habits of abstraction or "knowledge," which, in turn, ends up strengthening the noncognitive habits that involve a sensitivity to the qualitative aspects of perception. An embodied and relational understanding of the emergence of more complicated meaning in experience is outlined in both the *Daodejing* and the *Zhuangzi*. *Daodejing* 42 states that "Dao gives rise to one, one gives rise to two, two gives rise to three, and three gives rise to the ten thousand/myriad things. The ten-thousand things carry *yin* on their back and the *yang* in their arms, in the center the *qi* (vital energy) achieves harmony."[33] Experience/nature is primordially an indeterminate continuum. As soon as we make a discrimination, we foreground one aspect of the field of experience and therefore divide the indeterminate into two parts (foreground and background). This initial discrimination, one that is merely functional or aspectual, does not simply produce two distinct "things." Any "determinate thing," intelligible only in relationship to the background situation that it emerged from, is itself constituted by the context or the "not-this-determined-thing." *Yin* and *yang* (the "two" in the above passage) gain their significance from their interrelationship. The "two" dimensions of experience inevitably produce a third, which is the recognized interrelationship between an aspect and its context. Chapter 2 of the *Zhuangzi* arguably appeals to this same understanding of cosmology and an emergent understanding of meaning.[34]

> So even moving from nonexistence to existence we already arrive at three—how much more when we move from existence to existence! Rather than moving from anywhere to anywhere, then, let us just go by the rightness of whatever is before us as the present "this."
>
> Now, courses have never had any sealed borders between them, and words have never had any constant sustainability. It is by establishing definitions of what is "this," what is "right," that boundaries are made. [. . .] For wherever a division is made,

> something is left undivided. Whenever debate shows one of two alternatives to be right, something remains undistinguished and unshown. What is it? The sage hides it in his embrace, while the masses of people debate it, trying to demonstrate it to one another. Thus I say that demonstration by debate always leaves something unseen.[35]

The shift from "indeterminate experience" to making a "determination" produces three in the sense that all three, aspect, context, and relationship, are immediately recognized. There are no "sealed borders" and our determinations have no "constant sustainability" because our distinctions always have this background/foreground structure. When an aspect of experience is made "intelligible," that determination depends on the background situation for its meaning. I take that this story of the "one giving birth to the myriad things" is not a genesis story. It is an account of the plural ways meaning and significance are recognizable in experience and of how a more complex understanding of things (*you*, 有) emerges from nonbeing (*wu*, 無) or that which is fundamentally indeterminate. Immediate experience is not reducible to propositional forms of meaning because the latter emerges out of the irreducibly relational understanding of meaningful interaction. It is not that distinction making per se is a problem for the Daoist. Errors arise when the making of conceptual distinctions begins to obscure and ignore the context that such distinctions are a product of. What the Daoist is critical of is how the individuation of things in experience can contribute to misperception. Certain forms of conduct become viewed as being of value. Cultural norms emerge from this, values reify, and the qualities of experience become understood as independently existing realities. The Daoist sage maintains awareness of the meaningful but noncognitive context. Each distinction, both the cognitive and noncognitive kinds, involves the context it is embedded in. The sage simply recognizes this.

Once these habits are better cultivated, this is tantamount to being grounded and embedded in our natural, embodied, and animal condition. "Knowledge" then also becomes grounded in its natural context. Echoing passages from the *Daodejing*, Dewey claims that "Immediacy of existence is ineffable. *But there is nothing mystical about such ineffability* [my italics]; it expresses the fact that of direct existence it is futile to say anything to one's self and impossible to say anything to another."[36] For a certain kind of philosopher, the claim that experience is "ineffable" will sound simply like mysticism or irrationalism. Under their traditional Western metaphysical framework, language adequately describes the natural world. Dewey's claims only sound "mystic" when philosophers operate in their "question-begging" metaphysics. With Dewey's naturalist account of experience, the languages people use and the concepts they form are secondary and derivative aspects of nature/experience. They do not exhaustively describe the human relationship to nature because they are not meant to, and we do not need them to. Humans are reflexively and prereflectively related to the world such that we navigate the world meaningfully without necessarily needing to appeal to "reason." In other words, we can *reasonably* say that humans *make both cognitive and noncognitive distinction, and we do so intelligibly and meaningfully*. In light of this naturalistic account of mind and experience, making distinctions is not simply a matter of concept formation. Drawing on Dewey's later works, Johnson claims that each "situation is meaningful to us in the most important, primordial, and basic way that it can be meaningful—it shapes the basic contours of our experience. The situation specifies what will be significant to us and what objects, events, and persons mean to us at a pre-reflective level."[37] One of the most important themes in Dewey's *Experience and Nature* is that, traditionally, the world and the basic way human beings are related to that world were assumed to be meaningless and irrational. "Reason" was a capacity to impose order onto a world chaotic and unintelligible. The body, the emotions, and human desire were likewise assumed to be antithetical to "reason." Just as Dewey tried to show how the "ineffability of existence" was not something super-natural, scholars must recognize that the claims in Daoism are not claims about transcending empirical existence. Human beings have the capacity to be rational yet to define them *solely* as such would be a gross mistake. The nonrational dimensions of experience are equally meaningfully felt. It is *natural* and *reasonable* to be empirical. The Daoist would simply agree with pragmatists like Dewey in saying that the first attempts by Western philosophers to be empiricists just got off on the wrong foot.

Meaning and Intelligibility in Daoist Philosophy

The above distinction between two different kinds of meaning perceived in experience is important for making sense of how the Daoist viewed nature as like a "nameless uncarved block of wood" and how they can perceive the world "without knowledge" and "without desire." For the Daoist, both the "named" and "nameless" aspects of experience are qualitatively distinct, and Daoist cultivation practices illuminate how these features are related to each other. For example, the Daoist philosophers drew important distinctions between the different kinds of desires. These distinctions are drawn because the qualitatively different ways people interrelate to nature are intelligible, and the significance of these differences is not necessarily understood through the use of language and concepts. The Daoists focus on the cultivation of habits such that we no longer ignore the meaningful way we primarily interrelate to the natural world (i.e., through nonpropositional meaning). In their view, the problems of society are all rooted in this habitual ignorance of our interdependence. Nature is fundamentally overlapping and indeterminate. Our ignorance of this is due to cultural and political institutions. Because our culture has inculcated us with particular habits of cognition and reflection (what the Daoist calls "knowledge"), we become perceptually alienated from our relationships to nature and each other. We need to participate in the process of "forgetting" such that we can return attention to nature and our fundamental relationships to it. What this does is help us maintain attention to the noncognitive aspects of experience such that we realize how the cognitive aspects (i.e., "knowledge") depend on that which is noncognitive. What the Daoist hopes to do is cultivate habits of perception more fundamental to experience such that the contexts that all distinctions are made in are meaningfully recognized as contributing to such distinction making. In becoming more sensitive to the contexts that such distinctions are being made in, they can maintain a phenomenological distance from the habits of conceptualization that can obstruct our perception of situations. *Daodejing* passage 28 suggests this exact point. It prescribes:

> Know the male yet safeguard the female, and be a river gorge to the world, as a river gorge to the world, you will not lose your real potency [常德不離], and not losing your real potency, you return to the state of the newborn babe. [. . .] Know the clean yet safeguard the soiled and be the valley of the world. As a valley of the world your real potency will be ample, and with ample potency, you return to the state of unworked wood.[38]

To "know the male yet safeguard the female" is tantamount to perceiving things (beings, *you*, 有) while being able to perceive the context that said things emerge from (nonbeing, *wu*, 無). It involves an attention to the individuated aspects of experience (the "male" half of *yin/yang*) while being receptive to the background context (the "female" half of *yin/yang*). As Robin Wang states, the "relationship between *you* and *wu* also implies interplay between background and foreground that is crucial to how yin-yang theory functions as a way of skillfully operating in the world."[39] The Daoist links this capacity to perceive both foreground and background to skillful and perceptually sensitive conduct. In achieving such a state, this is what the Daoist considers virtuous or of not "departing from their constant potency" (常德不離). It is likened to an infant (innocent or not yet adulterated by cultural forms). As stated above, individuated aspects of experience are always related to values and desires. The goal is to cultivate and maintain attention to the context of experience while still perceiving the individuated things of nature. This is how one maintains an existential distance from "knowledge." Furthermore, to "know the clean yet safeguard the soiled" is precisely to see that which is of "value" (good, beauty, etc.) as being inextricably tied to the nonvalued (bad, ugly, etc.). It is to recognize how value and disvalue ("determinate" and "indeterminate") mutually generate each other. The Daoist is not trying to do away with any of these distinctions. Instead, they hope to contextualize all distinctions within the wider context of experience.

The description of the Daoist sage as being "without desire" (*wuyu*, 無欲) or to not desire (*buyu*, 不欲) certain values/things should be understood in a way similar to how scholars have understood *wuwei* (無為) or "without action." The *wu* or "without" does not completely negate all forms of action. The *wu* represents a negation of particular forms of coercive conduct. The same applies when thinking about being "without desire." Ames and Hall have described being "without desire" (*wuyu*) as "rather than involving the cessation and absence of desire, represents the achievement of deferential desire [. . . that is] shaped not by the desire to own, to control, or to consume, but by the desire simply to celebrate and enjoy things."[40] Instead of insisting that since *some* desires are bad, therefore *all* desires are bad or morally suspect, the Daoist philosopher focused on understanding the nature of our different desires. This important point is one missed by Hansen in *A Daoist Theory*. Hansen's account of Daoism argues, "The Laozi introduces the idea that we create desires by learning guiding discourse—gaining knowledge of what to do (know-to). [. . .] Instantly this model gives us a new conception of the roles of language and mind. Pragmatic (action-centered) rather than semantic analyses now make more sense. Language guides and controls behavior."[41] The distinction the *Daodejing* and *Zhuangzi* make between different kinds of desires is lost here. Hansen's monistic account of desires as merely learned from and determined by language only applies to the Daoist understanding of the dispositions that "have desire" (*youyu*) as opposed to the dispositions that are "without desire" (*wuyu*). Hansen's account is what can perhaps be called a monistic account of desires and value (or a monistic account of language's capacity to structure and shape conduct). Insisting that desires are learned merely through language is, like Dewey would claim, to mistake the abstract *products* of interaction that emerge at the *end* of a history as if they were somehow the *cause* or *source* of that history or process. As Dewey describes in *Experience and Nature*,

> In the assertion (implied here) that the great vice of philosophy is an arbitrary "intellectualism," there is no slight cast upon intelligence and reason. By "intellectualism" as an indictment is meant the theory that all experiencing is a mode of knowing, and that all subject-matter, all nature, is, in principle, to be reduced and transformed till it is defined in terms identical with the characteristics presented by refined objects of science as such. [. . .]
>
> The isolation of traits characteristic of objects known, and then defined as the sole ultimate realties, accounts for the denial to nature of the characteristics which make things lovable and contemptable, beautiful and ugly, adorable and awful. It accounts for the belief that nature is an indifferent, dead mechanism.[42]

What Dewey is criticizing is the tendency to reify conceptual aspects of experience as if they took precedence to or existed independent of relations, what he calls the "philosophical fallacy." By ignoring the process that creates the abstract objects of thought (i.e., "cognitive meanings") where things are conceptually individuated out of the (noncognitive) context of experience, people ignore features of existence that are important for both self-understanding and our ability to navigate the natural world. Daoists, as I understand it, maintain a position more like Dewey's in the sense that they recognize that experience is not merely theoretical and cognitive in content. To assume that "what is real is the rational,"[43] ipso facto, ignores the qualitative way humans intelligently or reasonably interact with the empirical world. Distinction making is not *merely* conceptual in character. Furthermore, Dewey does not mean to criticize all intellectual endeavors. His hope is to defend a broader understanding of intelligent conduct that recognizes the natural human capacity of judging the differences in function and quality of different desires and experienced qualities. As Youru Wang is right to claim, Hansen's account of the *Zhuangzi* assumes a kind of "linguistic determinism."[44] Hansen insists that human desire and freedom are *solely* constituted and structured by language (albeit a broader, naturalistic account of language). What Daoist philosophers actually argue is that desires are not merely learned and acquired through culture. Our bodily existence, so long as we are finite organisms and wish to survive in the world, requires basic needs to be fulfilled.

This is not to deny that language and culture play a significant role in shaping what people might end up desiring. Cultural traditions can inculcate their members with arbitrary desires. The Daoist tradition recognizes this and attempts to diagnose and remedy it. Passage 3 of the *Daodejing* claims that "it is for this reason that in the proper governing by the sages: they empty the hearts-and-minds of people and fill their stomachs, they weaken their aspirations and strengthen their bones, ever teaching the common people to be ["without knowledge"] (*wuzhi*) and ["without desire," i.e., without a "rarefied account of things desired] (*wuyu*). It is simply in doing things ["nonegoistically"] (*wuwei*) that everything is governed properly."[45] Passage 12 (which will be quoted in a later chapter) makes a similar argument as well. There are conceptual beliefs or "knowledge" (*zhi*) that emerge in cultural life long after the basic needs of a people are fulfilled. Regardless of how "transcendent" or "universal" a culture may believe its values are, theorizing about and possessing such values depends on basic human needs being fulfilled. Ziporyn similarly describes the practices in the *Daodejing* and the *Zhuangzi* as attempts to ground persons such that they recognize the natural or bodily source of their values and desires. "The recommendation of the text is not necessarily the complete elimination of everything that we experience as eye desires. It is more centrally concerned with the reintergration of the eye desires back into stomach desires, [. . .]. The problem with eye desires is that they become removed from the stomach, become autonomous and 'constant.' "[46] Strictly speaking, *some* desires are critiqued as harmful for the Daoist. It is not just that "eye desires" can potentially become uprooted from/ungrounded in stomach desires. Once they become ungrounded, they develop in highly abstract, imaginative, and unempirical ways (they become *ideology* or *ideological*). The longer certain abstractions like the belief in essences or substances are taken as real and the longer philosophical inquiry fails to reference empirical reality, the more these abstract beliefs and concepts come to inhibit our relationship to nature and our community. As soon as abstractions and values are believed to be independent of our basic human needs, they begin to take on a life of their own, and the only way to remedy this neurosis is to "forget" them (*wang*, 忘) and return attention to our embedded, natural existence. When we cultivate an ability to maintain an awareness of the noncognitive context of each experience, we make and understand distinctions in a way that is grounded and embodies nature as it truly is, like an "uncarved block of wood." Persons recognize that they are *of* nature (i.e., of the same interdependent and overlapping structures) because they too see themselves as fundamentally indeterminate like an "uncarved block of wood." When persons can ground their perception of situations in the indeterminate context of experience, they can be considered to be both "self-so" (*ziran*) and recognize all things as "self-so" as well.

Although there are quite a few Western philosophers that have theorized about embodied experience,[47] Dewey perhaps provides one of the most robust accounts of what an embodied existence involves. A few characteristics make Dewey radically different from the dominant Western understanding of mind and experience. First is the fact of "ontological relativism" or the insight that our ontological categories do not exhaustively correspond to reality. Existence is not constituted by independently existing things but, instead, processes. Second, meaning and value are immediately felt as qualities of interaction between organism and environment and are immediately recognizable as such. For Dewey, experience is both *in* and *of* nature. The way the human body is interrelated to its environment is continuously felt. Relations are just as real and just as immediate as things are for a pragmatist. The feeling that *this* experience is *my* experience is just another provisional way experience is undergone.[48] It is not a fundamental or necessary structure of it. "Experience" no longer refers to a private and individual occurrence. The main thesis of *Experience and Nature* is that we should not view experience and nature as two separate things and that experience *is* nature.[49] For Dewey, the distinction between the "objective" and "merely subjective" involves using question-begging assumptions about the nature of human experience. Traditionally, Western metaphysics holds that the relationships between things are secondary and merely "accidental" aspects of reality. Reality was something behind the veil of mere appearance. Dewey's project is not only an alternative to the traditional, representational account of experience. It is also a *reconstruction of* the nature of experience such that the traditional view is contextualized within a new framework. Although I may *feel* like this experience is *my experience*, this is really only one possible mode of human experience, and it is due to the (provisional but ignorant) way habits have been formed. Experience *is* nature in the sense that human relationships to nature are not a merely secondary property or "accidental" (they *are equally real*). The situation and the subject are aspectual or functional distinctions. The person in the situation is as much the situation as any other aspect of it. Through this reconstruction, Dewey hopes to outline how habits can be formed such that we are ignorant of our interdependence. Put another way, Dewey hopes to show how experience and nature can become (provisionally) divided due to ignorant habit formation.

Without the cultivation of other perceptual sensitivities, much of what occurs within the bounds of experience is not brought to the foreground of consciousness. The somatic, emotional, and aesthetic dimensions of experience are mostly ignored. For Dewey, it is a mistake to assume meaning is merely a private or subjective reality. As he states, "Many modern thinkers, influenced by the notion that knowledge is the only mode of experience that grasps things, assuming the ubiquity of cognition, and noting that immediacy or qualitative existence has no place in authentic science, have asserted that qualities are always and only states of consciousness."[50] Dewey is neither an objectivist nor subjectivist about meaning in the traditional sense. His emergent understanding of experience is one that attempts to dispense with this metaphysical dualism. Experienced qualities are qualities of interaction, and "the qualities were never 'in' the organism; they always were qualities of interactions in which both extra-organic things and organisms partake."[51] When a pragmatist like Dewey claims that relations are just as real as things, they are critiquing the idea that "qualities" are merely subjective realities. With the pragmatist's naturalist account of mind, no such ontologically determinate thing exists that can be called a subject that a quality could exist "in" (i.e., qualities are not "simply located"). As Lakoff and Johnson describe it, *both "objectivism" and "subjectivism" are myths.*[52] Interaction, or what the later Dewey would call a *transaction*, between organism and environment produces qualitative experience. The quality of experience is always novel and context dependent. It is one thing to argue that values are merely relative or subjective. It is a completely different issue to argue that, as I highlight in chapter 4, values *are* the immediately felt qualities of interaction with the environment and that values say as much about what kind of *being* this organism is as much as the objective conditions that give rise to such consummated values. With an embodied account of values, philosophers can overcome the traditional distinction between objectivism and relativism.

An embodied understanding of experience does not merely provide an alternative to the representational understanding of experience. Dewey's project in *Experience and Nature* is also an attempt to diagnose and recontextualize the (ignorant) set of habits that do not realize greater interrelationship and intercommunication with nature. It is an attempt to explain how habits can be cultivated such that we continually ignore the qualitatively immediate way all experience is constituted. The "objectivist" understanding of meaning fails to account for so much of human existence because it divides up processes that are continuous wholes and then confounds itself as to how best to put things back together. For example, the subject/object, mind/body dualisms are only assumptions made about experience. The "objectivist" account of meaning also relies on the assumption that nature and reality are divided into two domains; the intelligible, cognitive, and essential/necessary which are separate from and opposed to the unintelligible, noncognitive, and accidental/contingent. For Dewey, "knowledge that is ubiquitous, all-inclusive and all-monopolizing, ceases to have meaning in losing all context; that is does not appear to do so when made supreme and self-sufficient is because it is literally impossible to exclude that context of non-cognitive but experienced subject-matter which gives what is known its import. [. . .] unless there is breach of historic and natural continuity, cognitive experience must originate within that of a non-cognitive sort."[53] With claims like this, some Western philosophers might try to accuse Dewey of irrationalism or "anti-intellectualism," but this would simply miss Dewey's point. What is being disputed is the nature of intelligence and about how wide a range of experiences intelligible includes. For Dewey, every aspect of experience that is brought to the foreground is internally related to and dependent on the background that it emerges from. As such, this realization can be considered *a form of intelligibility* (*a kind of knowing*). Dewey in his later works draws from William James. Dewey, like James, would claim that the context of all experience involves feelings or relations that always help contribute to the meaning of a situation.[54] Consciousness makes determinate what is initially experienced as indeterminate. Ziporyn's account of Zhuangzi has argued a similar position. Ziporyn states:

> For Zhuangzi any meaningful and assertable being—any intelligibility, any coherence, anything that can be pointed out—is ipso facto a determinate being, with before and after. To be posited at all is to be posited together with its negation; otherwise, positing has not taken place, nothing has been said, nothing has been pointed out. [. . .] To set up any category, any coherence, any quality, is to set up the context of this coherence, the not-this. The context is thus internal to the coherence.[55]

When claiming that any posited or "determined" aspect of experience is internally related to what "it is not," Dewey and Ziporyn are not then claiming that this form of experience is a mysterious process that is impossible to understand. Recognizing that an abstract object of thought does not exhaustively correspond to the natural world is itself a kind of intelligibility (i.e., a *meaningful way* experience of the world is disclosed). "Ontological relativism," the *fact* that a single aspect of experience is being highlighted out from the indeterminate background of experience and that this isolation is not because there is a "reality behind appearance" that makes it so would perhaps only be a problem if abstract thinking was the only intelligent form of human conduct. Recognizing that the ontological distinctions humans form in experience are derivative and relative is itself a meaningful way of disclosing the world where the immediately felt quality of existence is perceived as not reducible to cognitive/propositional meaning.

Conclusion

For the Daoist philosopher and Dewey, the natural world is irreducibly communicative and interrelated. If we are to respond to and ameliorate social ills with greater levels of insight, it requires abandoning the epistemological perspective shaped by a substance metaphysics. As I will continue to highlight throughout the next few chapters, the Daoist critique of "knowledge" and their account of different desires, like the difference between "eye-desires" and "stomach-desires," is best understood in light of an embodied account of human experience and meaning. "Knowledge" can inhibit perception of situations. The way the Daoist addresses this problem is by cultivating other human potentials such that this undermines the potency and inertia of the cognitive habits that continuously foreground only certain features of experience.

Building on this account of experience and meaning, the following chapters will further elaborate on how "knowledge" and "desire" contribute to misperception of situations that, in turn, helps to normalize and encourage undesirable forms of life and human suffering. We can then see how and why a given ideology encourages oppressive behavior in the sense that certain sets of beliefs (especially nonnaturalistic and metaphysical ones) have an inherent logic to them. Although nonnaturalistic metaphysical beliefs do not accurately correspond to the natural world, they still can provide a formula that encourages oppressive behavior. In this way, the Daoist can reject that anything in nature has an "intrinsic" or independent reality but can still caution people away from particular metaphysical beliefs (like the belief in anything "intrinsic"). Metaphysics (substance ontology, moral realism) provides a conceptual framework that is both inaccurate and structurally oppressive when seen in light of this naturalistic and antirepresentational account of experience.

As the next chapter will show, the capacity to respond to situations with greater insight and sensitivity is a matter of cultivating dispositions. As an alternative to an ethical framework that depends on the idea of metaphysical substances, Daoism provides cultivation practices. These practices include "mind fasting" (*xinzhai*, 心齋) and "sitting and forgetting" (*zuowang*, 坐忘). The practices help us recognize the particularity of things (*ziran*) and how nature is like an "uncarved block of wood" (*pu*) because we can perceive things with clarity (*ming*, 明) and maintain equilibrium/tranquility (*jing*, 靜). Responding with greater sensitivity to situations demands we cultivate a receptivity and openness to the way all things are relationally constituted. When we finally abandon an account of ethical conduct based on the metaphysical assumptions of distinct individual things and replace it with Daoism, what we have left is a naturalistic account of values that illustrates how intuitively, so long as the nature of values is understood, this simultaneously involves an understanding of how to maximize valuable relationships and minimize unnecessary suffering. We do not need principles or "reason" (i.e., substances) to mediate situations from a nonnatural source.

Chapter Two

"Without Action" (無為)

Daoism on Theory, Cultivation, and Action

Wuwei in Daoist Philosophy

Perhaps the most important and studied idea from Daoist philosophy is the term *wuwei* (無為) or (to literally translate the term) to be "without action." Generally, the term *wuwei* is the name given to the kind of conduct where persons can spontaneously respond to situations in a noncoercive way. The ability to respond to situations *wuwei* is due to persons being constituted by a particular set of dispositions to act. Although there has been much said about the Daoist notion of *wuwei*, often the emphasis has been on describing the romantic or individualistic aspects of human conduct that could be considered *wuwei*. Previously, scholars have focused on these aspects at the expense of looking at the forms of conduct that are *not wuwei*. In doing so, scholars end up presenting Daoist philosophy in a decadent (bourgeois) and uncritical fashion. Daoist philosophy presents an alternative understanding of social and political life and of the human relationship to nature. This chapter introduces major themes found in both the *Zhuangzi* and the *Daodejing* in order to help address these problems in previous scholarship. I outline what being "without action" (*wuwei*) would be for the Daoist philosophers and how it is related to other important Daoist ideas. In particular, this chapter introduces the idea that being "without knowledge" (*wuzhi*, 無知) is an important dimension of the Daoist dispositions to act. The next chapter focuses on the relationship between acting *wuwei* and being "without desire" (*wuyu*, 無欲). Properly understanding what it means to be *wuzhi* and *wuyu* will help to further elucidate how it is that the Daoist sage can respond to situations *wuwei*.

Contrary to previous scholarship on Daoist philosophy, *wuwei* is not just a name given to action that is "spontaneous, effortless, and/or sensitive to situations." Most importantly, it is *not* to act *wei* (為) or *not* to be "coercively acting." *Wuwei* is explicitly a negation or absence of those forms of conduct that the Daoist considers to be *wei*. *Wuwei* is not just preferable to *wei*. A key line that I take to be of great importance and one that informs this book's thesis comes from the *Daodejing* passages 29 and 64: "Those who act ruin it" (為者敗之). For the Daoist, *wei* is a form of conduct that undermines itself. It is to act such that one's conduct does not cohere with situations because of how human beings are related to their own intentions, desires, and beliefs. A tyrant's actions can be considered *wei*, but what is more crucial is that the Confucians, Mohists, and Legalists (among others) are all, for the Daoists, considered guilty of acting *wei* as well.

As perhaps all scholars of Daoism know, *wuwei* is not the literal absence of all forms of action. The negation (*wu*) of *wei* signifies an absence of particular dispositions, desires, and forms of understanding. Responding to situations *wuwei* is possible through the cultivation of habits such that persons maintain the suspension of problematic conceptual structures limiting human experience. The habits of thinking that accompany these structures, which are themselves indebted to metaphysical assumptions, thus no longer inhibit the capacity to perceive situations. *Wuwei* is conduct that is not "self-imposing" in the sense that conceptual distinctions (*zhi*) are not projected onto the field of experience in a way that delimits people and things as if they were separate from their world. A key example is that the *wuwei* conduct of the Daoist is not informed by a sense of the self that is independent. In being able to perceive the indeterminate ("nameless") context of experience, we become free of the epistemological framework that clings to the conceptual individuation of things in experience.

Although being *wuzhi* and *wuyu* are two key features behind why the Daoist can respond to situations *wuwei*, the root source of the problem is the framework that imposes distinct "things" onto the flux and flow of experience. *Wuwei* is conduct that is without self-interest, nonimposing, and without a purpose externally imposed onto situations. If forced to give it a shorthand translation, perhaps "nonpurposive action" is the safest although Ames and Hall usefully translate *wuwei* as "noncoercive action." In light of how the Daoist suspends the epistemological framework that assumes independent things, another possibility is to translate *wuwei* as "nondelimiting conduct." There is no simple, shorthand way to translate the term *wuwei* when we consider the dimensions of Daoism that inform their account of action. From the Daoist perspective, non-Daoists are all more or less guilty of delimiting nature and imposing their own framework onto the field of experience in a coercive way. This cognitive tendency is itself indebted to the view of the self as taking precedence to or as independent of its world. Because the tendency to impose one's own metaphysical framework is related to the sense that they are an independent person, we can consider "nonegoistic action" to be another suitable philosophical translation for the term *wuwei*. From this point on, *wuwei* as "nonegoistic action" will be the preferred translation.

The Daoist critique of the Confucians and Mohists is not only a critique of their moral beliefs and behaviors. Their critique must also be understood as a critique of the metaphysical and epistemological assumptions that inform what it means to be "coercively acting" or conduct that could be labeled as being rooted in a sense of egoism and purposiveness. We cannot understand what forms of conduct are *wuwei* without also understanding how the Daoist sage is "without knowledge" (*wuzhi*) and "without desire" (*wuyu*). Furthermore, we can't understand what forms of conduct are *wei* without knowing why the Daoist critiques both "knowledge" (*zhi*, 知) and desire (*yu*, 欲). Acting *wuwei* is possible because the Daoist cultivates dispositions such that they do not cling to reified and "fixed" beliefs and desires. Conduct that is egoistic or *wei* involves clinging to reified conceptual distinctions and institutionalized moral discourses. The Daoist practices "forgetting" (*wang*, 忘) those culturally sedimented beliefs such that they can bring a renewed attention and awareness to nature in its indeterminacy and flux. Generally, the capacity to respond to situations in a way that is phenomenologically grounded and attentive is what can be referred to as being attuned to situations. Its opposite, the inability to wholly bring attention to situations due to sedimented habits of perception and belief is what this book calls "alienation." The Daoist sage is perceptually attuned to the world because they do not suffer under perceptual alienation.

Nonegoistic Conduct (無為) in the *Daodejing*

For the Daoist, an overly abstract and detached account of human life provides little assistance for dealing with the complexities of existence. The Daoist would further suggest that a "fixed" moral interpretation of situations is both misguided and self-undermining. An important lesson outlined in the *Daodejing* and the *Zhuangzi* is of recognizing how both language and the abstract concepts formed in experience can often (*ironically*) undermine their supposed efficacy. The same goes for abstract moral ideals and ethical principles. Culturally sedimented beliefs, like *institutionalized* morality and moral discourses, become corrupt and self-undermining as soon as they are raised to a certain status or class of judgment. This is not to say that the Daoist simply rejects every kind of human institution (theoretical, social, political, etc.). The Daoist critique of such institutions, by showing how they become self-undermining when developed to a certain point, is meant to remedy their ill effects. Ziporyn has previously argued this point as well with his account of "ironic coherence."[1] The Daoist critiques their contemporaries always with the idea in mind that, with a proper understanding of what moral discourses are *actually doing* and what they were *meant to do*, such a critique will help us understand what forms of conduct are actually ameliorative. In other words, the Daoist can be understood as providing a metaethical reflection on how institutionalized morality arose and why it has become problematic. The Daoist then provides a *functionally equivalent* but better set of practices. They do not simply critique their contemporary cultural institutions. Their critique promises to provide a *functionally better* but (*ironically*) different alternative in the sense that the Daoist provides a new paradigm for understanding human society. The Daoist is not simply "deconstructing" the ideas of their philosophical opponents and their respective cultural assumptions. They are simultaneously *reconstructing* a nonanthropocentric account of values and interrelationship.

The distinction between "coercive action" (*wei*) and "nonegoistic conduct" (*wuwei*) signifies the difference between who and what the Daoist critiques and the Daoist's own ironic solution to societal ills. The *irony* of acting *wuwei* is due to how the Daoist believes their own account of human conduct functions better than other philosophical alternatives. If the Daoist were merely rejecting that there was *any* way of evaluating and valuing behavior, they would say that explicitly. What we have instead is the promise that the *real* way to achieve what the Confucians and Mohists desired is to reject their respective projects and to adopt the Daoist's understanding of nature and values. The *determinate* and "purposive" way of the Confucians and Mohists is misguided, yet the desire to achieve harmony and alleviate social ills is still shared by the Daoist. The Daoist ideal of *wuwei* is not a nihilistic or reclusive one. The Daoist sage is one at home in both the context of human relationships and within the larger context of nature in all of its constant fluctuation and indeterminacy.

The distinction between *wuwei* and *wei* represents two different predispositions to act and two different ways of relating to the conceptual aspect of human experience. *Wuwei* involves spontaneous conduct because particular habits of thinking and belief no longer obstruct the capacity to understand and respond to situations. One reason behind why "knowledge" can end up inhibiting conduct is that certain culturally sedimented beliefs are simply misinterpretations of what things are and of what their relationship is to the rest of the world. Another reason is that certain habits of thinking and belief do not immediately adjust or shape the human capacity to respond to and perceive situations. The Daoist aspires to be "without knowledge" (*wuzhi*). Just as *wuwei* is not a literal absence of action, *wuzhi* is not the complete rejection of conceptual "knowledge." *Wuzhi* realizes an experiential distance from cognitive distinctions by contextualizing them within the noncognitive context of human experience (as explained in chapter 1). When it comes to the relationship between theory and practice, we can best understand the Daoist as holding that *practice takes precedence to theory*. An example of the Daoist's irony promising to *function* better than their opponents can be seen in *Daodejing* passage 38.

> The highest virtue is not [intentionally] virtuous, therefore it has virtue; The lowest virtue does not lose [sight of its] virtue, therefore it is without virtue. The highest virtue is "without action" and "without intention" [i.e., without means of *wei*, 無以為]. The highest benevolence [*ren*, 仁] "acts imposingly" but is without the intention of "acting imposingly"; The highest "right conduct" [*yi*, 義] "acts imposingly" and has the intention of "acting imposingly." The highest "social customs" [*li*, 禮] "acts imposingly" and [when] it does not resonate, thus they seize the arm and force it.[2]

For the Daoist philosopher, those who act *wei* or "have the intention to *wei*" (有以為) are not truly virtuous. They act in a way that is uncompromising, imposing, and ultimately politically motivated (as it bears some relationship to power and hierarchy). It is a form of conduct that is tied to a sense of self as independent (egoism). As is the case with acting *wei*, the person that always has virtue (*de*) on their mind does not actually possess virtue. It is only when one loses conscious sight of virtue that one can say they embody virtue. Those who act *wei* bear a relationship to their beliefs and habits of thinking that inhibit their ability to understand situations. They believe they are performing an act that is moral, but such conduct is in reality coercive as it is ultimately tied to a separate sense of self and power. The passage above suggests that "those of highest benevolence (*ren*) act imposingly (*wei*) but do not have the intention of acting as such" (上仁為之而無以為). Although intentionally imposing an external order onto other people is problematic (as is suggested with *yi* and *li*), the *root* of the problem is not that persons act purposively and thereby intend to impose their own sense of order onto others. Daoists critique the central Confucian virtue of "benevolence" (*ren*) because they take the Confucian *attitude* as an *interpretation of nature* that is coercive and misguided. As the passage suggests, the Confucian is *predisposed* towards acting coercively regardless of their intention to act on their beliefs. It is an unintentional or spontaneous form of coercive conduct. It is the Confucians' *interpretive framework*, "final-vocabulary," and "horizon of relevance,"[3] that predisposes them to *mis*interpreting situations, and this is the root cause of their *wei* conduct. For example, it is the belief that they are a self of great merit that undermines their supposed benevolence. The conceptual and interpretive framework that informs the conduct of persons acting *wei* is what is ignorant. Furthermore, it is precisely the *moral attitude* (in its current manifestation) that further inhibits the ability to understand why such "moral" conduct does not help to alleviate social ills. It is important to note that, for the Daoist, there is still a distinction made between those of the "higher virtue" and "lower virtue" (that is, the Daoist is *clearly evaluating forms of conduct*). The Confucian virtues simply are not the "highest virtues." The highest Confucian virtue (*ren*) is critiqued as imposing, yet the Daoist does not think the Confucian has the intention of acting coercively. From the Daoist perspective, the real problem is that human society has departed from Dao or the "way" and this represents a form of ignorance. The Confucians' desire to ameliorate social disharmony is not completely wrong-headed. The problem is that their project is informed by a misinterpretation of social reality.

The Daoist has the same desire to ameliorate social ills but recognizes that the Confucian social project is undermining itself. The key to understanding why the Confucian (or really, any moralist project) is self-undermining can be seen from the first few lines of passage 38. Those persons that have lesser virtue are not able to "lose their virtue" (不失德) because they have a reified understanding of persons and of their virtues or lack thereof. Virtues become valued objects ("virtues") to possess, reified as secondary qualities that belong to individuals, when persons are themselves interpreted as distinct and taking precedence to their relationships. When this happens, persons are ignorantly made into distinct things where virtues are understood as desirable and valuable properties instead of being understood as what they truly are: dispositions that predispose persons such that they flourish in their relationships and respond to situations in ways that maximize their ability to *cocreate valuable interrelationships*. When the Confucian (or any moralist) takes virtues and reifies them, this is one reason why "virtue" and the resultant moral discourse that emerges from such reification becomes self-undermining. The idea that there are "virtues" and "persons of virtue" leads to an egoism and moral narcissism, a topic that will be addressed further in chapter 6.

There is a sense that what the Daoist is describing in passage 38 of the *Daodejing* is a historical or genealogical account of the emergence of moral discourse and the institutions that accompany them. Such institutional forms of morality become self-undermining because they do not identify the source of our problems. What is best, for the Daoist, is to not depart from Dao. The Confucian project is one that attempts to address social ills but ends up only perpetuating the same patterns of behavior that were problematic to begin with. Passage 38 continues:

> Thus, when *Dao* is lost there is "virtue" (*de*); lose "virtue" and then "benevolence" (*ren*) emerges, lose "benevolence" and then "right conduct" (*yi*) emerges, lose "right conduct" and then "social customs" (*li*) emerge. That which is "social customs," this is a sign of weak loyalty and trustworthiness and is the first sign of chaos. For the person of foresight, this is [merely] the decorations of Dao and the beginnings of stupidity. Therefore, the great gentleman resides in [Dao's] thickness and does

not dwell in the thin; resides in Dao's true/solid and does not dwell in its [mere] ornaments. Thus, abandoning the former and obtaining this.[4]

The Daoist describes how social practices can develop to such an extent that we further depart from Dao. When moral discourses and practices become institutionalized, they are developed into a reality that departs from their naturalistic and empirical roots. They become cultural forms and practices that are no longer grounded in empirical, causal interrelationships. These practices and beliefs then become related to the concrete problems that they were initially meant to address in a way that obscures the ability to understand how and why they have become problematic. As with how "virtues" can become aesthetically pleasing to the reflective sense of self, ossified values can become self-referential to the point of becoming "flowery" or aesthetically pleasing as well. When a moral discourse becomes thick or "fixed," the Daoist believes this is when we should become the most apprehensive. The Confucian practices and cultural institutions are guilty of both departing from Dao and of promoting moral obtuseness. This is because people end up focusing on the merely aesthetic and superficial aspects of what is *actually valuable* about the *maintenance of valuable ways of interrelating*. They believe that their social practices and the accompanying institutions are sufficient for instilling the right dispositions in people. When mere formulaic participation in cultural institutions becomes the determining factor in explaining whether conduct is deemed valuable or good, this is the beginning of ignorance and the undermining of social institutions. This is precisely when persons of "lower virtue" can easily maintain their false sense of merit. For example, ritualized mourning is done to help give form to the emotions that arise with the loss of loved ones.[5] When such social practices become formulaic and rigid, they obscure the relationships that they were initially meant to elucidate. Instead of helping persons understand loss, they reinforce arrogance, moral narcissism, and distract us from understanding death. The idea that a person could be *good* at mourning should strike everyone as misguided and even backwards. To be *good* at mourning is to be *good* at experiencing loss of value (i.e., to be good at experiencing absence of the valuable interrelationships that constitute who we are). Although the Daoist believes that death should not be hastily given the label good or bad, the death of a loved one involves the meaningfully felt absence of valuable relationships. Grief undergone without the misguided, rarefied beliefs about what the process *should* involve would be just that: mourning. It is the unfettered capacity to understand what this particular absence means and of being predisposed such that one knew it was inevitably coming. Death and change are inevitable parts of existence. Because of the particularity that emerges from nature, the death of friends and family members should not be given uniform expression. A formulaic expression of what death *should* involve would not do justice to or fully express the particularity of such relationships. Textually speaking, the *Zhuangzi* does not suggest that we are stoic in the face of death and change.[6] Being "known" (*ming*, 名) as a "good mourner" becomes desirable (and problematic) because it has become tied to power and social hierarchy. A "good mourner," in the sense that one does it inauthentically and egoistically, is someone that is showing the appearance ("decorations") of understanding life and death while not really having cultivated the emotional sensitivity that such institutions and practices were meant to create. The root of these problems is the reification of values and egoism. In other words, the Daoist is apprehensive of the tendency to dwell and cling to the "named" (*ming*, 名) aspects of experience and to the reified products of thinking (*zhi*, 知). We need to forget (*wang*, 忘) these aspects of experience such that we achieve a perceptual and existential distance from them. In doing this, we return to Dao and are no longer alienated from our embeddedness in nature. In not clinging to "names" and "knowledge," we develop the dispositions that are *wuzhi* which, in turn, encourages *wuwei* conduct.

"Nonegoistic Conduct" and Spontaneity in the *Zhuangzi*

The Daoist sage is described with an unconventional vocabulary that will sound strange to philosophers accustomed to thinking about human subjectivity within the framework of a representational account of mind. Why the dispositions of the Daoist sage would be appealing will be unclear. Perhaps the best example of how the Daoist describes the dispositions of the Daoist sage but an example that will be unclear to many readers is one found near the end of chapter 7, "Sovereign Responses for Ruling Power) (應帝王) of the *Zhuangzi*. As it suggests, it is best to cultivate these dispositions: "In this way, embody the endlessness and roam where there is no sign, fully living through whatever is received from Heaven without thinking anything has been gained, thus remaining a vacuity, nothing more. The Utmost Person uses his mind like a mirror, rejecting nothing, welcoming nothing, responding but not storing. Thus he can overcome all things without harm."[7] To embody (*ti*, 體) the endless and to roam (*you*, 遊) where there are no signs are not simple prescriptions to follow. As is often the case in the Daoist texts, the Daoist is described as being of particular predisposition to act. They *embody* particular sensitivities and interrelationships. These dispositions involve greater levels of attention and awareness than non-Daoist sages usually possess. There are two aspects of experience that, from this passage, the Daoist would be without when they "use their mind like a mirror." First, the Daoist would roam where there is "no sign." This is a reference to the "names" (*ming*, 名) and rational symbols projected on to experience by the human mind. Second, the Daoist would preserve the life they were "allotted" (*ming*, 命) and not think that "anything was gained" or achieved. They would not think they possessed a distinct characteristic that would likewise be projected onto experience by the human mind (that is, they would not interpret themselves as a "thing" that possesses certain named properties). In being without these features while perceiving the world, the Daoist would be an emptiness, uninhibited by aspects of cognition that play a role in obstructing perception. It is because of this emptiness that their perception of situations is likened to a mirror uninhibited by obstructions and capable of impartially reflecting all things. Although the belief that people can perceive situations more or less accurately or efficaciously is not by itself a controversial claim, from the Daoist perspective, the conceptual aspects of human experience can play a role in obstructing perception of the world. Merely having the right concepts does not, by itself, promote greater understanding of situations. Cultivating the sensitivity to respond to situations involves different practices. For the Daoist, the capacity to best perceive situations involves the freedom from becoming "fixed" on the aspects of experience that are reflective or that involve the imagination *re*-presenting experience through the formation of concepts. It is not that thinking and concept formation per se are problematic. Our perception of situations is inhibited when awareness dwells solely on these secondary, cognitive aspects of experience.

The *Zhuangzi*, like the *Daodejing*, is critical of the moralist perspective. This is not because of morality per se, but because of the paradoxical way that a "purposive" moral attitude undermines itself and produces the opposite of what was intended. Chapter 4 of the "Inner Chapters" (especially the first story) and in the "Primitivist" "Outer Chapters"[8] are places where this theme is most explicit in the *Zhuangzi*. In the first story of chapter 4, *Confucius (*denotes when the character "Confucius" is a mouthpiece for Zhuangzi) reminds his student that "the Consummate Persons of old made sure they had it in themselves before they tried to put it into others. If what is in yourself is still unstable, what leisure do you have to worry about some tyrant?"[9] Another way of framing this, different from arguing that *practice takes precedence to theory*, is that the cultivated dispositions and the sensitivity to situations that results from such dispositions take precedence to theory and the formation of beliefs. For the Daoist, "knowledge" and the naming of reality will inevitably be an incomplete process as there will always be "something uncut and unshown."[10] What the rest of this *Zhuangzi* story carefully tries to describe is how prescribing antecedent ethical principles is corrupting, self-defeating but, most importantly, *not what persons needed to be focused on to begin with*. For the Daoist, a nonrelational, nonprocessual account of persons and values is both a misinterpretation of the world and a set of beliefs that obstructs our ability to respond to and understand situations with greater levels of receptiveness and care for detail.

The first dialogue of chapter 4 of the *Zhuangzi* provides a step-by-step account of how the Daoist is sensitive to situations. The story starts with one of *Confucius's students asking *Confucius for guidance. There is a tyrant governing a foreign kingdom, and the student wants to take what he has "learned from you [i.e., *Confucius] and to derive some standards and principles from it to apply to this situation. Perhaps then the state can be saved."[11] This is when *Confucius responds by saying that the "consummate Persons of old made sure they had it in themselves before they tried to put it into others"; that is, they cultivated the dispositions before they went out to preach to others. "Having it in yourself" is more complicated than it first might seem. For *Confucius, you cannot show yourself to be too virtuous near a tyrant or it would become obvious that the tyrant was a corrupt person and then he would just kill you. At the other extreme, you cannot just go along with "what other people want you to do," or they would question your sincerity and no longer trust you. The story continues with the student theorizing about how he can go about changing the character of the tyrant for the better. The student twice suggests ethical prescriptions for this situation. *Confucius rejects them and provides reasons why they might not work. When *Confucius finally offers an answer to this question of "what principles or standards can be prescribed to this situation," he answers with an account of "mind fasting" or *xin zhai* (心齋).

> If you merge all your intentions into a singularity, you will come to hear with the mind rather than with the ears. Further, you will come to hear with the vital energy (*qi*) rather than with the mind. For the ears are halted at what they hear. The mind is halted at whatever verifies its preconceptions. But the vital energy is an emptiness, a waiting for the presence of beings. The Course alone is what gathers in this emptiness. And it is this emptiness that is the fasting of the mind.[12]

By cultivating noncognitive habits, one becomes more sensitive and receptive to the meaning of situations they encounter. Instead of merely bringing attention to language ("listening with the ears") or abstract conceptualization ("listening with the mind"), we need to bring as much of the qualitative field of experience to the foreground of consciousness. The problem that the Daoist is trying to deal with in this passage is that being "fixed" and clinging to the cognitive aspects of human experience (*zhi*) while ignoring the noncognitive background is precisely what is involved with conduct that is *wei* and "rule following." *Confucius's student comes seeking "principles and standards" (則) to address this situation. *Confucius's response is (ironically) that we must not cling to prescribed standards and "fixed" ethical principles, and instead we should cultivate a perceptual receptiveness to the indeterminate (empty) or aesthetic "thus-so-ness" quality of situations (i.e., to be attentive to the natural world as irreducibly cocreative and interdependent). Prescribing fixed ethical standards and following "rules or conduct" ends up undermining the ability to bring adequate attention to situations. Just as with the *Daodejing*, a reified account of "value" and "virtue" obfuscates the concrete interrelationships persons share with each other. We need to, instead, maintain greater levels of attention to the immediate and concrete way things are meaningfully interrelated.

The *Zhuangzi*, as with the *Daodejing*, is focused on identifying the dispositions that are best attuned to the world. There are many phrases in the *Zhuangzi* like "making use of clarity" (以明) and "resting in what is not known" (知止其所不知) that should be understood as suggesting that cognitive habits within the field of experience need to be pacified such that attention is increasingly brought to the noncognitive dimensions of experience (*wuzhi*, 無知). Phrases in the *Zhuangzi* such as "sitting and forgetting" (坐忘) and "heart/mind fasting" (心齋) describe cultivation practices. Each involves the practice of quieting (forgetting) the habits of thinking by focusing on breathing, the body, and maintaining attention to the qualitative aspects of experience such that we maintain a renewed and continued attention to the immediate quality of situations.

In the next story of chapter 4, the dialogue introduces another dilemma that is similar to the previous story. The Duke of She, Zigao, is designated as an envoy to the state of Qi. Failure in his mission will bring him trouble. Success in this mission will be difficult. The service Zigao must fulfill to his superiors is bringing him great levels of anxiety, and he has not yet departed. He asks *Confucius (as mouthpiece) for advice on what to do. First, *Confucius describes how there are two great constraints in the world; the first is "fate" (*ming*, 命), and the other is duty or responsibility (*yi*, 義). These features of social reality are two distinct kinds of constraints that will always situate human conduct. It is "fate" to be bound to our parents and to be limited in lifespan. There are then also political and social obligations that have their own respective weights. The first part of Confucius's answer here is that we must be attentive to what is unavoidable in situations. Like the previous story, the story then provides Zhuangzi's answer to this dilemma. Just as with the "fasting of the mind," the solution involves a greater attention to and absorption in the present situation. As the Zhuangzi claims, "Being a son or a subordinate, there will inevitably be things you cannot avoid having to do. Absorb yourself in the realities of the task at hand to the point of forgetting your own existence. Then you will have no leisure to delight in life or abhor death. That would make this mission of yours quite doable."[13] Apart from understanding what can and cannot be avoided in a given situation, the text suggests that we perceive situations in such a way that it is tantamount to forgetting our own existence. Underlying this story is an understanding of the self as interdependent and *internally related* to its environment. For the Daoist, the process of "forgetting" the self is simultaneous with an attunement to nature because human conscious life on the most fundamental level discloses and internalizes the world (the self is not "simply-located" and is always also what "it is not," that is, its environment). The belief that persons are independent selves is both wrong and an example of how beliefs and abstractions can become ossified such that persons are predisposed to acting *wei*. As with the *Daodejing*, the tendency to make things or people into independently existing objects contributes to misunderstanding situations. When we can "forget" and break down the former habits of perception that limit our ability to perceive situations, we then act *wuwei*.

Daoist Irony as a Functional Equivalent to Morality

If we read stories in the *Zhuangzi* like the ones above and believe that they only describe the capacity to respond spontaneously and effortlessly to situations, this misses one of the most significant aspects of Daoist irony. Daoist irony promises to *function* in a way that still fulfills the promises that their philosophical counterparts cannot. Traditionally, both in Chinese and Western philosophy, moral discourse is developed with the intent to provide a framework or *reasons* to act moral where moral conduct is usually understood as contrary to selfish interest. For example, Michael Slote describes the distinction between prudence and morality as a difference between self-regarding and other-regarding forms of conduct.[14] In the Christian religion, agape is a love for another being that is (strictly speaking) *not* pleasurable for or felt by each individual. When scholars usually discuss altruism and whether such conduct exists, genuine altruism is described as conduct that does not necessarily result in any benefit for the person performing such action. They describe such conduct as not contributing to the fitness of the individual person.[15] One important feature of sui generis moral conduct is that, at its best, it is conduct that is self-less or done with a genuine concern for other people even at the (possible) expense of one's own well-being. Usually, moral conduct is informed by or grounded in a reality or purported "truth" that is often considered contrary to human biology, desire, and self-interest. Although Daoist irony rejects that there is a sui generis "moral order" to the world, Daoists still describe the cultivation of human dispositions as potentially involving spontaneous, self-less conduct. Functionally, the Daoist rejection of a "moral order" is simultaneous with an account of human conduct that is "without self-interest" (*wusi*, 無私).

The Daoist's capacity to act without self-interest is due to perceiving nature with the absence of "knowledge" (*zhi*) or what can be referred to as nonnaturalistic metaphysical assumptions. The *Zhuangzi*, for example, claims that the "Utmost Person has no definite identity, the Spiritlike Person has no particular merit, the Sage has no one name,"[16] and this is not due to sui generis moral reasons. For the Daoist, to believe that there are distinct persons or things in the world is to cling to the cognitive and secondary aspects of experience (*zhi*) while ignoring the primary, indeterminate continuity of all things. If truly moral behavior, for the moralist, is supposed to be "other regarding" and "self-denying," then the Daoist responds by highlighting how such framework is question begging. There is no distinct and independent self to deny. So long as the Daoist cultivates the capacity to perceive situations without "knowledge" (*zhi*), the Daoist can respond to situations without the sense that they are a self with merit, name, and identity. They forget the independent sense of self and become melded with the world.

The most important story in the *Zhuangzi* about "forgetting the self," of realizing how all things are interdependent, and what the meditation practices of Daoism involve comes from the beginning of chapter 2. It states:

> Sir Shoestrap of Southernwall was leaning against his armrest on the ground, gazing upward and releasing his breath into the heavens above—all in a scatter there, as if loosed from a partner.
> Sir Swimmy Faceformed stood in attendance before him. "Who or what is this here?" he asked. Can the body really be made like a withered tree, the mind like dead ashes? What leans against this armrest now is not what leaned against it before."
> Sir Shoestrap of Southwall said, "How good it is that you question this, Yan! What's here now is this: I have lost me. But could you know who or what that is? You hear the piping of man without yet hearing the piping of earth; you hear the piping of earth without yet hearing the piping of Heaven."[17]

Daoist cultivation practices involve breathing and attention exercises that are meant to promote an ability to perceive nature as an undivided continuum. All forms of experience, even the forms of experience that are fixed on "knowledge" (*zhi*), are situated within this context of nature as fundamentally indeterminate. What is lost in this passage is the reflective and abstract independent sense of self. In the Daoist view, the faculties of reasoning and cognition (as secondary aspects of experience) are still a part of the entire field of experience. They are not ontologically separate realities. The problem that the Daoist is diagnosing is that attention can be such that conceptual individuation (the process of "carving up" experience) ends up obfuscating the way experience is disclosed. When this happens, the processes and products of thinking are then experienced *as if* separate from the natural processes of the body interacting with the environment. When human society and culture are developed to the extent that they begin to promote this perceptual alienation from nature, persons experience the world in such a way that they no longer bring their attention to the immediate relationships between themselves and nature. It is *as if* the processes of the body and mind are two separate and distinct realities. What the Daoist is also suggesting in this story is that reflective consciousness, that is, the processes of consciousness that reduplicate and *re*-present aspects of experience, need not be present for all possible forms of experience. As soon as "I have lost me" (吾喪我), we have cultivated a perceptual distance from "knowledge."

With the claim "I have lost me," the *Zhuangzi* is highlighting how experience does not fundamentally involve the experience of a self already individuated from the environment. "Knowledge" and the individuation of things is a secondary process of experience. The Daoist understanding of *wuwei* must also be understood as a kind of self-less conduct. In acting *wuwei*, the Daoist is predisposed to situations such that they do not interpret the persons involved as separate and distinct. Although we can say that the Daoist rejects the existence of sui generis "moral reasons" (as modern science would also reject), they provide a *functionally equivalent* way of addressing situations that addresses selfishness and egoism yet also adds to that list "moral narcissism." The Daoist project is not merely a rejection of sui generis moral facts. They are addressing the same problems their contemporaries are trying to ameliorate. The solution, for the Daoist, is that part of the problem has been that "knowledge," our reified account of things, has become ossified. Only after people are predisposed to interpreting situations as they truly are (fundamentally indeterminate and interdependent) can they behave in ways that are spontaneously without a sense of self as independent. Although moral discourses and transcendent metaphysical realities are most often used to justify conduct that is self-less, the Daoist alternative is to properly perceive nature as a continuous, interdependent flux. The first story of chapter 2 continues with an account of nature as interdependent. It states:

> When the Great Clump belches forth its vital breath, we call it the wind. As soon as it begins, raging cries emerge from all the ten thousand hollows, and surely you cannot have missed the rustle and bustle that then goes on. [. . .] A light breeze brings a small harmony, while a powerful gale makes for a harmony vast and grand. And once the sharp wind has passed, all these holes return to their silent vacuity. [. . .] It is the gusting through all the ten thousand differences that yet causes all of them to come only from themselves. For since every last identity is only what some one of them picks out from it, what identity can there be for their rouser?[18]

Whatever the wind represents (either nature, life, or the *qi* that runs through all things), it allows the cries or voices of the "ten thousand hollows" to emerge. When it stirs, they stir. When it halts, they return to being silent, empty hollows. The empty hollows depend on wind to come to life, yet when they stir, their "emerging comes only from themselves." They are spontaneously particular and unique, and this is because they are *constituted* by the wind in their own unique way. Each *ironically* comes from itself because the voice coming from each hollow is in a state of dependence with the rest of the world.

Taken without considering what Daoist irony promises, scholars might believe that the Daoist vision of human life provides little hope for effecting social change. This is far from the case. As later chapters of this book aim to clarify, the Daoist project provides a more accurate understanding of social and political reality. Through this better understanding of social and political reality, the Daoist project can better ameliorate social ills. Human society has departed from Dao, and departing from Dao involves a unique kind of ignorance. One aspect of this ignorance is the belief in an independent self. If persons are interdependent selves that are functions of their environment, then the usual, moralist ways of interpreting situations and social ills is fundamentally misguided. The Daoist ideal of *wuwei* conduct is grounded in an understanding of interdependent selves. Conduct that is *wei* would be action done from a feeling that persons are independent things.

Institutionalized Morality and Metaphysics as Self-Undermining

From the Daoist perspective, when moral beliefs are informed by a substance ontology or the belief that any thing can be reduced to a "simply located" reality (e.g., like a *causa sui* or "cause in and of itself"), this is a misinterpretation of the natural world because it ignores relational interdependence. As later chapters further illustrate, a substance metaphysics plays a significant role in perpetuating and even justifying suffering and oppression. We could say that "moral fundamentalism" and "moral Manicheanism" constitute a narrow "horizon of relevance or significance" that hinders the ability to understand and respond to problematic situations. There are scholars that ignore these key features of Daoism when they critique it. A good example of this practice appears in "Zhuangzi's Ironic Detachment and Political Commitment" by Bryan Van Norden. In the article, he argues that the *Zhuangzi* cannot provide anything in support of a moral life because Van Norden makes these problematic assumptions.

> (1) First, as thinkers in the hermeneutic tradition have stressed, human beings are creatures who can only make choices against the "horizon of significance" that a final vocabulary supplies. [. . .] (2) When individuals have no final vocabulary in which to articulate deep values, they are easily prone to certain kinds of wrongdoing. Specifically, whether one has any deep values or not, one can see the force of satisfying immediate and superficial desires, such as desires for food, sex, wealth, prestige, and power. [. . .] (3) A third problem is that, in the absence of a final vocabulary, it is far too easy for those who wield power to do so in an arbitrary or self-serving manner.[19]

To assume this much is to demonstrate exactly what Rorty warns us against in *Contingency, Irony, Solidarity*: that with final vocabularies, "their user has no noncircular argumentative recourse"[20] when trying to justify their position. Making such assumptions, as Van Norden does, is equally to make assumptions about the mind, experience, and what motivates human action. To then appeal to these unjustified assumptions when critiquing another philosophical tradition is question-begging argumentation. The *Zhuangzi* directly challenges the belief that language and abstract ideas exhaustively and accurately correspond to the natural world. In fact, the Daoist is explicitly critical of the very real threat that "knowledge" and "learning" predispose us towards acting in ways that are completely arbitrary. There is nothing more arbitrary than metaphysical beliefs that are nonnatural and unempirical in quality. Even worse is that (*as history has shown us*) such metaphysical beliefs maintain their aesthetic and affective character in spite of the fact that they do not improve the lives of people. People cling to such aesthetic ideals regardless of their inability to bring about any change in their condition.[21] The aesthetic and political effect of nonnatural metaphysical beliefs helps to normalize and rationalize coercive social practices by providing an epistemological framework *in spite of* empirical reality.

Traditionally, the way the moralist has framed moral issues in the West has gone like this: persons have bodies with (irrational) desires. Some traditions even believe that humans are born with various degrees of "bad" or "evil" aspects to their nature. Selfish desire or the innate "badness" is often considered a cause of social ills. Desire or our "bad nature" needs to be kept in check or inhibited with a causal force or higher "reasons" to act.[22] It could be "god's law" or an aspect of our natures that needs to be "nourished" or "perfected" (for example, being justified with the idea of a *telos*, or final end to be fulfilled). Humans could be the kind of being that, built into the nature of our subjectivity, also possess the capacity to transcend our bodily (conditioned or mere animal) existence. For example, one tradition believes we can interpret the world as being peopled by "ends-in-themselves" and thus able to participate in knowledge that is unconditional. Regardless of what form it has taken, metaphysics of this kind has dominated moral discourse. In reality, their framework is question begging as it obscures the nature of social ills, coercion, and how oppression *becomes normalized*. The more important question that we should be asking is how and why the vast majority of peoples living on this earth, historically and presently, do not get the opportunity to achieve the satisfaction of most any kind of desire. Most people struggle to get their basic needs for food and water fulfilled. Before we even get to the question of desire, we have the more fundamental question of why, for well over the past two thousand years, has basic animal fitness been so difficult to achieve? The moral philosopher might come along and insist that human nature is to blame. Selfish desire is to blame, and somehow, desire for wealth, privilege, and power are "immediate and arbitrary." Human nature is to blame for roughly 1 percent of the human population overexploiting, coercing, and oppressing the vast majority of the human community. In doing so, a minority of humans can fulfill their own desires while the remaining majority either struggle for survival, rarely get to participate in culture (the main avenue for channeling desires), or are overexploited such that the majority of their labor goes to benefit the ruling class and so perpetuates hierarchical social and political relationships. If desire and human nature were really the problem, if morality centrally involved the inhibiting of our natures or the suppression of (irrational) desire with a power that was rational and nonnatural, it strikes me as highly implausible that human society (either historical feudal societies or the neofeudalism of Western capitalist imperialism) would emerge in the form that it has. In reality, a small human minority has been able to suppress, coerce, and inhibit the desires and tendencies of their fellow humans while maintaining the freedom to not be held to the same social constraints. Entire social and political institutions and the cultural forms that reinforce said institutions enable this level of inequality to perpetuate. The *conditions* are such that the ideas and institutions that inform and limit human conduct make the levels of inequality and control of material reality even possible. Although selfish desire might play a role in perpetuating these hierarchical political relationships, there are numerous other cultural (and *culturally provisional*) factors that play an even greater role.

How does human society manage to get to the point where the power and wealth of a small minority of the population surpasses that of the vast majority? How does human society end up developing into deeply stratified class and social divisions but also manage to perpetuate such economic and material hierarchies? The story that the moralist tells us is that nature, greed, and desire are to blame. In the absence of overt physical force (a practice that also benefits from a cultural ideology that normalizes violent conduct), in order to sustain an inegalitarian social and political arrangement, this economic and material hierarchy must be made to look natural, reasonable, and even "moral" to the rest of the population. The problem is not necessarily due to human nature. A cultural and ideological apparatus and the enculturation of a population with said "conceptual framework" (*zhi*) are necessary to legitimize these social and political relationships. For the Daoist philosopher, "knowledge" (*zhi*) is needed in order to normalize forms of life that are undesirable, unfree, and involve greater levels of suffering. Simultaneous with the development of a political ruling class that maintains economic, cultural, and material privileges above and beyond the majority of the population is a cultural ideology that helps to make sense of these political relationships. In other words, a "final vocabulary" (which provides a "horizon of relevance") is necessary to normalize undesirable forms of life. The best "final vocabularies" for doing this are those that are unempirical and explicitly antiempirical in the sense that they preach that empirical experience and the immediate, natural relationships humas bear to their world are either irrational and/or immoral. Religions have often played a role in normalizing forms of life that involve passively accepting greater levels of suffering. When the population is told to deny their desires while maintaining forms of life that involve their desires be limited by the ruling class, the majority of the population is taught to reject exactly the *nonarbitrary, sense-giving* relationships organisms use to make sense of their world. Whether it is through a moral or religious discourse, when the population is taught to be satisfied with the suffering that they incur due to the way that society is organized, this helps the ruling class perpetuate such hierarchical relationships.

If philosophers play loose with what they demand of a moral discourse, it is easy to see how the same demands that might seem to be necessary characteristics of moral behavior play the same role that "knowledge" plays in making coercion and oppression seem normal. Altruism, for example, is often described as the kind of conduct that is done without any benefit to the agent doing the action. It is conduct that is (potentially) to the benefit of others with either no benefit to oneself and/or even (possibly) a detriment to one's own well-being. In another context, we could call this the "protestant work ethic" or the way capitalist society involves the alienation of labor such that the products and fruits of our individual labor are not granted to the individual performing such work (an even more egregious case being full blown slavery). With the overexploitation of workers, any discourse that functions to inhibit or extinguish the self-interest and desire of persons fulfills the role in normalizing unegalitarian social and political relationships. Put another way, the most powerful tools for anyone hoping to "wield power" in an "arbitrary and self-serving manner" would be "knowledge" or the institutionalized (*mis*)education of the population. At its best, this (*mis*)education would teach the population that our "deeply held values" are necessary in order to inhibit our desires, deny our natural and embedded existence, and would further justify these social practices with a conceptual framework that was nonempirically verifiable or, worse, *virtuously* nonempirically verifiable. There is absolutely no better conceptual framework for normalizing arbitrary social practices and coercive political relationships than nonnatural and nonempirical metaphysical assumptions such that the population learns to misinterpret the world and, in spite of empirical and natural relationships with the world, this way of seeing the world is equated with moral behavior. The problematic and self-undermining moralist attitude tries to attribute the cause of social ills to metaphysical substances like individual "agents" or "human nature." This ignores how the epistemological framework that systematically shapes and informs society is what really enables and normalizes suffering and oppression.

For the Daoist, the arbitrariness of cultural forms is due to them becoming dislodged from and no longer grounded in empirical and natural interrelationships. "Knowledge" plays a role in "blotting out" or filtering human experience in ways that inhibit our understanding of the world. When such forms of "knowledge" persist, this produces a unique form of ignorance or what this book calls "alienation." This point is missed by the traditional moral philosopher in the West. As the Daoist is right to point out, language and the formation of concepts can play both inhibiting and liberating roles in human life. The problem that the Daoist is diagnosing is of a context far wider than the theory we get from academic philosophers about "right conduct" and the right antecedent principles to act. Why do whole communities come to believe that certain beliefs and forms of life are of value when they simply are not? The Western philosopher believes that with the right facts and antecedent principle, we can achieve greater understanding of social ills. The reason for "bad" or "immoral" conduct is then attributed to an "agent" that bears *sole* responsibility for said conduct. Apart from these ideas simply being question begging as they assume that human mind can potentially "reflect" reality with the right concepts (it certainly does *not* do this), from the Daoist perspective, the most important form of education we can get involves the cultivation of attention and awareness of the immediate relationships people embody with respect to their environment. This also entails a transformation in how we relate to the cultural aspect of human experience or, really, a return to naturalness and our original spontaneity. When we can achieve this, we no longer cling to "knowledge" and the "names" we attribute to things. It is tantamount to a perceptual distance from the products of conceptual thinking such that these habits no longer inhibit perception of situations.

Philosophical Irony, Dewey, Rorty, and Lao-Zhuang Daoism

Before moving on, it is important to revisit works that have argued that Daoism bears a resemblance to American pragmatism and, in particular, the neo-pragmatists Rorty and Quine. There are also scholars that are skeptical that the *Zhuangzi* and Daoist irony could provide any kind of moral guidance. As a few scholars have also suggested, the *Zhuangzi* could arguably be understood as a position like the "ironist" that Rorty describes in *Contingency, Irony, and Solidarity*.[23] To help clarify and defend philosophical Daoism against claims that it is morally dubious, it will be useful to see how the Daoist philosopher is not quite Rorty's "ironist." For the Daoist, values are rooted in our experience of the natural world. Furthermore, nonnaturalistic accounts of values are forms of "knowledge" (*zhi*) that simply perpetuate alienation from nature and the ability for persons to understand what forms of interrelating with the world are even valuable. Following Johnson's *Morality for Humans*, we can also consider most nonnaturalistic accounts of values as espousing a form of "moral fundamentalism." The Daoist takes it that sui generis moral facts cannot possibly exist. They can also be understood as rejecting all forms of morality that fall under what can be called "moral Manicheanism" or the interpretation of situations such that complex causal relationships are naively reduced to "simply located" realities such as essences, persons acting from a *will* or faculty of reason that is believed to be *causa sui*, and the belief that conduct can be interpreted in an ontologically bi-furcated and mutually exclusive way (like "good and evil"). When moral discourses develop into "moral fundamentalism" and "moral Manicheanism," this is the point where such discourses become self-undermining in producing and legitimizing the same suffering they were developed to ameliorate ("those who *wei* ruin it," 為者敗之). "Moral Manicheanism," as a misinterpretation of social reality, is also a form of ideology that makes persons and cultures precisely what they themselves condemn (evil, monsters, barbarians, etc.). As Nietzsche warned, "those who go searching for monsters should make sure they do not become monsters themselves."[24] A moral interpretation of social ills that relies on intellectually suspect (nonnaturalistic) metaphysical assumptions is precisely what the Daoist is critiquing when they criticize conduct that is *wei* or "purposive." To act *wuwei* is more than acting spontaneously. To act *wuwei* is to be predisposed such that persons are not framing their understanding of situations through a problematic moral metaphysics.

Although Rorty's work has much in common with the *Zhuangzi*, there are important differences that separate the two traditions. When previous scholars have compared Daoism to Rorty's work, it is Rorty's description of the "ironist" that they reference. Rorty defines the "ironist" in *Contingency, Irony, and Solidarity* as follows:

> (1) She has radical and continuing doubts about the final vocabulary she currently uses, because she has been impressed by other vocabularies, vocabularies taken as final by people or books she has encountered; (2) she realizes that argument phrased in her present vocabulary can neither underwrite nor dissolve these doubts; (3) insofar as she philosophizes about her situation, she does not think that her vocabulary is closer to reality than others, that it is in touch with a power not herself.[25]

If we were not careful when reading Rorty and simply searched for those passages that sounded "dubiously relativistic," this just cited passage would appear to be a great find. Divorced from the rest of Rorty's project in *Contingency, Irony, Solidarity*, Rorty seems to be merely arguing for a form of skepticism. Such an accusation misses the main thesis of his work. As Rorty claims in the beginning of the work, the project he envisions is the ongoing task of cultivating solidarity that "is to be achieved not by inquiry but by imagination, the imaginative ability to see strange people as fellow sufferers. Solidarity is not discovered by reflection but created. It is created by increasing our sensitivity to the particular details of the pain and humiliation of other, unfamiliar sorts of people."[26] Rorty's project of cultivation will not make much sense if we assume a traditional understanding of action and its relationship to theoretical knowledge. Just as is the case with earlier pragmatism, Rorty's project is primarily focused on both what can be called "philosophy of action" and an account of human beings as more than merely cognitive, language using mammals. As Shusterman describes it, "Rorty firmly refuses to ground ethics in reason. Instead he champions feeling as the underlying ground for the ethical consensus that generates our commitment to human rights and other central moral principles."[27] This is because, for the pragmatist, thought and reason are not what motivate human beings to act. Thought and reflection, by their very nature, inhibit and delay action. For Rorty, Dewey and James, emotion and desire are what motivates human action. "Thinking in itself does not produce doing. Reflection, deliberation, and reasoning indeed inhibit action, as Dewey (again after James) insists: "all thinking exercises by its very nature an inhibitory effect. It delays the operation of desire, and tends to call up new considerations which alter the nature of the action to which one felt originally impelled (*E* 189)."[28]

Furthermore, thought and cognition are secondary and derivative aspects of experience. Theory is useful for guiding the cultivation of habits but the possession of theory by itself simply cannot replace moral cultivation (or growth of *any* sort). In other words, *practice/cultivation takes precedence to theory* for pragmatists like James, Dewey and Rorty. For the pragmatist, as well as for the Daoist, the possession of a "final vocabulary" does not immediately adjust the conduct of human beings. What is most important for becoming an ethically sensitive human being is to cultivate a perceptual (noncognitive/nonconceptual, i.e., qualitative or aesthetic) sensitivity to the particularity of situations. Rorty's project at times does depart from the earlier pragmatists, yet in this respect, he is still consistent with his predecessors. James, for example, "urges a meliorism of perception, the need to liberate ourselves from 'a certain blindness' we have concerning the tastes and feelings of 'people different from ourselves.'"[29] Pragmatists have a fundamentally different understanding of what is required to be an ethically sensitive human being. To use Gadamerian vocabulary, Rorty argues that without a *wider* "horizon of relevance," people are less likely to *even recognize the suffering of others* (i.e., to even *interpret* situations such that they recognize or acknowledge the suffering of others). With the pragmatist's account of *lived* experience, the habits of perception and cognition disclose different aspects of the field of experience. The meaning of experience and the isolation of objects in the world from their contexts are not already a given datum of experience. Instead, habits (both noncognitive and cognitive) structure and restructure the content of experience. Certain features in the total field of experience are brought to the foreground, while other features recede to the background. This is precisely what Rorty implies when he states that (mere) reflection on and theorizing about moral theory will not produce a "reason" or "motivation" to care about the suffering of others. Though this might sound suspect to some philosophers, their concerns are structured by question-begging assumptions. For Rorty's "liberal ironist," the main concern is an issue of attention. It is about cultivating an *absence* of certain ways of thinking/believing that prevent us from even noticing the suffering of others when it occurs. A "final vocabulary" can limit attention by making particular aspects of experience appear insignificant or meaningless.[30] The capacity to respond to situations with greater sensitivity and receptiveness demands the cultivation of dispositions. Stubbornly clinging to one's own "final vocabulary" would simply limit our horizon of relevance. Fortunately, we are not merely language-using, concept-forming mammals.

The purpose of this book is not to exhaustively defend Rorty against his critics. There has been much said about Rorty, and there have been more charitable yet still critical accounts of Rorty's work. In distinguishing Rorty from Daoist philosophy, I want to suggest that what Rorty is lacking, what he still needs for his own project yet explicitly denies, is a radical empiricist understanding of experience. As Shusterman is right to point out, Rorty "differs radically from the classical pragmatists by vehemently rejecting the whole concept of experience, a concept that is undeniably crucial for Peirce, James, and Dewey. Rorty instead substitutes language as philosophy's essential medium and substance."[31] Alexander has criticized Rorty on this as well. As Alexander states, "Rorty's view [. . .] reflects the heritage of positivism's radical dualism between cognitive meaning and emotive meaninglessness, only Rorty has given up the cognitive side of the doctrine, leaving him with little but emotivism. He recognizes the need for some kind of viable, humane social order, but he has no way of explaining how a moral imagination is educated or how it works."[32]

Both Alexander and Shusterman are right to point out that what is missing in Rorty's work is an account of aesthetic or noncognitive meaning that is so important for Dewey's own project. For Rorty, "final vocabularies" can obstruct and obfuscate experience such that we fail to recognize the occurrence of suffering. What is left unsaid by Rorty is an account of *what* is obstructed by clinging to our own "final vocabularies." For Dewey, it is the immediate quality of experience that is obstructed which is the primary "stuff" that constitutes our lives. These are the aesthetic or qualitatively and immediately felt dimensions of experience underlying cognitive habits. As Dewey describes it in *Art as*

Experience, the noncognitive dimensions of experience are immediately felt as meaningful yet in a way different from abstract ideas and linguistic meaning. The meaning or significance of aesthetic experience is not reducible to propositional statements. For Dewey, "If all meanings could be adequately expressed in words, the arts of painting and music would not exist. There are values and meanings that can be expressed only by immediately visible and audible qualities, and to ask what they mean in the sense of something that can be put into words is to deny their distinctive existence."[33] The immediately felt quality of experience is a *function of* the way human organisms are related to the natural environment. For Dewey, *these qualities are immediately knowable and intelligible as such*. Johnson describes this Deweyan understanding of meaning as "grounded in bodily experience; it arises from our feeling of qualities, sensory patterns, movements, changes, and emotional contours. Meaning is not limited only to those bodily engagements, but it always starts with and leads back to them. Meaning depends on our experiencing and assessing the qualities of situations."[34] The ability to highlight certain relationships (always provisional) foregrounds select aspects of the total situation we are experiencing. From Dewey's perspective, we habitually neglect the immediate quality of existence in favor of our own habits of abstraction and thinking. This is, in large part, due to the impoverished state of education in our (Western) culture. Drawing on Dewey, David Hall suggests that the "normal processes of education, [. . .], are sufficient to destroy aesthetic sensitivities by the age of twelve. [. . .] If this is so, it is at least partly because the 'normal processes of education' [. . .] involve the distortion of the aesthetic sense through an overconcern with the moral and scientific sensibilities."[35] Of the numerous ways human beings make sense of the world (and they are not mutually exclusive), of the many different capacities that can be cultivated, Western culture has been encouraging the cultivation of a limited set of habits while neglecting others. What Western education is missing is the cultivation of aesthetic and perceptual sensibilities. For Hall, "aesthetic experience is meant to turn us in the direction of the just-so-ness of things, to give us a sense of the uniqueness of details as constitutive of wider harmonies. This lesson is difficult to learn if our ostensibly aesthetic experiences are distorted by an appreciation of harmonies of a strictly logical or moral kind."[36] The pragmatists would never insist we *merely* cultivate a sensitivity to the qualitative dimensions of experience. What they do suggest is that a lack of cultivating other human potentials is bound to inhibit the ability to respond to situations. We are not merely "rational animals." In Daoist philosophy, the distinction that is made between "knowledge" and being "without knowledge," as I clarified in chapter 1, is similar to Dewey's account of embodied experience in his later works. In light of a radical empiricist understanding of human experience, Rorty does not adequately provide an account of how cognitive habits (*zhi*) can potentially obfuscate perception. The Daoist's naturalistic account of mind will help to explain how the ability to respond to situations involves being sensitive to the noncognitive or qualitative meanings of experience.

Before moving on, it is important to clarify one last major difference between Rorty and Daoism. Rorty's position often appeals to noncognitive dimensions of experience, yet he never clarifies what this involves. For example, Rorty claims "The idea that we all have an overriding obligation to diminish cruelty, to make human beings equal in respect to their liability to suffering, seems to take for granted that there is something within human beings which deserves respect and protection quite independently of the language they speak. It suggests that a nonlinguistic ability, the ability to feel pain, is what is important, and that differences in vocabulary are much less important."[37] There is a sense that what Rorty is arguing is that the noncognitive or nonlinguistic dimensions of existence are what is most valuable or constitutive of the human being. There is also a sense that he is making a claim, *a truth claim*, about the natural causal order and that "something in human beings" is an aspect of human existence that would not be reducible to propositional knowledge. As Rorty also claims, for the "ironist," our "final vocabularies" are not what unites us with other human beings nor is it the capacity to speak languages. What unites humans is the concrete capacity to experience and be susceptible to pain which is not reducible to the languages we speak.[38] Critics of Rorty often miss that, for Rorty, "pain is nonlinguistic: It is what we human beings have that ties us to the nonlanguage-using beasts."[39] Strictly speaking, these are claims about the natural, causal order of the world, that is, *what is real*. The problem is that, in my view, Rorty's antirealism is still partially stuck in the older, representational account of mind. "Meaning" and "truth" are merely the properties of sentences. "Truth," for Rorty, only takes a propositional form. Descriptions of reality with the use of language are the only things that can have truth value.[40] Rorty's antirealism is leveled against analytic philosophers (in particular, the logical positivist). His emphasis on language and his rejection of the pragmatist account of experience confine Rorty to a kind of emotivism (as Alexander claims).

Contrary to Rorty, in *Nature and Experience*, Dewey illustrates how the traditional distinction between "idealism" and "realism" is one that completely misrepresents the nature of experience and reality. Such a dualism assumes that reality is bifurcated. What is "rational" is transcendent and "real," and what is "irrational" is "accidental" and mere appearance. The mind is fundamentally disconnected from reality and only "accidentally" bears a relationship to it. If meaning is not merely a property of propositional statements, then the relationship between human consciousness and nature/reality is not a mere "accidental" or secondary aspect of experience. In *Experience and Nature*, Dewey claims that experience is both *in* and *of* nature. What this means is that the mind's relationship to reality is *equally real*, that is, that the mind's relationship to nature is equally nature. Put another way, this aspect of nature that is called the "mind" is related to nature *through* nature. We could also say, like Stambough when describing Heidegger and Buddhism, that what *is real is no longer assumed to be merely the rational*.[41] This is not then a metaphysical claim about reality "in-itself." What these philosophers have done is change the conversation in such a way that the realist/antirealist distinction is recognized as misguided. Understanding Daoism will require first that we understand its naturalistic account of the mind and the mind's relationship to nature. With their understanding of experience, as is the case with Dewey, the Daoist's processual understanding of nature and experience cannot be characterized using the traditional realism-versus-antirealism dualism.[42]

Conclusion

The Daoist ideal of *wuwei* conduct is not simply "effortless" conduct. The capacity to respond to situations *wuwei* requires a different epistemological orientation. It requires that problematic, ossified beliefs or "knowledge" no longer obstruct our perception of situation. The Daoist critique of "knowledge" is not critical of all forms of knowing but is, instead, a critique of the ossification of conceptual distinctions. Human society can develop in ways that, though initially the social and political institutions had a liberating effect, the same institutions become reified and develop to a point where they play a role in inhibiting human freedom and understanding. Such ideological formations obscure the capacity to both understand the nature of social ills and help to perpetuate the same coercive social practices. Daoist cultivation practices help to mitigate a certain "blindness" that humans acquire due to how they perceptually cling to conceptual aspect of experience. By bringing renewed attention to the dimensions of experience that underly cognitive and abstract thinking, this helps to recontextualize those habits within the wider field of experience, thus allowing us to maintain a phenomenological distance from such abstraction. It is the Daoist capacity to widen the context of experience and of what aspects of experience are brought to the foreground of consciousness that grants them the ability to more wholistically respond to and understand situations. As the rest of this book will continue to highlight, it is practices like "sitting and forgetting" (*zuowang*, 坐忘) and "the fasting of the heart/mind (*xinzhai*, 心齋) that grant persons the habits of perception necessary to respond to situations *wuwei*. In particular, being "without knowledge," "without desire," and "without heart/mind" (*wuxin*, 無心) are key dimensions of the Daoist's predisposition to act.

In the beginning of *Experience and Nature*, Dewey suggests that the "transcendental philosopher has probably done more than the professed sensualist and materialist to obscure the potentialities of daily experience for joy and *for self-regulation* (my italics)."[43] By this, Dewey means that the Platonists, the Cartesians, the Kantians, and logical positivist, have all neglected the empirical relationships to the natural world because of the uncertainty and insecurity that intimidates finite beings like us. The assumption that nature is both "morally suspect" and "unintelligible" is one that runs deeply throughout Western culture. What is more blasphemous is Dewey's suggestion that social problems might naturally regulate themselves if we were brave enough in rejecting nonnaturalist accounts of mind and morality; that there is already something *anarchical* at work that humans can tap into simply by virtue of being continuous functions of nature. For the Daoist, it is the nonnaturalist accounts of mind and morality (metaphysics) that obfuscate our understanding of nature and our relationship to it. Clinging to mental abstractions and ideals as if they were accurate representations of reality is to live in a myth. As the *Zhuangzi* puts it, we are all like "clumps of earth."[44] All of the joys and sufferings of the human condition emerge from the natural interrelationships with the world. Torn between the realm of ideas and the natural world, the transcendentalist metaphysician is doomed to schizophrenia. Far from being liberatory, metaphysics, nonnaturalism, and a failure to be truly empirical in method have only hindered the ability to both understand the human condition and ameliorate social ills. For the Daoist, acquiring an understanding of how all things are interdependent processes gives us the insights we need to ameliorate our problems best. With an embodied understanding of experience both the cognitive (propositional, named, abstract) and noncognitive aspects of experience (desires, perception, the aesthetic aspects of experience) are meaningfully felt or "sense giving" and therefore within the bounds of intelligible and reasonable experience. In other words, the noncognitive aspects of experience provide the living organism with *meaningful* information about their world. In the next few chapters, I will provide further, textually grounded accounts of how and why this is the case for the Daoist philosopher.

Chapter Three

On Being "Without Desire" in Lao-Zhuang Daoism

The Problem of Desire

Building on the previous chapter, this chapter clarifies why the Daoist is critical of desire and why "having desire" (*youyu*, 有欲) inhibits the ability to respond to situations as *wuwei* or with "nonegoistic conduct." The Daoist critique of desire is itself informed by a processual understanding of nature and a phenomenologically informed account of the nature of desires. For the Daoist and contrary to how desire has been characterized in Western philosophy, desires are *culturally learned and cultivated*. They are more abstract and conceptual in character and cannot be understood as merely reflexive, mechanical, and bodily. The Daoist is critical of desire and of a society that is encouraging the creation and accumulation of desires (*yu zuo*, 欲做). This is because desires change how persons observe (*guan*, 觀) and interpret their world. Desires (of the "eye") are indebted to "knowledge" (*zhi*, 知). Desires indebted to "knowledge" contribute to *misperception* (what the Daoist refers to as an anthropocentric or "human" perspective) because these desires are informed by the prior conceptual framework that mistakenly views things as independent. This "human" perspective inevitably leads to ignorance when it comes to the self and self-understanding as well. The conceptual individuation of nature into independent things that are valuable encourages competition which further encourages us to *mis*interpret persons as distinct, atomistic individuals. In reality, each person is *internally related* to nature and to others. The epistemological framework that results from accumulating desires creates the problem of seeing the self and other as externally related and mutually exclusive.

In Daoist philosophy, problematic desires are indebted to "knowledge," which specifically refers to the epistemological framework that contributes to misperception and further inhibits the ability to respond to situations *wuwei*. This epistemology is problematic because persons cling to how aspects of nature have been individuated into independent things. The concepts we form and the "names" we have given to things filter perception in a way that obstructs the ability to perceive situations which, in turn, produces a perceptual and existential form of alienation from nature (as I discuss more in chapter 5).[1] When cultural institutions are shaped by "knowledge," this encourages people to depart from their original spontaneity (*ziran*, 自然). Any society that teaches the population to view and interpret the world through "knowledge" is one that can be said to depart from Dao. The Daoist is critical of only those forms of cultural "knowledge" that make persons ignorant of nature's original spontaneity or *ziran*.

The Daoist understanding of nature and of the human relationship to it presents us with a novel way to critique social and political institutions. It is for this reason that Daoist philosophy does not fit nicely into Western categories and philosophical traditions. The Daoist critique of "desire" and "knowledge," and their understanding of nature as primordially an "uncarved block of wood" (*pu*, 樸), also provides a different account of altruistic behavior. For the Daoist, to be "without desire" and "without knowledge" is simultaneously to be of the dispositions that would behave "without self-interest." The Daoist account of conduct that is "without self-interest" is (*ironically*) in the best interest of each "self-so" aspect of nature. It is a form of life that is in accord with Dao and sensitive to how all things are empty "centers" of nature because persons are unfettered by the problematic values and "knowledge" related to egoism (like the desire for "name" and "merit"). When the abstract features associated with an independent sense of self are absent in experience, this is like realizing that each aspect of nature is an empty center as well. The Daoist sage, as emulating this empty center, can then respond to situations in a morally attuned way. These insights are equally expressed in the Daoist descriptions of the sage as being "without heart/mind" (*wuxin*), "without self-interest" (*wusi*) and as being a "genuine person" (*zhenren*). Contrary to recent scholarship, the Daoist explicitly critiques desire and then provides an alternative evaluation of human conduct that does not rely on problematic Western metaphysical assumptions.[2]

Desire and Misperception: The Daoist Critique of Desire

The Daoist sage, as described in the *Daodejing*, takes desire and greed to be one of the main causes, if not *the* cause, of social calamity and chaos. For the Daoist, accumulating desires is not in accord with our original spontaneity or how we are naturally endowed. Steve Coutinho states that "desires, as understood in the *Laozi*, however, seem to refer to something that is inconsistent with a natural life. They appear to be constructed by human artifice, and thereby also essentially involved in insatiable cycles of acquisition."[3] It is through being "without desire" (*wuyu*) that the Daoist sage is free of misperceiving situations. Such a key claim about perception is alluded to in the opening passage of the *Daodejing*. As it claims in *Daodejing* 1, "to be constantly without desire [*wuyu*] is how to observe the subtleties of things; To constantly have desire [*youyu*] is how to observe their boundaries."[4] At minimum, the Daoist is claiming that being "without-desire" (*wuyu*) changes how one observes (*guan*) the world. "Having desires" is how one observes the boundaries between things, while being "without desire" is how one can observe the "subtilities" in situations.[5]

Recently, there have been a few scholars that have tried to push back against the reading of the *Daodejing* as being critical of desires.[6] I have provided a more textual analysis of this and why such readings are problematic in a previous publication.[7] By drawing on Wang Bi's comments and other passages of the *Daodejing*, the early sections of that article illustrated how, for the Daoist, possessing desires (*youyu*) is related to being imposing in one's conduct or *wei* (為).[8] To respond to situations "without egoistic conduct," a Daoist sage must also be "without desire." This is because when we "have desire" we dwell on the objects of perception. These distinct objects are only projections onto experience and do not accurately represent nature and our relationship to it. The human mind is what individuates things, and this is related to desire.[9] The Daoist does not merely critique desire per se. We misperceive situations because we fail to see that the way we "carve" up nature into "types" is provisional. When we cling to desires, we are clinging to a substance metaphysics and the attendant epistemology that obscures our perception.

The *Daodejing* describes desire as doing more than just contributing to misperception; desire also shapes affect. As *Daodejing* passage 12 claims, when the way we perceive the world is shaped by desire, this means that our predisposition is one of bad emotional affect. "Having desire" inhibits the ability to perceive the world as *pu* or like an "uncarved block of wood," but this "knowledge" also upsets our emotional predispositions. "The five colors blind the eye; the five tones deafen the ears; the five tastes disrupt the mouth; The galloping of horses hunting in the field causes the heart/mind to go mad; goods that are difficult to obtain cause personal conduct to become obstructed. Therefore, the Sage acts on the stomach and does not act on the eye, thus taking away that and accepting this."[10]

The Daoist juxtaposes two different features of human culture and existence. On the one hand, the Daoist is apprehensive of desires that they associate with the "eye" or those aspects of human life that are not directly related to our basic needs as animals.[11] On the other, the Daoist suggests we stick to the "stomach." A useful way of thinking about this distinction is by seeing this as a distinction between what Brook Ziporyn helpfully calls "eye desires" and "stomach desires."[12] It is also important to ask here whether or not those features of existence that are associated with the "stomach" should be considered desires at all. At the very least, the Daoist assumes that certain cultural forms are directly related to problematic desires and thus obstruct the ability to perceive situations. On my reading, the distinction drawn between the "stomach" and the "eye" should be treated as two distinct features of existence. Contrary to basic animal needs, desires are *cultural and cultivated*. Basic biological needs are not culturally cultivated (but can arguably be adjusted by different cultural forms). Desires, as cultural, go above and beyond how biological organisms are naturally predisposed. In terms of lived experience, the phenomenon of feeling hungry and then trying to satisfy that biological urge to eat is a vastly different experience from the desire to participate in cultural institutions (like the desire to excel or gain recognition [*ming*, 名] for participation in society).[13] An important distinction needs to be made between the drives or urges of the body and the social and culturally learned forms of human conduct. The Daoist is, rightly, drawing that distinction in passage 12 of the *Daodejing*. In light of Daoist philosophy, we need to see the experience of most desires as far more abstract and conceptual in character. Biological needs are not.

For the Daoist, desires are problematic because they encourage people to depart from their naturally endowed spontaneity—*ziran* or as they are "self-so." Apart from *ziran*, the Daoist also describes nature as like a "nameless uncarved block of wood" (無名之樸). The metaphor expresses that the natural world is fundamentally an indeterminate continuum (*wu*). In light of *Daodejing* 12, the Daoist critiques the "five colors" and the "five flavors" because these are cultural abstractions that have become reified and mistakenly taken as accurate representations of reality. Reality is an indeterminate continuum of overlapping processes where there is *no single way* to correctly divide it up into "kinds" or "types."[14] Reified abstractions within experience can be considered *ossified* when they obstruct our ability to perceive nature as indeterminate and primordially "uncarved." All possible experience takes place within the context of nature as indeterminate and "nameless" (*wuming*, 無名). As humans develop more desires, we individuate different aspects of experience and give them names (*ming*, 名). If we can maintain attention to the primordial, indeterminate context of experience while still using language and forming concepts, we will perceive how the "boundaries" between things are provisional and secondary aspects of experience as a whole.[15] Thus, the inability to perceive the indeterminate context of experience is related to how we have reified the value of things as well.

With the Daoist's antirepresentational account of experience, the products of abstraction (*zhi*) are merely provisional realities. They are tools that help us navigate the world, but they do not exhaustively represent the world to us. What the Daoist cultivates is the capacity to disclose nature as fundamentally "uncarved" and "nameless." Such cultivation allows them to maintain a phenomenological distance from the products of abstraction and conceptual individuation. They do not completely abandon such habits but, instead, cultivate a capacity to recontextualize them within a wider sphere of lived experiences. This is a feature that the *Daodejing* and the *Zhuangzi* have in common. Chapter 2 of the *Zhuangzi* states:

> The understanding of those ancient people really got somewhere! Where had it arrived? To the point where there had never existed any definite thing at all. This is really getting there, as far as you can go. Where no definite thing exists, nothing more can be—added! Next there were those for whom specific things existed, but no sealed boundaries between them. Next there were those for whom there were sealed boundaries, but never any rights and wrongs. When right and wrong are bright, the Course begins to wane. What sets the Course to waning

is exactly what allows preferences for one thing over another to succeed in reaching its full formation.[16]

The progression of seeing the world as "uncarved" to seeing it as being constituted by things necessarily involves seeing these things as being of value and disvalue. Distinction making is tied to the perspective, desires, and intentions of the being that is conceptually individuating nature. When persons cling to the "names" and cognitive distinctions they draw (*zhi*), they are simultaneously clinging to a limited and narrow set of desires structuring perception while ignoring the background continuity of experience. Desiring involves the use of the imagination, abstraction, and concept formation. It is not a mere reflexive or bodily act but is, instead, one that is reflective as it involves the imagination *re*presenting objects (that is, depends on the *prior*, conceptual individuation of things in experience). This is not the case for the needs or drives that are of the "stomach." The biological organism is internally affected in ways that are not reducible to propositional meaning or concept formation. These drives or needs rooted in the biological organism are not constant. They come and go depending on the fleeting needs of the organism.[17] When Dao declines, this is because certain cultural forms obscure our ability to recognize what forms of life are even of value (i.e., the "eye desires" are inhibiting perception and distracting us from seeing the value in keeping our stomachs full). The reason why such a distinction is important is that it highlights an important problem with desires. Desires don't need to be related to the needs of the stomach. It is for this reason that manufacturing desire (*yu zuo*) is a useful tool for those with political power. "Eye" desires serve as wonderful distractions from the basic needs of people (i.e., filling up their stomach). Things get dangerous when desires and cultural institutions are no longer grounded in the concrete, biological needs of the organism.

Animal Fitness, the "Center," and "Ontological Relativity"

Together with the tendency in recent scholarship to suggest that the Daoist philosopher is merely guided by desire, some scholars have argued that the Daoist has no possible resources for dealing with the morally suspect desires that philosophers find problematic.[18] Considering that both the *Zhuangzi* and the *Daodejing* criticize desire, claim that having many desires is how one departs from Dao, and even suggest that desires are the root source of societal ills, scholars seem to be glossing over important aspects of Daoist philosophy. If scholars believe that the Daoist is led by desire or has nothing to offer in the way of critiquing desire, then they must reconcile and explain how this is so when Daoist texts frequently critique greed and desire.[19]

Far from having nothing critical to say about problematic desires, the Daoist sees these desires as related to the ossification of the individuation of things. The Daoist understanding of nature holds that each thing is a coalescence of relationships or a *function of* their environment. Although there are not independent things in nature, each *ziran* or "self-so" aspect of nature is unique because it is *caused and determined* by the rest of nature. Alternatively, we can think of each "self-so" aspect of nature as a unique focal point in a larger field of relations[20] and can then be understood as a "center" of nature as well.[21] By being a "center" of nature, this does not mean that each thing is then *the* center. Arguing that *each* thing is a center of nature implies a nonanthropocentric egalitarianism as well as perspectivism.[22] All things are equal in the sense that each is limited in scope and always constituted by its world. There is no such perspective that is *the* perspective. It is for this reason that the Daoist texts consider residing in the center to be the position that is epistemologically in accord with nature. Recently, other scholars have provided an account of this in Daoism. Drawing on the *Zhuangzi* and Guo Xiang, Mercedes Valmisa argues that we can consider the center to be epistemically the most advantageous position from the perspective of adapting to situations. "The center allows one to understand the grounds on which agents make choices, to approach the infinite network of possibilities wherein one is embedded while not committing to any one of them."[23] The ground for the Daoist is *ziran* and nature's indeterminacy (*wu*). This connection has also been drawn by Jung Lee. He states:

> Like the mirror and still water, the Daoist sage allows the concrete circumstance to manifest itself in all its specificity and particularity before undertaking the timely action. Accordingly, by "using illumination" the Daoist sage can respond in the most *fitting* manner. Often imaged as the "center of the circle," the "hub of the wheel," and the "point of rest on the potter's

wheel of heaven," Daoist responsiveness entails the ability to literally transform with the situation and to act in a way that is "inherently so" (*ziran*).²⁴

In terms of how the Daoist perceives situations, their goal is to become sensitive to how each situation is particular and unique. They can achieve this because they have themselves become empty of "knowledge" and "desire" and thus, like a mirror unadulterated, are receptive to each situation in all its changing particularity. This particularity (*ziran*) is frequently what the Daoist appeals to when they describe their alternative to Confucian and Mohist morality. The goal is to both recognize and embody nature as indeterminate. It is through cultivation (namely, breathing exercises) that the Daoist suggests we become detached from obfuscating desires. The *Zhuangzi* juxtaposes everyday people with the sage as grounded and frugal to make this point. "The Genuine-Humans (*zhenren*, 真人) of old slept without dreaming and awoke without worries. Their food was plain but their breathing was deep. Genuine-Humans breathe from their heels, while the mass of men breathe from their throats, submissive and defeated, gulping down their words and just as soon vomiting them back up. Their preferences and desires run deep, but their Heavenly impulses run shallow."²⁵ The passage suggests that the "Genuine-Humans" or "true persons," *zhenren* (真人), are both existentially grounded and frugal in their lifestyle. That they "breathe from their heels" suggests that they are rooted or at the root (*ben*, 本) and are plain with their diet (as *Daodejing* 12 suggests). The non-Daoist masses are juxtaposed with this frugality. The common people chaotically use language, as if trapped (alienated) by their own words and the "names" (*ming*) of things. Their "desires run deep," but that which is what heaven has endowed them with, the "heavenly impulses," is shallow. In the *Zhuangzi*, both language (and, by extension, "knowledge" due to the individuation of nature) and desire play a role in adulterating that which we are naturally endowed with by Heaven.

When the Daoist talks about desires and the lessening of desire, one does not find the same metaphors that shape Western understandings of desire. What we get in Daoist philosophy is an account of desires that fits with their account of things as "self-so" aspects of nature. In different philosophical and cultural traditions, words and phrases are often associated through different webs of meanings. Perhaps the most peculiar association found in the Daoist texts is how being "without desire" (*wuyu*) and "without knowledge" (*wuzhi*) is related to residing in an empty center. Departing from the original spontaneity of things is tantamount to departing from this empty center. As with the *Daodejing* passage 5 when it states to "hold to the center," the *Zhuangzi* describes desires in the same way. *Zhuangzi* chapter 3 begins with the following important story:

> The flow of my life is always bound by its banks, but the activity of the understanding consciousness is constrained by no such limits. When something thus bounded is made to follow something unbounded in this way, it is put into danger. And to try and wielding further understanding to redress this danger only puts it into deeper danger still. It may do good, but not to the point of getting anywhere near a good name; it may do evil, but not to the point of getting anywhere near punishment—for it tends toward the current of the empty central meridian [緣督] as its normal route. And this is what enables us to maintain our bodies, to keep the life in them intact, to nourish those near and dear to us, and to fully live out our years.[26]

This passage presents an issue at the root of many philosophical projects: the question of a bound and limited empirical experience having to grapple with the reality of reasoning and imagination being unhindered by the same limitations. As Youru Wang's study describes it, like the Kantian project of determining the "bounds of sense," the issue presented here is of understanding the "limits of language" and, consequently, the limits of experience.[27] Organisms are bound and limited. The languages that humans create and the concepts they form do not share the same limitations. If asked, based on this passage, what the Daoist believed was the reason behind why people were predisposed towards being in danger, their diagnosis is that it was because that which is bound and limited (life, organisms) is being led by the unbounded ("knowledge," *zhi*). Furthermore, the attempt to increase "knowledge" only further inhibits our ability to address our problems. If "knowledge" is the problem, then one cannot further "knowledge" with the hope of ameliorating social ills. What the Daoist prescribes is that we stick to the "central meridian" (緣督), which is a term in Chinese medicine. It refers to "the current of energy that runs vertically through the middle of the human back."[28] By dwelling in the epistemic center, this enables us to perceive how each *ziran* thing *embodies* a changing network of relationships. Furthermore, the Daoist believes that dwelling in the center will also involve nourishing "those near and dear to us." Avoiding the (ossified) moral extremes and the (cultural) "values" that society tries to entice its population with is how to become best predisposed towards preserving both one's own life and the lives of those near to them. If it is flourishing that the Daoist is promoting or valuing, this form of flourishing would involve both the absence of many cultural desires but also involve the flourishing of others as well.[29]

The *Zhuangzi* chapter 3 relates dwelling in the empty center to maintaining basic animal needs in another passage of the text when describing the difference between "what is of heaven" and "what is of man." For the Daoist, when a feature is of "man," this implies that it is provisional and not an aspect of our original spontaneity in the sense that it adds more to the processes of life. Having the epistemological framework or perspective of a "human" (as a *type* of "thing") involves making and clinging to both "knowledge" and "desire." In this passage, the Daoist links three ideas: 1) the particularity of things (that is endowed by Heaven), 2) humans are the kind of "thing" (*wu*, 物) that "group things together" (they make ontological distinctions that do not exhaustively correspond to nature), and 3) this is related to fitness or the basic needs an animal might have. The passage claims:

> It is of Heaven, not man. Heaven, in its generation of each thing as "this," always makes it singular, unique, alone. Man, in characterizing each thing by its appearance, always groups it with something else. Thus I know that whatever it is, it is Heaven, not man. The marsh pheasant finds one mouthful of food every ten steps, and one drink of water every hundred steps, but he does not seek to be fed and pampered in a cage. For though his spirit might there reign supreme, it would do him no good.[30]

First, the passage draws the distinction between what is of "heaven" and "man." Then, it claims that it is the human being that "groups things together" (which suggests that "what is of heaven," that is, the natural world, is not made up of independent "things" or "types" and "classes" but is instead made up of unique particulars). Finally, the text discusses a pheasant achieving its basic needs for survival and contrasts this with being fed yet locked in a cage. At first glance, the first half of the passage does not readily relate to the other half. With respect to the Daoist account of the nature of experience, when the "human" clings to the products of cognition, grouping things into "sameness" and "difference," and fails to perceive the original continuity of all things due to "knowledge," they depart from their original spontaneity (*ziran*) which is given by heaven. The cultural abstractions become ossified, and persons become perceptually "fixed" in how they perceive the world. The passage suggests that if each "human" did not depart from that which is of "heaven," they would behave more like the pheasant in only maintaining their animal needs. When the "human" clings to "knowledge," they become limited by their epistemological framework such that they fail to see their existential condition for what it is; a cage that inhibits their freedom and agency in the world. This metaphorical "cage" that the *Zhuangzi* speaks of is not a literal cage that merely inhibits the physical body. Kings and (non-Daoist) sage are equally in this cage which is existential and epistemological in nature as it inhibits the ability of those that suffer under such illusions from seeing the arbitrariness of many of society's cultural institutions.

Zhuangzi on the "Genuine Person"

Although the *Daodejing* is more explicit on this point, the *Zhuangzi* describes the Daoist sage as lacking a "fixed" self that then possesses the capacity to see all things as parts of the larger whole of nature. Apart from the stories mentioned above, the *Zhuangzi* describes the "true persons" or *zhenren* as embodying the capacity to maintain their naturalness in light of them still participating in the cultural institutions of society. The "true persons" are described in chapter 6 of the *Zhuangzi* as possessing the capacity to distinguish that which is endowed from "heaven" and that which is the doing of the "human."

> To understand what is done by Heaven, and also to understand what is to be done by the human, that is to reach the utmost (至矣). [. . .] However, there is a problem here. For it is only through its relation of dependence [待] on something that our

understanding can be considered correct, but what it depends on is always peculiarly unfixed [未定]. [. . .] Let us say instead, then, that there can be "a Genuine Understanding" [真知] only after there is such a thing as someone who is himself genuine even while being human—human yet genuine, genuine yet human: the Genuine-Human [真人].[31]

Our understanding (*zhi*) exists in a state of dependence and is one that is conditioned. Whenever an aspect of experience is individuated and foregrounded, there is always something left "uncut"; that is, the indeterminate context of experience is never fully perceived by consciousness. Each act of individuation then participates in the same structure (foreground/background or *you/wu*). Individuation then always depends on that which is "unfixed" or "not yet fixed" (*weiding*, 未定). Realizing the difference between that which is "endowed by heaven" and that which is the "doing of the human" is similar to the process described in the *Daodejing* of being "without knowledge" (the ability to contextualize "knowledge" within the indeterminate *wu*). As the previously quoted passage from chapter 3 of the *Zhuangzi* suggests, "man, in characterizing each thing by its appearance, always groups it with something else. Thus I know that whatever it is, it is Heaven, not man."[32] It is the human that organizes "knowledge" into types and classes. The natural world, as radically interdependent and fluctuating, cannot be exhaustibly captured by the processes of individuation and conceptualization, yet "genuine understanding" (真知) does not involve completely abandoning "knowledge" either. It involves disclosing situations such that "knowledge" is perceived as a secondary and provisional aspect of experience (i.e., of realizing that propositional forms of meaning are grounded in the nonpropositional forms of meaning). "Knowledge" and how it depends on (*dai*, 待) the indeterminate context of experience is then immediately perceived (the cognitive/propositional aspects of experience are perceived as dependent on the noncognitive/nonpropositional).

"Genuine understanding" is not the perception or apprehension of "facts." "Genuine understanding" comes *after* the "true person" (*zhenren*) is realized, and it involves the capacity to disclose all "knowledge" (*zhi*) and "right-wrong" (*shi-fei*, 是-非) distinctions as situated in the indeterminate (*wu*). Drawing on Western religion and existentialism, Poul Andersen describes the *zhenren* as existentially embodying Dao where Dao is the nothingness (*wu*). In realizing that we embody nothingness (*wu*), this enables the *zhenren* to manifest "genuine understanding." He states that "Daoism is about constituting oneself as a manifestation of a being of truth. One might be tempted to say that it is about "creating" oneself, but this is not the term that a Daoist, or indeed a Western existentialist, would use. The true self of Daoism is a state of being that emerges within, out of the nothingness of the Way."[33] It is not accurate to call this process one of "creation" because the Daoist is "forgetting" that which was already created (the doings of the human) in order to return to the naturalness that constitutes our most fundamental relationships with the world. As with the first story of the *Zhuangzi*, chapter 2, forgetting the independent sense of self reveals that experience is fundamentally an openness to the world. The process of forgetting the "human" lets what is "endowed by heaven" become disclosed in experience, but the goal is not to completely abandon all that is the "doing of humans." To recognize that one is fundamentally like an "uncarved block of wood" or a *zhenren* means one's dispositions are attentive to how the "doings of the human" depend on "that which is of heaven." A *zhenren* does not then perceive reality as it is "in-itself" (because there is no reality "in-itself"). The *zhenren* perceives how "names" and the individuated things of experience depend on some-other-thing and this is simultaneous with the realization that the person (*zhenren*) embodies the same overlapping continuum of nature as well. Knowing that which is "done by man" and that which is of "heaven" is to see the provisional aspects of experience (human conceptual artifice, "names" and "knowledge") as a function of nature as an indeterminate continuum (*wu*).

Like Andersson, Robin Wang has provided an account of the relationships between the "true self" and the "provisional self" in the *Zhuangzi*. This "true self" is the self of an "empty heart/mind."

> *Zhuangzi* articulates two levels of the heart/mind (*xin*). One is the heart/mind that knows external objects. It makes distinctions and has a yes or no (*shi-fei* 是非) point of view on the world. In this activity, the heart/mind cannot get the *Dao*. The other heart/mind is no-mind, or the heart of the *Dao*. It transcends all distinctions and dualistic views and is connected with the heart/mind of the universe. The true person with an empty heart/mind can transcend the limits of physical forms and allow his or her mind to wander in complete freedom.

> We could say that this is a movement from an empirical ego (*ziwo* 自我) to an ontological true self (*zhenwo* 真我).[34]

When we dwell on the cultural conventions and "names" attributed to things, we fail to bring our attention to the wholeness of nature. The Daoist takes our more fundamental heart/mind to be of "no-mind" or, as described in the *Daodejing* 49, being "without heart/mind" (*wuxin*). As with the above analysis, the *zhenren* is an empty center of nature that allows the fluctuating world to fill up and alter perception in an unadulterated manner. Although scholars might be tempted to interpret the "real self" of Daoism as like a substance or as participating in a transcendent, nonnatural metaphysical reality, this would neglect the naturalistic and immanent dimensions of the Daoist's account of the self and its relationship to the rest of nature. Dao is nothingness or nature as "uncarved." The provisional heart/mind that makes and clings to distinctions is not abandoned by the Daoist. In order to deal with how distinction making (*zhi*) can become coercive, we need to contextualize these distinctions within the larger whole (to see *shi-fei* in light of *wu*). The following is how chapter 6 of the *Zhuangzi* continues:

> Thus their liking of something was a oneness with it and their disliking of something was also a oneness with it; what they liked and disliked, their liking and their disliking, were all the oneness. Their oneness was oneness, and their non-oneness was also a oneness. In their oneness, they were followers of the Heavenly. In their non-oneness, they were followers of the human. This is what it is for neither the Heavenly nor the human to win out over the other. And that is what I call the Genuine-Human [真人].[35]

The goal is not to extinguish the "humanly" in favor of that which is "heavenly." This too would be to cling to *shi-fei* distinctions. If *shi-fei* distinctions are perceived within the context of the oneness of nature, then their limiting perceptual effects are mitigated. If people are not actively attentive to their continuity with nature, this does not change the fact that they form a "oneness" with it. Their perceptual "nononeness" is only their perceptual ignorance of their immediate, qualitative relations with the world. By not letting one part win out over the other, the Daoist sage becomes best predisposed to dealing with the precariousness of life. Although it is the "doings of humans" that cling to and create the *shi-fei* (right-wrong), the Daoist possesses the capacity to contextualize such distinctions by dwelling in and realizing that they, like all things, are empty centers of nature.

In a later chapter of the *Zhuangzi*, the *zhenren* is described as being without those values associated with the egoistic or provisional self. It states in chapter 17, "Autumn Floods," of the *Zhuangzi*, not allowing the "humanly" to destroy that which is "heavenly" involves the absence of "purposiveness" and of seeking for merit.

> Ruo of the Northern Sea said, "That cows and horses have four legs is the Heavenly. The bridle around the horse's head and the ring through the cow's nose are the human. Hence I say, do not use the human to destroy the Heavenly, do not use the purposive to destroy the fated, do not sacrifice yourself for the sake of mere names in the hope of gain. Hold onto this carefully and you may be said to have returned to what is genuine in you."[36]

In preserving that which is "genuine" (*zhen*, 真), persons are not simply becoming authentic or realizing their "true self." Such a reading is in fact antithetical to the Daoist spirit. By extirpating the features of experience related to clinging to purposes and merit, one is "forgetting" the reflective sense of self that is believed to be independent. Maintaining what is "true" (真) is to abandon egoism and the features associated with it. Chapter 6 of the *Zhuangzi* describes this as well, saying that the "Genuine-Humans of old did not revolt against their inadequacies, did not aspire to heroic accomplishments or perfection, made no plans to be distinguished persons. In this way, they could be mistaken without feeling regret, could be correct without self-satisfaction."[37] It is through emptying experience of the provisional self (as the *Zhuangzi* chapter 2 states, *wu sang wo*) that we come to embody the truth of nature as fundamentally indeterminate. Most importantly, there is something paradoxical at work in this "Autumn Floods" passage. In abandoning desire, purpose, and merit, the *Zhuangzi* is suggesting that this is also how to best preserve one's life. Desires actually involve harm to oneself. This is because they are related to a false sense of the self as independent.

The description of the Daoist sage as empty of a self or as emulating the nothingness of Dao is a description that is pervasive throughout the Daoist text. Being without this "knowledge" is precisely what the Daoist sage hopes to emulate. The provisional heart/mind, when clinging to "knowledge," is hindered by *shi-fei* distinction making in the sense that *shi-fei* (right and wrong) are interpreted as substantial and independent. Seeing the oneness underlying all things enables one to no longer cling to any *shi-fei* distinctions ("knowledge") insofar as these distinctions are seen in the context of nature as indeterminate (*wu*). Such rigidity with respect to what is "right" and "wrong" is, in fact, undermining the desire to make things "right" and avoid the "wrong." In part, this is because when we cultivate the capacity to see the underlying oneness of all things, we would see the many *shi-fei* distinctions as arbitrary in light of the larger context. Both sides are viewed as arbitrary and ignorant. Another reason is that desires are harmful in the sense that they contribute to ignorance. Egoism, too, and the pursuit of merit and "name" are likewise harmful as they pervert and distort our heavenly endowed spontaneity. Although scholars might read some of these claims as Daoist versions of individualism and egoism, chapter 5 will return to this point more by looking closely at how the *Zhuangzi* critiques both egoism and moralism. The Daoist position, as one that preserves life, is (ironically) in the self-interest of persons only in the sense that we are not independent selves to begin with. We can "preserve those near and dear" when we abandon the belief in an independent sense of self and all of the reified "values" associated with it (merit, fame, etc.). In this sense, the Daoist position of realizing that each "thing" is an empty "center" of nature fulfills most of the roles that a "moral discourse" was supposed to fulfill. Instead of an appeal to some transcendent reality, the Daoist simply negates the existence of a separate and independent self. This helps to mitigate both selfish desires and the narcissistic tendencies of the moralist sages. The key here is that, for the Daoist, such an accurate account of nature as involving overlapping processes that form continuous wholes is not just more epistemologically advantageous; seeing all things as "self-so" also involves seeing how all things are connected. It is for this reason that being "without self-interest" ironically helps to fulfill the interests of the community at large.

"Without Desire" as Sticking to Need and the Daoist Egalitarian Society

The *Daodejing* suggests that it is through being "without desire" that the Daoist sage can noncoercively promote an egalitarian society. Ironically, acting from "without desire" is in everyone's best interest. It is in each person's best interest to recognize that there is not an (independent) self and to act "without self-interest" such that society is organized where all people can fulfill their basic needs. *Daodejing* 37 claims that the accumulation or "creation of desires" is both discordant with the natural predispositions of things and is antithetical to the Daoist egalitarian society.

> *Dao* is really nameless (*wuming*), were nobles and kings able to respect this, all things (*wanwu*) would be able to develop along their own lines. Having developed along their own lines, were they to [create desires, *yu zuo*, 欲作], I would realign them with a nameless scrap of unworked wood. Realigned with the nameless scrap of unworked wood, they would leave off desiring. In not desiring [*buyu*, 不欲] they would achieve equilibrium [*jing*, 靜], and all the world would be properly ordered of its own accord [*ziding*, 自定]" (with minor changes).[38]

Perhaps of all the different positions and claims of the Daoist philosopher, these claims are the most difficult for the Western philosopher to accept and understand. The Daoist describes the "creation of desires" (*yu zuo*) as a way of departing from how we are naturally predisposed. In not desiring, we could achieve a kind of clarity or equilibrium (*jing*, 靜). From the Daoist perspective, cultural and political institutions have been encouraging the creation of desires in the population.[39] Far from believing that desire is a natural occurrence or simply a natural offshoot of our biology, the Daoist is suggesting that the "creation of desires" is a form of conduct that is *wei*, or politically coercive. As *Daodejing* 3 claims, the Daoist sage is capable of properly governing society because the sage sticks to fulfilling the needs of the population and does not manufacture "knowledge" and "desire."

> Not treating goods as valuable will causes the common people to not fight; not valuing difficult to obtain items/commodities will cause the common people to not be thieves; not manifesting or presenting many potential desires will cause the heart/mind to not become confused. Therefore, in the governing of the sage, they empty their [i.e., the common people's] heart/mind and fill their stomach, weaken their intentions and strengthen

their bones. Constantly promoting the common people to be "without knowledge" and "without desire." Encouraging those who [believe they] "are wise" to not dare to act. Acting "without coercive action," thus everything is governed.[40]

Promoting superior character and "valuable goods" is not simply a way of ignorantly "carving up" nature. For the Daoist, such practices lead to combative and resentful conduct which, in turn, further necessitates seeing other people in our communities as independent of and against "us" and "me." Competition and the desire to obtain social status or valuable goods (ironically) help to perpetuate these same hierarchical relationships because of the obfuscating role "desire" plays in perception. The Daoist satisfies the *needs* of the population. When society is structured in a way where people cannot easily (or ever) fulfill their basic animal needs (of the stomach), it is actually desire that plays a role in obfuscating perception and distracting the population. A *cultural* framework must be employed to morally legitimize a society that prevents peoples from fulfilling basic animal needs. "Desires" are manufactured so as to distract the population. The arts, music, and "rare goods" (as *Daodejing* 12 suggests) can be understood as playing this role to various degrees. However, "rare goods" and the concentration of wealth in society are not only there to act as distractions. The possibility of escaping the unfreedom of this political system also provides incentives to keep the entire system going. For example, a soldier in feudal society both defends the system of feudalism and is rewarded for doing so in being elevated out of the lowest social class. Competition for higher political rank and honor functions in the same way. The higher up one goes in the political hierarchy, the more people achieve a kind of freedom from the precariousness of life. The victors in the competition for higher rank, insofar as they do not see the whole system as the source of societal ills, are helping to maintain the same coercive political relations.

Poverty is not a basic feature of nature. It is a socioeconomic condition that has been *imposed* on the population so as to limit the possible forms of life available to them. Maintaining poverty and great levels of economic inequality then limits the possibilities of the population. It limits their power, freedom, and capacity to form solidarity as overexploitation robs people of the basic resources (like time) that would are needed to address their condition. The political system itself is an act of *wei* or "coercive conduct" whenever it leads to overexploitation and manipulation of desires of the common people. *Daodejing* 75 states that "the people's hunger is because those above are eating too much in taxes—This is why they are hungry. The people's lack of order is because those above manipulate them."[41] Political institutions can become coercive once those "above" see the imposition of scarcity and poverty as a means of control. "Knowledge" then takes (*at least*) two coercive forms. "Knowledge" can be called upon to defend the social hierarchy (as if such a hierarchy was *merited*, for example), or people can become "clever" such that they become better at stealing from each other (stealing an entire state would then be the most efficient form of theft).[42] When the Daoist sage helps the population fulfil the basic needs (of the stomach), apart from this helping to mitigate political corruption and theft within the community (because the conditions that help to encourage theft are now gone, as I explain more in chapter 6), this helps the population in another sense. In not being distracted by "desire" and no longer miseducated through "knowledge," the population would be predisposed towards viewing themselves and nature in their naturally endowed spontaneity or as "uncarved" (*pu*), When persons recognize that they are primordially "uncarved," this means they recognize themselves as constituted by nature as a web of relationships. If we were not aware of what the Daoist specifically meant by "knowledge," the claims of *Daodejing* 3 might sound politically coercive. In not "creating desires" and in "abandoning knowledge," the Daoist sage is actually helping the population perceive themselves and others as interdependent members of their communities by removing the "knowledge" that contributes to social ills and the formation of dispositions that depart from how we are naturally endowed. They are helping the population return to their naturalness (*ziran*).

Daodejing 32 similarly describes the politically ideal society as one that does not depart from nature as "uncarved" and "nameless." A key to understanding this passage is that conduct and political organization that are "imposing" (*wei*) are not principally about how a ruler or other people would or would not *physically* interfere with other persons and/or nature. This is first and foremost a critique of "knowledge" or the epistemological and phenomenological "carving up" of nature. The social and political relationships that shape a society governed *wuwei* would not promote "desires," "knowledge," and the entire epistemological framework that predisposes the population to act *wei*. Without keeping this in mind, it is not readily apparent how being in accord with Dao and acting *wuwei* involves the common people ordering society equitably, which is precisely the claim of *Daodejing* passage 32. Society governed *wuwei* or nonegoistically would be spontaneously egalitarian.

> Dao is really nameless.
> > Were the nobles and kings able to respect this [i.e., *pu*],
> > All things (wanwu) would defer of their own accord.
> > The heavens and the earth would come together
> > To send down their sweet dew,
> > And without being so ordered,
> > The common people would see that it is distributed equitably.
> > When we start to regulate the world, we introduce names.
> > But once names have been assigned,
> > We must also know when to stop.
> > Knowing when to stop is how to avoid danger.[43]

The Daoist is claiming that the forms of life that do not depart from nature as an "uncarved block of wood" are the *more valuable* forms of life. The Daoist admits that there are pragmatic reasons for "carving up" nature and experience. Language and distinction making has its uses but not knowing when to stop (知止) is what the Daoist takes to be the source of social ills. At the most fundamental level, humans are relational, interdependent selves. The belief that persons are ontologically independent selves is one that requires unempirical and metaphysical beliefs.

The Daoist Account of Being "without Self-Interest"

The Daoist critique of desire does not rely on a transcendent, universal "order" or "law" that is superimposed on nature to justify why desire is bad. The Daoist's naturalistic, processual metaphysics instead provides an account of desires that in grounded in human experience. There are empirical reasons to "forget" both "knowledge" and "desire" or, in other words, to behave in a way that is "without self-interest." Being "without self-interest" is not only in proper alignment with nature (each "self-so" aspect of nature being recognized as a center), the dispositions the Daoist cultivates are also (*ironically*) the best ways to achieve success and fulfill our biological needs. The Daoist egalitarian society is informed by this interdependent, relational account of persons. There are two more key passages of the *Daodejing* where these particular arguments are made explicit. The first comes from *Daodejing* 7, which states the following:

> Heaven is long lasting and earth is enduring. That which is why heaven and earth are capable of longevity and also enduring, it is by means of their not living for themselves; thus, they are capable of long life. Therefore, the sage puts their own body behind them [i.e., out of sight], yet their body is first; puts their own body outside them [i.e., out of mind], yet the body is sustained. Is it not by means of their being "without self-interest" (無私)? Thus they are capable of completing their "self-interest" (私).[44]

The key aspects of this passage are 1) nature is enduring because it does not "live for itself," 2) the Daoist sage emulates such behavior, and 3) it is through "not living for the self" that the needs of the "self" can be achieved. This is arguably a kind of altruism, but the Daoists go the further step and argue that this is (paradoxically) the form of human conduct that best helps persons achieve their own interests. If we start from the (*question-begging*) assumptions of liberal individualism, then such claims by the Daoists are not readily plausible. In light of the Daoist account of interdependence and of nature as an "uncarved block of wood," this form of conduct is easier to understand. We are not independent selves. Such beliefs only emerge from a culture where competition and the creation of desires are being promoted. When the common people view themselves as distinct individuals that are not internally related to each other, they maintain the further ignorant belief that their needs and welfare are not intimately related to the welfare of the community. To put it another way, the kind of competition and desire that the Daoist finds to be problematic is of the kind that encourages the creation of an entire cultural framework where values are fit into a "zero-sum" framework. For the Daoist, abandoning "private ends" (*si*, 私) is (*ironically*) the most efficient way to bring about both individual and communal ends because there are no such things as "private individuals" that could actually possess their own individual ends. Another key passage that presents the Daoist account of social problems comes from *Daodejing* 49:

> The sage is constantly without a heart/mind [*wuxin*, 無心]; he takes the heart/mind of the common people as their own heart/mind.
>
> Those who are good he holds to be good. Those who are not good he holds to be good. Thus, he attains goodness. Those who are trustworthy he trusts. Those who are untrustworthy he also trusts. Thus, he attains trustworthiness.
>
> When the sage resides in the world, he fuses himself with it. For the world he merges hearts. All the people fix ears and eyes on him, and the sage regards them as smiling children. [*with minor changes*][45]

The Daoist sage is "without heart/mind" when they recognize all things as "uncarved" (*pu*) and thus equally constituted by the same interdependent continuum. Being "without heart/mind" is to recognize that all persons are "without heart/mind" as well. The sources of our problems are not reducible to "simply located" realities like "substances." Chapter 6 of this book will return to this passage, but what is important to stress here is that the Daoist sages merge themselves with others and help to promote the same merging and fusing together of the members of their community by removing those obstructions (i.e., "desire" and "knowledge") that inhibit persons from recognizing their interdependence. The political and social *wuwei* functioning in this situation is of liberation from those cultural forms that alienate us from both nature and our fellow human beings. By getting rid of such cultural (*metaphysical*) fictions and myths, those forms of life that are *actually* desirable, valuable, and in accord with nature as fundamentally indeterminate can be brought about. Being *wuxin* or "without heart/mind" is tantamount to residing in the epistemic center and of being "without desire" and "without knowledge." It is to respond to situations "without self-interested" behavior because the Daoist sage perceives situations as a function of interdependence.

Conclusion

In the introduction of this book, I suggested that the Daoist account of *wuwei* conduct was not merely spontaneous or effortless. Instead, *wuwei* better realized the same ends that the Confucians and Mohists were hoping to achieve through their respective moral discourses. In looking at why a Daoist is "without desire," we can see how this is the case. The Daoist position is one that provides solutions for most of the concerns of the moral philosopher. It provides reasons for abandoning desires and also provides an alternative to egoism. Both of these are related to their view of the ideal society as being egalitarian and of promoting the needs of the population. By dwelling in the empty center, the Daoist sage becomes capable of perceiving the natural world as fundamentally indeterminate and overlapping. It is this capacity that explains how it is in each person's best interest to get rid of superfluous desires and to promote the needs of others. In both the *Zhuangzi* and the *Daodejing*, dwelling in the (metaphorical) center involves returning to how each of us is "self-so" (*ziran*) or how we were naturally endowed by "heaven." By dwelling in the empty center, the Daoist perceives things not as mere beings (*you*) but as constituted by the "indeterminate" (*wu*) continuum of nature. The Daoist is critical of desires because they promote an epistemological framework that views the things of nature as independent. In ignorance, we merely bring our attention to the "named" aspects of experience while ignoring the background, "uncarved" continuity of nature. If we are "without desires," then we are of the best epistemological predispositions. We can maintain attention to the "indeterminate" while engaging with "names" and "knowledge." From such a perspective, the Daoist sage can perceive the abstract aspects of experience for what they are, namely, provisional "signposts" that do not accurately correspond to reality in all of its flux and overlap. When we see all things as parts of a larger whole, this promotes greater interpersonal care in the community. In maintaining how we are each "self-so," we are also maintaining the dispositions that promote social harmony, alleviate arbitrary suffering (like the hunger imposed on us by the ruling class), and reduce the deleterious effects of "knowledge" or the ideologies of those in power. Most of the key aspects of a "moral discourse" are accounted for when we adopt Daoist metaphysics.

Although we can think of the Daoist position as providing a functional equivalent to the moral discourses of their contemporaries, it is important to stress that this position is not just another way of determining and creating *shi-fei* distinction. If it were, it would be susceptible of corruption. (*Those who act ruin it.*) To cling to *shi-fei* distinctions would mean that perception dwells only on "knowledge." People would then only perceive determinate things while ignoring the overlapping oneness of nature. When Daoists dwell in the empty center, they perceive both the individuated things (*you*) and the larger context of experience (*wu*). Being "without heart/mind" (*wuxin*) and "without self-interest" (*wusi*) are two key examples of how the Daoist sage is "without knowledge." In the *Zhuangzi*, similar descriptions are presented when the Daoist is described as capable of seeing the larger oneness or wholeness underlying all things. This process of seeing the self as a part of a larger continuum is what fulfills the role of a moral discourse for the Daoist philosopher. In chapter 5 of this book, I will continue to illustrate how the *Zhuangzi*, just like the *Daodejing*, provides further examples of why the Daoist is critical of both the traditional moralist and the egoists.

Scholars might wonder why the Daoist does not just simply provide a more straight-forward philosophical position similar to that of the Mohist and Confucians. From the Daoist perspective, to do so would be inherently self-undermining because such a position is informed by a reified account of things. The philosophical zigzagging of the Daoist's irony is not merely a style of prose. If the source of social ills is the tendency to cling to reified objects of experience, then the Daoist alternative cannot be straightforward. In being sensitive to life's complexities, Daoist philosophers hope to avoid the pitfalls of their more straightforward philosophical critics. In other words, there is no reason to trust moral philosophers when they claim that they and their theories are the only thing standing in the way of arbitrary oppression and great levels of suffering when the question-begging metaphysics that informs their ("moral") theories has much in common with the coercive and immoral systems of thought that have been employed to justify and normalize oppression. Racism, antisemitism, misogyny, and any other metaphysical theory that has been employed to help fulfill these purposes depends on a substance metaphysics that organizes the world into a "knowledge" of "classes" and "types." Not only can the Daoist provide a functional alternative to the "moral theorists" of their time, but they can do so in a way that does not need to assume that reality is constituted by the same or similar metaphysical structures. The Daoist sage is one that is ever wary of how those people that are "moral" or "good" can often revert to or realize the behaviors of exactly the kinds of monsters they had set out to condemn. Far from believing that a nonnatural metaphysics is necessary in order to mitigate suffering and oppression, the Daoist provides an alternative to the rigidity of the moral philosopher. The next chapter of this book transitions to this topic of how the "moral metaphysician" has far more in common with metaphysical totalitarianism than they are willing to admit. The Daoist, on the other hand, can provide us a way to critique them both.

Chapter Four

The "Nonnaturalistic Fallacy" in Lao-Zhuang Daoism

A Daoist Account of Values

This chapter continues the previous discussion by outlining how the Lao-Zhuang Daoist account of nature provides what can be called (anachronistically) the "nonnaturalistic fallacy." Based on the Daoist insights into nature and experience, "qualities" and "values" are always the product of interaction, and any attempt to isolate qualities from the contexts that they are unique products of would commit an epistemological fallacy, what I call the "nonnaturalistic fallacy." The Daoist would further claim that qualities are properties of interrelationship and are always context dependent and novel occurrences. In other words, there is *no such "thing" or quality like a good/value/end-in-itself*. Epistemologically, the intelligibility of a quality is due to the context that situates it. Qualities are only meaningful *as* situated in particular contexts or *as* functions of larger wholes. Furthermore, the Daoist account of mind and nature would claim that it is actually nonnaturalistic accounts of value that are the sources of excessive suffering in human society. For Daoists, the forms of life that commit the nonnaturalistic fallacy maintain an ignorance about the nature of value and what is actually of value. Through this ignorance, they suffer and also become desensitized to the suffering of others. Such metaphysical objects do not exist, and they have done far more harm than good. When perception is shaped by the conceptual framework that posits the existence of metaphysical realities that would allegedly transcend or exist prior to conditional, empirical reality, these forms of "knowledge" obstruct our capacity to understand oppression and suffering. "Intrinsic value," far from being an assumption necessary for grounding ethical conduct, provides a formula for and helps to normalize coercive and oppressive behavior. Put another way, the Daoist would reject that there is a "moral order" to the cosmos that is independent of the natural world but would simultaneous point out that the belief that there are propositional statements about morality that are true regardless of whether humans exist would have a detrimental effect on human society.

The intent of this and the following chapters is to further clarify how and why the Daoist understanding of mind and morality is radically naturalistic such that it simultaneously critiques nonnaturalistic accounts of values as the source of social ills and disharmony. In looking at how "intrinsic value" is attributed to a rational being, this chapter concludes by showing how it is a nonsense idea to believe people can value "intrinsic value," and it presents other examples of why the nonnaturalistic fallacy helps to justify and normalize suffering and violence. Although it will not be an exhaustive account of how and why "intrinsic value" is an inherently oppressive idea,[1] I focus on how attributing metaphysical "substances" to the natural world is a similar practice to that of the "anti-Semite" and the "antiblack" racist and their ideology. The conscious relationship one would have to such metaphysical objects encourages resentment and presents us with a highly problematic account of values. Clinging to such metaphysical objects only inhibits our ability to understand and respond to situations. "Intrinsic value," when applied to a desired "end," also helps to justify "any means necessary" conduct such as war. War can only be considered of *positive* moral value if we assume the existence of "intrinsic value." For the Daoist, war is never a possible means to a morally good end. Committing the fallacy bifurcates the experience of nature in such a way that it becomes possible to justify "any-means-necessary" conduct such as war.

Dewey's "Philosophical Fallacy": Daoism's "Nonnaturalistic Fallacy"

The Daoist account of mind and experience is one that is naturalistic and empirical in a way similar to the works of John Dewey.[2] Like Dewey, the Daoist tradition is best understood as one that critiques the fallacious account of "knowledge" and human experience that reduces the meaning of situations to the propositions formed in language. These misguided beliefs are rooted in an ignorance about the relationship between the concepts we form and nature. The Daoist understanding of nature involves an account of the limits of propositional knowledge, yet this is grounded in a broader understanding of meaningful and intelligible experience.[3] Furthermore, the Daoist can be understood as providing an account of how *any known or intelligible aspect of experience is internally related to and dependent on the context it is a function of.* There is no such thing as a quality or value "in-itself." To believe otherwise is to commit the "nonnaturalistic fallacy": *the belief that any known "qualities" or "values" exist independent of a natural context.* All perceived "qualities" and things of experience have this meaningful structure and *are only knowable and intelligible as functions of the contexts they are products of.* Although I draw some inspiration from Dewey's ethical naturalism, it is perhaps best to consider Daoist naturalism to be a bit more radical than Dewey's own. Dewey's critique of the Western philosophical tradition is grounded in his radical empiricist account of experience. Pappas explains: "Dewey thought that the general failure to be empirical in philosophy amounted to a failure to acknowledge primary experience as the non-cognitive context of philosophical inquiry. Philosophers often denied the practical experiential context of their own investigations and took the products of their inquiries to replace experience as it is lived."[4]

The content of experience, for Dewey, is not merely cognitive and conceptual. The noncognitive features of experience help to constitute the meaning of any foregrounded and abstract aspects of experience. Throughout his later works, Dewey formulates and reformulates his description of this fallacy, and he never seems to be satisfied with his earlier formulations.[5] In the beginning of *Experience and Nature*, he describes three fallacies in the tradition of philosophy that can be understood as different dimensions of his "philosophical fallacy." He states, "The three [fallacies] are the complete separation of subject and object, (of what is experienced from how it is experienced); the exaggeration of the features of known objects at the expense of the qualities of objects of enjoyment and trouble, friendship and human association, art and industry; and the exclusive isolation of the results of various types of selective simplification which are undertaken for diverse unavowed purposes."[6]

Although isolating certain aspects of experience at the expense of others is what constitutes conscious life—that is, *selective emphasis* and the foregrounding of certain relationships is a natural process of consciousness—we mistakenly believe the products of such processes are independent realities when we ignore the way they are embedded in a noncognitive context. In a sense, the first two fallacies are derivative of the third as they are simply particular instances of "selective simplification." The "philosophical fallacy" was later formulated as the "analytic fallacy." As Pappas explains, for Dewey, "the key to this fallacy is that the rich and concrete context from which distinctions are abstracted is forgotten and the results of inquiry are given a status that they do not and should not have."[7] Any feature of experience that is isolated out of the background continuity of experience is *internally* related to and constituted by that context. The belief that a thing or quality is independent of context is simply nonempirical.

Although the Daoist account of nature and experience can be understood as similar to Dewey's "philosophical fallacy," it is possible to restate the Daoist position even more clearly by critiquing the metaphysics and epistemology behind ethical nonnaturalism. G. E. Moore's ethical nonnaturalism is one such extreme view of knowledge and morality. His "naturalistic fallacy," a position that is rightly criticized by Putnam as simply a form of Platonism,[8] is a position I take as antithetical to Daoism. Moore's famous claim about the "good" runs like this:

> "Good," then, if we mean by it that quality which we assert to belong to a thing, when we say that the thing is good, is incapable of any definition, [. . .] and in this sense "good" has no definition because it is simple and has no parts. It is one of those innumerable objects of thought which are themselves incapable of definition, because they are the ultimate terms by reference to which whatever *is* capable of definition must be defined. [. . .] [T]here is, therefore, no intrinsic difficulty in the contention that "good" denotes a simple and indefinable quality.[9]

The first thing to note, and a point I will return to later in this chapter, is that Moore's "nonnaturalism" asserts that qualities are properties of objects. Under this framework, a quality like the "good" is merely the attribute of a single object. The quality "good" does not *constitute the being* of the thing in question. Before it is even argued that the "good" is a quality that is nonnatural, assumptions are made about the nature/*being* of qualities and things. As Putnam describes it, Moore's ethical "nonnaturalism"

> announced that what ethical judgments are really about is a single, supersensible quality called *good*. (Moore called it a

"non-natural" quality.) Not only is *good* supposed to be invisible to the senses and undetectable by the natural sciences, it is also "simple," according to Moore's theory—that is, not analyzable in terms of other properties or qualities. In this respect, it was supposed to be like the color yellow, although (as Moore pointed out) yellow is a natural (in fact a sensible) quality, whereas the allegedly unitary and simple quality of *good* is not.[10]

Moore assumes that some qualities are knowable and intelligible in ways that are "not analyzable in terms of other qualities" and that some qualities are intelligible independent of context. As Mark Johnson describes Moore's views, "Any attempt to define 'good' commits what Moore christened the 'naturalistic fallacy,' because *good* is not a natural object or property. Moore notoriously illustrated the notion of a non-natural property with the property *yellow*, which he claimed we do experience yet which cannot be defined in terms of anything else. Likewise, Moore asserted that *good* is a property possessed by certain states of affairs that we can experience but not define in terms of any natural properties."[11]

With this account of the "good," humans would possess both the capacity to perceive natural properties and, through transmundane recognition, experience the quality "good" which would bear no relationship to said natural properties. Ethical judgments would bear no relationship to the natural world in a way that can be understood through natural, causal relationships (the only relationship the "good" could participate in would be one of standing in relation to a "mind" that can apprehend it as 1) a (nonnatural) property of a distinct object or situation or 2) as a nonnatural, metaphysical object itself that was related but external to the natural world). Contrary to these metaphysical claims that bifurcate reality into two distinct realms of existence, Daoists would claim that everything known and made intelligible is done so in relation to "some-thing-other"; that is, any known and posited "A" is only knowable and intelligible in relationship to "not-A." Daoists would agree with Johnson when he argues that, "no concept is understood 'in itself.' Concepts get their meanings in relation to other concepts and to historical situations and frameworks in which the concept develops and gets its temporary application. Concepts grow and change as changing conditions require us to find new ways of ordering and making sense of our experience."[12]

Contrary to Moore, the Daoist account of experience would hold that "yellow" was a "color" and only knowable in the context of its family of resemblances to other "colors." Each "color" is a provisional name denoting a wide variety of various experiences had by human organisms. The color understood as "yellow" is recognized and isolated out of a background of many different experiences of "color" and is always initially isolated out of this continuum because of our practical concerns.[13] There is no such ability to understand "yellow" devoid of context and interrelationship. The Daoist account of nature goes one step further. "Colors" are not properties of objects or things, nor are they subjective experiences. "Color" is the *product* of the interaction between the human organism and its environment. It is the unique way the chemistry of this biological organism interacts with waves of light of different frequencies that further interact with different aspects of the environment. To use a Whiteheadian phrase, "color" is not "simply-located."[14] G.E. Moore is simply guilty of Whitehead's "fallacy of simple location" and Dewey's "philosophical fallacy." The same thing applies to the quality "good." There is then no such thing as a "quality" that is nonnatural because every known quality depends on and is an emergent function of a natural, continuous context or "whole." Based on the Daoist account of experience, a "good-in-itself" is an epistemologically suspect phrase. A phrase like this is simply the result of mistakenly reifying the products of cognition as if they existed independently of that process. Qualities are properties of interrelationship and are not the sole possessions of either objects or subjects. The remainder of this chapter will continue to illustrate how the Daoist philosophers provide an account of experience that is antirepresentational. This, in turn, can help explain how this account of experience would involve the nonnaturalistic fallacy, how "intrinsic value" provides justification for "any-means-necessary" conduct such as war and how such metaphysical objects help to legitimize systematic oppression.

Daoist Philosophy: On Values and Valuing

A central theme in Daoism involves the idea of "returning" attention to the fundamental way humans interrelate with nature. This process is achieved through cultivating a greater sensitivity to the natural world and our relationships to it. If people do so, then the extraneous suffering that human society creates (due to their ignorance) will be mitigated. This "returning" involves undercutting the epistemological framework that produces alienation from nature. The problem is that, for the Daoist, certain cultural and political institutions encourage the formation of certain habits and beliefs that obfuscate our ability to understand our relationship to nature. Daoists do not insist that persons remove themselves from human society completely. Daoism diagnoses (what they believe to be) the source of extraneous suffering in human society. Doing so involves understanding and accurately perceiving the natural world. As passage 52 of the *Daodejing* makes clear, "Making out the small is real acuity (*ming*), Safeguarding the weak is real strength. Taking into account the way things reveal themselves, If you go back again and rely upon your acuity, You will stay clear of calamities. This is what is called [inheriting the constant, 襲常]."[15] What the Daoist is suggesting is that we are not attentive to the natural, more fundamental way we interrelate to the world.[16] We cannot stay clear of problems because we are not of the most sensitive and receptive dispositions to act. What is obstructing our experience of situations, and how does one return to the "uncarved block of wood" (*pu*), and what is "self-so" (*ziran*)? The answer, I take it, is that the Daoist is suggesting that people habitually ignore the *actual process of valuing* nature in favor of abstract "valuation" or post facto "evaluation" of experiences of valuing, that is, that we mistake the second-order evaluation of nature *as* the first-order process of valuing and interacting with nature. Furthermore, "valuing" is the qualitative way things are immediately located in relation to the natural world. This is because valuing, *as* the interaction between various aspects of nature, is always a "primary property" (traditionally, as with Moore, "value" is assumed to be a "secondary property"). To borrow Dewey's term, abstract "valuation" is a secondary/derivative aspect of experience and, like the Daoist account of "names," does not exhaustively correspond to the concrete way beings interrelate with the world. "Valuation" is the abstract *evaluation* of concrete experiences of valuing nature. When we commit the nonnaturalistic fallacy, this conceptually (and provisionally) bifurcates nature in a way that it denies relational connections.[17] With the Daoist's naturalism, it is epistemologically suspect to believe that we value abstract objects or "simply located" entities. Yet because of the nature of consciousness, it is possible (and unfortunately, frequently the case) that we neglect the concrete and unique way we are immediately and meaningfully related to the world. Valuing, *in concreto*, always involves the immediately felt quality of experience. The belief that one values abstractions (like valuing "the Good") is misguided. Furthermore, these same misguided habits and beliefs also end up obstructing the experience of the immediately felt quality of existence; that is, they obstruct our attention to concrete particulars/things. Passage 2 of the

Daodejing is one of many passages that can be understood as outlining this understanding of values. "When all under heaven knows the 'beautiful' as being beautiful, thus there is already foulness. When all know the 'good' as being good, thus there is already the 'not good.' Thus, the 'determinate' ('有') and the 'indeterminate' ('無') mutually generate each other [*xiang sheng,* 相生]."[18] What the Daoist is diagnosing is the tendency to cling to the abstract or named (*ming,* 名) aspects of experience as if the abstractions we project onto experience exhaustively correspond to nature. The Daoist is critical of the tendency to reify qualities in experience as if they were independent of context. Any posited thing, quality or value (*you,* 有) simultaneously involves the concrete context that it is a *function of*; that is, non-being (*wu,* 無). Being (*you*) is the secondary and provisionally posited aspect of experience and nature. Regardless of the kind of evaluation, the posited (*you*) is only meaningful and intelligible in relation to the nonposited (*wu*). Passage 40 of the *Daodejing* claims that "the events of the world arise from the determinate (*you*), and the determinate arises from the indeterminate (*wu*)."[19] A posited thing is not separate from the rest of nature. It maintains a connection or "oneness" with the rest of nature because each posited thing is a *function of* the larger whole. The names we give to things and the concepts we form are provisional. They are functional and not ontological distinctions.

There are some scholars that consider the *Zhuangzi* to be espousing basic moral relativism.[20] What these accounts miss is that, traditionally, "values" have been understood as secondary properties of objects.[21] Under the Daoist view (as espoused in this book), values are now "primary properties." Both "values" and "things" are no longer understood as "simply located" because values emerge from a cocreative process between environment and organism. The *Zhuangzi* needs to be understood in the same naturalistic way as the *Daodejing* passages above. Chapter 2 claims:

> There is no being that is not "that." There is no being that is not "this." But one cannot be seeing these from the perspective of "that": one knows them only from "this" [i.e., from one's own perspective]. Thus, we can say: "That" emerges from "this" and "this" follows from "that." But by the same token, their simultaneous generation is their simultaneous destruction, and vice versa. Simultaneous affirmability is simultaneous negetability, and vice versa. Thus the Sage does not proceed from any one of them alone but instead lets them all bask in

the broad daylight of Heaven. And that too is only a case of going by the rightness of the present "this."[22]

This passage expresses the same insight that is articulated in the *Daodejing*. Any posited "value" or thing depends on the context or the "nonposited" aspects of experience. To be clear, each "perspective" is not "right" in a normative sense. The claim that each "knows them only from 'this' perspective" is a descriptive claim about the natural world. It is not an endorsement of each way a perspective provisionally affirms "values" and things. What is normative in this passage is how the sage is described. The "Sage does not proceed from any one of them" in the sense that the sage recognizes the natural interdependence and historical contingency of all posited values and things.[23] There is no reason to "proceed from any one of them" because each "nonsage" perspective, in so far as these perspectives do not possess the insights of the Daoist sage, would all be guilty of the nonnaturalistic fallacy. They are positing their "values" as if they were independent of context (as the previous chapter suggested, they view *shi-fei* distinctions while unable to see the wider context of these distinctions, *wu*). As soon as a perspective recognizes how values and things are not "simply located," they would be considered a Daoist sage in the sense that they would not be guilty of the nonnaturalistic fallacy.

Another naturalistic account of values in the *Zhuangzi* is introduced through a series of questions in chapter 2 of the "Inner Chapters." Although the questions might at first appear to be basic skepticism, there is an ironic answer to many of Zhuangzi's questions. Methodologically, Zhuangzi's questions are often intentionally framed such that the (ironically) "right" answer to the question is that "this question is the wrong question to ask" or "this question presupposes certain kinds of answers, and all these answers are wrong." The text playfully highlights how the framing of questions can be question begging. As the story goes,

> But now let me take a stab at asking you about it. When people sleep in a damp place, they wake up deathly ill and sore about the waist—but what about eels? If people live in trees, they tremble with fear and worry—but how about monkeys? Of these three, which "knows' the right place to live? People eat the flesh of their livestock, deer eat grass, snakes eat centipedes, hawks and eagles eat mice. Of these four, which "knows" the right thing to eat? Monkeys take she-monkeys for mates, bucks

mount does, male fish frolic with female fish, while humans regard Mao Qiang and Lady Li as great beauties—but when fish see them they dart into the depths.[24]

This story should not be read as mere skepticism about values. Biological organisms are related to certain kinds of environments. Furthermore, certain ways of relating to the environment are immediately felt as more valuable. There is a "fit" or "coherence" achieved with certain forms of interactions. With respect to the *Zhuangzi*, we should not impose a dichotomy between facts and values. *Valuing* is how all facts are known; that is, in a processual framework, it is impossible to extricate epistemology from axiology. The point of this passage is that the qualities felt in experience are not "subjective qualities" or "subjective realities." Qualitative experience emerges from the interaction between organism and environment (again, a *cocreative* process relying equally on both organism and environment). Asking the question "Which perspective is right?" is question begging because it assumes the "rightness" is somehow an "isolatable quality-in-itself." Keeping this in mind, the lesson of another famous story in the "Outer Chapters" of the *Zhuangzi* is easier to understand. The story is the "happy fish" story, and it involves a dialogue between Zhuangzi and his logician friend Huizi.

Zhuangzi and Huizi are observing a fish above the Hao River when Zhuangzi, upon seeing a fish dart about in the waters below, remarks that "such is the happiness of fish." Huizi responds with skepticism, questioning Zhuangzi on how it is possible that he can know the "happiness" of fish (i.e., what we should consider a "subjective" or "private" feeling) when Zhuangzi is not himself a fish. What we get with Zhuangzi's reply is not just a witty reply back to his logic-loving friend. The capacity to know something is, for Zhuangzi, tied to one's intimate relationship to the world (being on a bridge over the river Hao, in this instance).[25] For Zhuangzi, existence is irreducibly communal and collaborative. There is no "private self" that exists prior to the relationships that *constitute* experience. "My" experience of the world is constituted by that world. It is always *from* "*here*" ("this") that I recognize and disclose a world. "Happiness" here denotes the particular way the fish is related to a world, and it is not simply a "subjective state." "Happiness" is never completely "private." It is Huizi, the logician/rationalist, who assumes there is an independent "private inner life" that takes precedence to the way nature is relationally constituted.

Ames claims that "for Zhuangzi, the language itself used to express the event on the bridge is a basis for assuming that there is shared experience between the human beings themselves and with other sentient animals even as remote from us as fish. Zhuangzi, far from putting these two seemingly disparate things together, is registering the depth of their interrelatedness."[26] Experience is primordially interdependent and intersubjective. We fail to bring our attention to the primary aspects of existence (i.e., *valuing*) because we cling to the "names" and concepts that we form about nature. The concepts formed about experience are functions of the "valuing" that *constitutes all possible experience.*

Both the *Daodejing* and the *Zhuangzi* frequently shift from a discussion of values to a discussion of "beings" and vice versa. When the relationships between things are no longer taken as secondary or "accidental" aspects of experience, this changes how we understand the nature of values. Traditionally, it makes sense to talk about how people possess values. There are dispositions or objects that we deem to be "good" and favorable, and we do so in the sense that these are properties of the objects in question (for example, healthy food is "good," or the "healthy" that is the "good" of the food is thought to be a property of the food.). Under this view, values are merely possessed and do not constitute the possessor in question because things take precedence to their relationships. As soon as we give up the idea that determinate objects exist prior to the contingent way said objects are related, then we can no longer claim that values are "secondary properties" of things. Values, in part, constitute the *being* of the beings under consideration. The "healthyness" of food is dependent on both the biology of the organism eating it and the relationship it has to other kinds of food.[27] The value of certain foods is not because the food possesses some "quality-in-itself." "Health" as valuable is a dynamic and ongoing interaction with the world.

The *Daodejing* 11 claims: "Thirty spokes converge at one hub, but the utility of the cart is a function of the nothingness (*wu*) inside the hub. [. . .] Thus, it might be something (*you*) that provides the value, but it is [the] nothing[ness] that provides the utility [*yong*]."[28] In a processual account of things and values, it would be correct to equate the two. A thing is a function of its context, and as such it is a *form of valuing*. Values simultaneously constitute the things in question because the interrelationship between a thing (*you*) and its context (*wu*) is qualitative. A quality is the "non-simply-located" interaction of various aspects of nature. In this sense value denotes a much broader domain. A provisionally posited abstract "valuation" is only intelligible in the context of that which has already been *evaluated*. Any isolated thing we might claim as valuable has been recognized as such only in the background context of our *ongoing and constant valuing* (again, epistemology and axiology are inseparable).

The difficulty in clarifying a processual account of values lies in the fact that "value" ambiguously denotes both nouns and verbs. We use the same word to denote both "particular values," that is, nouns like "justice" and "freedom" that might be "values I possess," and certain ways of acting, that is, the verbal "we value each other" or "to value their property." Any posited thing would simultaneously be a kind of valuing in the sense that each interaction is also a kind of evaluation. A value would then not be a static possession but would instead be the dynamic way this continuum called "nature" is interrelating and transforming. The ability to recognize and posit a thing is inseparable from the ability to see its value in a given context, that is, the concrete way it is a function of a situation. We may point to a being (*you*) as valuable, but it is simply a function of the whole continuum (*wu*) that is the ongoing *valuing* that constitutes nature.

Although it is possible to interpret both the *Daodejing* and the *Zhuangzi* as espousing a kind of transcendent mysticism (admittedly, the Daoist religion that later emerges in China goes this route),[29] an interpretation like this is problematic because it neglects the naturalistic language that runs throughout both the *Daodejing* and the *Zhuangzi*. Instead of taking Daoist meditation practices as aiming to achieve transcendence, they are better understood as involving the cultivation of greater awareness to the qualitative particularity of nature. When we do not recognize the natural source of all values, we ignore how what is sacred is what is natural for the Daoist.[30]

The attitude that the Daoist is critical of is of those peoples and cultures that believe they are independent of (and then superior to) the natural world. The world, metaphorically described as an "uncarved block of wood," is a complex network of interrelationships. This understanding of nature should not be confused with Western notions of "natural law" or "natural rights." When consciousness imposes a "simply located" account of things and values onto nature, this will inevitably backfire. Any form of human conduct that tries to manipulate nature in a coercive way simultaneously fails to acknowledge their natural interdependence and how they are internally related to it.[31] They fail to see that they, their culture, their people, are equally aspects of nature. The meditation practices of

Daoism are an attempt to ameliorate experience such that the effects of nonnaturalistic forms of belief and desire on our perception of situations is disempowered or, to borrow a term in phenomenology, desedimented.[32] What such meditation practices lead to are the insights that were outlined above and in previous chapters with the Daoist naturalistic accounts of experience. With these meditation practices, we cultivate habits of attention and practice "forgetting" (*wang*, 忘) nonnaturalistic and reified "knowledge" (*zhi*). In doing so, we properly understand the nature of "values" and thereby no longer commit the nonnaturalistic fallacy. Daoist philosophers are concerned with maintaining attention to the immediate quality of our situations for this very reason. As passage 64 claims, we should "deal with a situation before it happens; Bring it under control before it gets out of hand. A tree with the girth of a person's embrace grows from the tiniest shoot. A pavilion nine stories high rises from one basket of earth. A thousand-foot wall begins from the soil under one's feet."[33] The habits that inhibit our ability to be receptive to the concrete and immediate particularity of situations inhibit our ability to respond to said situations. Whether it be certain forms of abstract and ossified desire (*yu*) or reified "knowledge" (*zhi*), Daoism focuses on cultivating habits such that nonnaturalistic forms of belief and desire no longer obstruct our interactions with the natural world. Daoists recognize that cognitive habits can obstruct our ability to be attentive to our immediate, natural interdependence. As passage 64 continues, "it is for this reason the sages, in leaving off desiring, do not prize property that is hard to come by, and in studying not to study, *returns to what most people have passed over* (my italics)."[34] What "most people pass over" is the immediate way they are interrelated to the natural world.

The ability to see things unadulterated by preconceived notions (*zhi*) is described by the Daoist using a wide range of vocabulary. There is the positive vocabulary used to describe this cultivated capacity named "clarity" (*ming*, 明) and as "making use of clarity" (*yiming*, 以明), but most often the Daoist sage is described using a negative vocabulary like the "*wu*-forms": three of the most important being "without knowledge" (*wuzhi*), "without desire" (*wuyu*), and "without egoisticaction" (*wuwei*). In early Daoism, clarity means a cultivated, perceptual sensitivity to the concrete particularity of things. The negative vocabulary of the "*wu*-forms," on the other hand, stresses that certain dimensions of experience no longer obstruct the conduct of persons. When someone is "without" these habits of experience, they have cultivated the capacity to perceive nature as a "nameless uncarved block of wood" (*pu*) and how all things are novel confluences of relations (*ziran*). Near the end of the first story of chapter 4 of the "Inner Chapters" (the important story I covered in chapter 1 of this monograph), *Confucius as mouthpiece for Zhuangzi suggests that

> you have learned the wisdom of being wise [知], but not yet the wisdom of being free of wisdom [無知]. Concentrate on the hollows of what is before you, and the empty chamber within you will generate its own brightness.
>
> Good fortune comes to roost in stillness. To lack this stillness is called scurrying around even when sitting down. Allow your ears and eyes to open inward and thereby place yourself beyond your mind's understanding consciousness.[35]

The Daoist sage is "without knowledge," but this is in the sense that they perceive situations without the epistemology indebted to a substance ontology. Because the sage has cultivated a perceptual capacity to observe the particularity of all things, they are without a fixed understanding of things and values. They are "without knowledge" in the sense that they no longer commit the nonnaturalistic fallacy. Cognitive habits no longer obscure experience when attention is brought once again to the quality of immediate existence. The Daoist does not cultivate a state of mind where all propositional knowledge is abandoned forever. Cognitive habits and propositional knowledge are functional and by their very nature involve isolating certain features of experience while pushing others to the fringe of consciousness. Maintaining attention solely to the abstract dimensions of experience is to spend one's conscious life living in one's overactive rationalizations and imagination or, for Zhuangzi, to "scurrying around even when sitting down" (*zuochi*, 坐馳). Although the phrase is mentioned only once in the entire *Zhuangzi*, it is an accurate and comical way of describing the problem the Daoist philosophers are diagnosing, that is, the problems of "propositional knowledge" (*zhi*) or the nonnaturalistic fallacy. It describes those persons (philosophers like Huizi) that have not cultivated the ability to perceptually distance themselves from cognitive habits. *Wuzhi*, or being "without knowledge," is a kind of knowing and perceiving that is not merely of the linguistic and cognitive form. *Wuzhi* is the felt awareness that one's conceptual categories (*zhi*), and the names (*ming*) attributed to things are secondary dimensions of experience and do not exhaustively represent our relation to nature.

When we fail to be "without knowledge," we can then be considered to have cultivated a "provisional private life" where, simply because of our lack of attention to our basic interactions with the world, we fail to recognize our interdependence with nature. Simultaneous with the inability to see the provisional character of each individuated thing is an inattention to the concrete and indeterminate context of experience. A lack of attention to the immediate way we are interrelated to the world is then not only a failure in the understanding, but also precisely what further inhibits our ability to spontaneously interact with nature's various potentials. If people are of the disposition where they fail to recognize the underlying continuity of nature (*wu*), this could be understood as having cultivated a false, independent "sense of self" and a false sense that they exist as isolatable "subjects." Dispositions would be insufficiently grounded in noncognitive relationships with the environment (i.e., Huizi has, in a sense, cultivated a "private self" and functions in an antisocial manner as he is not attentive to the immediate way all experience is constituted by its context). There is no such way of undergoing experience that is *completely* private or separate from the world, yet there is always the possibility that human consciousness neglects the immediate relations with the world. For both Dewey and Daoist philosophy, it is always a possibility that persons do not recognize the meaningful way they are situated in the world. From the Daoist perspective, the majority of people are inattentive to the relationships that constitute us. Radical subjectivism, in the sense that people exist as distinct "minds," is not a real possibility, but there is a sense that the habits we cultivate can be such that we are inattentive, careless, and neurotic about our embodied existence. With ignorant forms of habit formation, people can become little Cartesians in the sense that they continuously fail to be attentive to their immediate, qualitative existence.

Valuing without "Intrinsic Value" in Daoist Philosophy

With the Daoist's naturalistic account of valuing, it is not empirically possible to value that which is metaphysical; that is, just as the idea of a "good-in-itself" is epistemologically suspect, the idea that a person could value abstract "values" is deeply fallacious. It is a mistake to think there are such things as "intrinsic values" as this is a misunderstanding of the *being* of values and things. We do not value "values" or things. Valuing is how things are interrelating to the world or the quality of interrelationship. On this model, conduct is then adjusted such that *greater valuing, that is, greater degrees of interrelationship,* is realized. If we take seriously the idea that value is interrelationship, then the more various aspects of nature are interrelating, the greater the value that emerges. If interactions involve mutual exchange where this exchange realizes a new set of relationships, then persons are adjusting their relationships to the world such that more value is realized. Achieving greater interrelationship with the world means more value is being cocreated. Different relationships are of a different quality as well. If certain qualities of relationship are of greater value than others, then human conduct can be adjusted to realize these forms of interrelationship more. Most important, real values involve an *internal relationship* to our environments. To be related to other people in an external way is not the same as the quality of relationship that can be considered an internal relationship. For example, a merely physical interaction can never be considered an internal relationship to another conscious being. Violent coercion also cannot be considered a cocreative act because it does not involve different aspects of nature mutually constituting and enriching each other in the process of change. In light of human relationships, this is not difficult to understand. If we develop relationships with others that involve emotional, intellectual, and physical qualities, this is a more valuable relationship than a one-dimensional interaction as it involves each person being internally related to the becoming of the other in a deeper sense. Comparable to Daoism, what Dewey's theory of valuation calls for is an empirical account of the *concrete valuing* persons are *actually* undergoing. Critical of nonnaturalistic accounts of value, Dewey claims:

> The extreme instance of the view that to be intrinsic is to be out of any relation is found in those writers who hold that, since values *are* intrinsic, they cannot depend upon *any* relation whatever, and certainly not upon a relation of human beings. [. . .] The views of this extreme nonnaturalistic school may, accordingly, be regarded as a definite exposure of what happens when an analysis of the abstract concept of "intrinsicalness" is substituted for analysis of empirical occurrences.[36]

It is impossible, empirically, to value in a way that is free of all relations. As soon as an entity is valued, it would literally bear a relationship to human consciousness and to any means used to attain such a valued "end."

A value that is properly "had" by a person must be of a possible kind of interaction with nature. The "reasonableness" of any form of valuing depends on the empirical context and the concrete means that are available for achieving the desired ends. Anything rationalized as a valued "end" is intelligible only in relationship to the "means" that can be utilized to achieve such an end. When we believe there is such a value "in-itself," we are quite literally admitting that the concrete context of experience, the possible means used to achieve such an end, does not adjust the value of a self-defined "value-in-itself." We are, by definition, also rejecting the fact that value is a product of relationship thus ignoring how value is a cocreative process that inevitably alters the particularity of each aspect of nature (and especially, the particularity of each person).

In light of this account of values and the nonnaturalistic fallacy, asking about "what transcendent facts/principles guide our valuing" is question begging as it assumes that "what" guides conduct needs to be external to concrete instances of valuing. Any concrete instance of valuing itself is only intelligible and knowable in concrete situations; that is, only lived, concrete experiences of valuing contextualize other concrete forms of valuing. The more experiences of valuing we undergo, the greater ability one has for *intelligently* adjusting to the different ways we can interrelate to the natural world. It is only by interrelating differently to the world that we understand how certain ways of interrelating are more fitting than others. Without concrete changes in the ways human beings interrelate with and understand their world, there is no "sense" (i.e., "meaning") to how one way of valuing might be more desirable or fitting than others. It should also be clear that this form of naturalism avoids that kind of relativism that implies "anything goes" (although, that argument was perhaps always a "red herring" with respect to the *Zhuangzi*). The claim that relativism implies "anything goes" depends on an account of values as "secondary properties" of things where values must either be merely "subjective realities" or correspond to a reality that transcends nature (the "myth of subjectivism" and the "myth of objectivism"). As the Daoist account of nature argues, valuing is always as expressions of our interdependence and intercommunication. Values say as much about the environment as they do about the people in question doing the valuing because the emergence of value is a cocreative process. Certain ways of interrelating to the world are not as valuable as others because any given way of valuing is inevitably related to other experienced forms of valuing. Furthermore, the ability to recognize value is not necessarily reducible to the formation of propositional statements and their meaning (although it could play a part in it). With this kind of naturalism, it requires that we maintain attention to the concrete ways interrelating with the environment differ in quality. The more harmonious interactions are with the natural world and our fellow living beings, the more value we realize in our interdependence. We do not need to appeal to an antecedently existing or transcendent, nonnatural reality.

Although this epistemological "error" has been called a fallacy up to this point, we can also see how the tendency to cling to metaphysical objects is related to the possession of certain existential and psychological dispositions. As a false sense of value, there are still reasons why people might feel psychologically motivated to cling to these metaphysical objects and commit the nonnaturalistic fallacy. For those familiar with the works of Jean Paul Sartre, a similar position to the nonnaturalistic fallacy is put forth when Sartre describes the person in "bad faith" and the "serious man." Like committing the nonnaturalistic fallacy, being in "bad faith" involves maintaining dispositions that are consciously "fixed" on metaphysical objects. To be in "bad faith" is to be of dispositions that do not coalesce with the world in any meaningful or valuable way, and in this way, we can say it inhibits our capacity to understand and respond to situations. As Lewis Gordon summarizes, for Sartre, "a serious man is in bad faith because he denies his freedom. He regards his values as objects to be *known*, not constructed."[37] To believe that one's "values" are distinct objects "out there" is to be in "bad faith." One key difference between Daoism and Sartre is that persons of "bad faith" are those who reduce their values to metaphysical substances in order to *evade* reality. They cling to these objects in order to avoid taking responsibility over their lives. For an existentialist like Sartre, it is a *choice* to be in "bad faith" and to cling to petrified, metaphysical "values" so as to deny responsibility for the values humans have *created*. The nonnaturalistic fallacy, conversely, is committed whenever we reduce any "thing" or "value" to a "simply located" reality like a metaphysical substance. The process of reifying concrete relationships to the world obscures our perception of situations. This process limits our freedom in the sense that people do not exhaustibly bring their attention to the world and their relationship to it. As will be outlined in the next chapter, cultural and political institutions help to shape the dispositions of people such that they view the world through "knowledge," thus producing perceptual alienation. For the Daoist, it is not simply a choice to believe that one's values are distinct objects "out there." Cultural institutions contribute to the formation of such beliefs. Unlike Sartre, Chinese metaphysics presents us with an account of agency that is always situated in the context of interdependence. The cultivation of greater levels of freedom is always situated within conditioned interrelationships.[38] People must change how they qualitatively relate to their world in order to recognize how clinging to metaphysical objects is not of real value. One way to do this is through cultivation. Another way is through a change of environment and the social institutions that shape the dispositions of people. Without concrete changes in the quality of interrelationship, people will continue to cling to metaphysical objects for their sense of fulfillment.

There is a clear difference between the forms of life that cling to metaphysical fictions and those that do not. It is both an epistemological and axiological error to cling to these reified objects as if they were of value. From the Daoist perspective, these ignorant forms of life also help to legitimize and encourage violent and coercive political projects. Making the world into distinct things is precisely the attitude that those with political power want to inculcate into the common people when they wish to preserve nonegalitarian and imperial forms of life. "Eye desires," "moral merit," and "metaphysical monsters" are all examples of the kind of objects that are valued or cognized when committing the nonnaturalistic fallacy. The Daoist critique of nonnaturalism and Sartre's idea of "bad faith" helps to highlight why metaphysical beliefs are epistemologically suspect and morally dubious. We must be wary of the moral metaphysician because, as McCumber puts it, "in the West, where the political rests upon the metaphysical, the most concrete struggles presuppose the most abstract arguments"[39] The most violent forms of human behaviors have been informed and justified through nonnatural metaphysical systems of belief. Remaining "fixed" on these reified "values" is ignorant, plays a role in shaping human affect, but most importantly, helps to provide an interpretive framework for coercion and oppression. With respect to human experience, it is the very structure of the metaphysics of "substance" that is problematic. Liberal metaphysics and the ideology of racial resentment share these same metaphysical assumptions.

"Intrinsic Value" Is Not Possible to Value

Critics of Daoism cannot cling to nonnaturalist metaphysical assumptions as if these beliefs were what constituted being an ethical human being. In fact, this is a perfect example of exactly the attitude Daoists are critical of when they suggest that "those who act ruin it." When morality is reduced to the possession of a certain kind of (propositional) "knowledge" or mere participation in cultural institutions, it contributes to moral obtuseness because these practices are not, in fact, equivalent to the actual possession of dispositional sensitivities that said practices were supposed to help form. From the Daoist perspective, to insist on the existence of "intrinsic value" is to cling to an outdated and confused piece of metaphysical thinking. Such ideas would necessarily involve the perceptual neglect of important features of situations that are needed for understanding their meaning. An "end" or "good-in-itself," far from being necessary for ethics, is a remnant of Greek metaphysics that should have been abandoned a long time ago. Without "intrinsic value," most philosophers in the West believe that there are then no constraints that can be placed on forms of life and values. With a processual account of nature and experience, limits can be placed on forms of life that can be considered highly problematic and not of real value. These same forms of life further inhibit persons from being able to recognize what forms of life are *actually* valuable and desirable (i.e., cultural institutions can encourage alienation in the population).

Considering how a processual framework provides constraints on possible values, it is important to show why abandoning "intrinsic value" is really not as great a loss as philosophers might insist. As I clarify in the rest of this chapter, there are a few key reasons why "intrinsic value" should be viewed with suspicion. One reason to be critical of the idea of "intrinsic value" is that the notion is virtually meaningless as it is impossible to actually value "intrinsic value." Since that which is "intrinsically valuable" is not possible to value, it can be considered merely "intrinsic" like an "essence" or other nonnatural metaphysical reality. Apart from "intrinsic value" being impossible to value, the relationship between the human mind, "intrinsic value" as a conceptual object, and how it would or could affect human experience bears great resemblance to the logic of anti-Semitism (as pointed out by Jean Paul Sartre) and other forms of racialized oppression such as "antiblack racism." "Intrinsic value" operates in a way similar to how a racial ideology operates within human conscious life. Another reason to be weary of "intrinsic value" is that the distinction between "intrinsic value" and "instrumental value" helps to justify totalitarian, unilateral, "any-means-necessary" conduct. Conduct that neglects the means used to achieve "valued ends" is highly coercive and inevitably self-undermining. These nonnatural metaphysical beliefs help to illuminate why the Daoist is critical of both war and the "moral attitude" as well. Metaphysical ideals such as these help to encourage passivity, docility, and resentment as there is no concrete way for people to value or develop interrelationships in a way coherent with these metaphysical objects. Far from believing that making this hard distinction between things having "intrinsic value" and "nonintrinsic value" is a good idea, philosophers should be apprehensive of any metaphysical system that ontologically bifurcates nature because doing so places certain features of existence as beyond the bounds of relevance and concern. Below, I first highlight how the notion of an "end-in-itself" is a phrase that is basically empty of any real meaning before moving into how we should understand "intrinsic value" within the Kantian framework. Following this, I then clarify why these metaphysical ideas contribute to oppressive ideologies.

When philosophers mention the phrase an "end-in-itself" and conflate it with "intrinsic value," they are in fact borrowing from a metaphysical tradition that has ignored and taken for granted highly problematic beliefs. There are two senses to what it can mean to be an "end-in-itself" and therefore be of "intrinsic value." In one sense, it emphasizes the "end" in the means/end relationship. An "end-in-itself" is the final, highest, most complete "end" of a process (a "final cause"/*telos*). It is a valued "end" that is not the means to a further valued "end" (i.e., no longer has "instrumental value"). This use of an "end-in-itself" will be discussed more in a later section. The other use of the term "end-in-itself" is how Kant uses it when trying to determine what kind of thing has the kind of value where, regardless of the relationship it may contingently possess, it will remain unchanged. What Kant defines as an "end-in-itself" (a rational being or subject) is precisely that which is criticized by Dewey in a *Theory of Valuation*.

> The words "inherent," "intrinsic," and "immediate" are used ambiguously, so that a fallacious conclusion is reached. Any quality or property that actually belongs to any object or event is properly said to be immediate, inherent, or intrinsic. The fallacy consists in interpreting what is designated by these terms as out of relation to anything else and hence as absolute. For example, *means* are by definition relational, mediated, and mediating, since they are intermediate between an existing situation and a situation that is to be brought into existence by their use.[40]

Regardless of the kind of valuing, value is immediately felt (in the process of successfully using a tool, for example, you immediately recognize its value. Instrumental value is inherent to the process of using a tool). An end is always related to the means used. Furthermore, as Dewey is right to point out, an "end" is always inherent in the process of using a means to an end or what Dewey calls an "end-in-view." As an instrumentality, an "end-in-view" (the concept or image the imagination projects onto the field of experience) helps to constitute the meaning of human conduct in the sense that such abstractions help to guide conduct towards a desired end. When philosophers conflate the notions of "intrinsicness" and "finality," they establish a bivalent account of reality that places anything that is not "intrinsically valuable" as merely possessing an "accidental" or "secondary" character. Means become "accidental" in relation to an "end" that is an "end-in-itself."

The metaphysicians that still dominate Western philosophy departments might take issue with these claims. From their understanding of it, they still insist that "rational beings" can or should recognize other "rational beings" as equal insofar as they are also "ends-in-themselves." This, purportedly, would place moral constraints on each "rational being." It is important to further deconstruct these claims in order to help make clear why they are basically tautological, at best, and carry almost no real descriptive or prescriptive weight. It is also not at all clear how a "rational being" as an "end-in-itself" could be the possessor of "intrinsic value" because there is the more fundamental problem that this Kantian account of agency and "freedom" presents us with a fictional account of human agency (and at least Kant admitted that this kind of "freedom" was an assumption). Kant's formula claims that you ought to "act [such] that you use humanity, whether in your own person or in the person of any other, always at the same time as an end, never merely as a means" when formulating desired ends.[41] Each rational being is an "end-in-itself" because they can exercise a *one-way causal influence over nature* (exercise an *unconditioned* power over nature). As such, rational beings are the only viable candidates for possessing the kind of value that possesses a one-way causal influence (i.e., "intrinsic value"). Because an "end-in-itself" cannot be the means for another end, it is an "objective" end in the sense that this thing cannot be adjusted due to any conditioned or conditional relationship to anything else. Based on this framework, if there is an object that can possibly have objective value or a kind of value that could be "intrinsic," it would need to be a kind of thing that has a one-way causal influence on the world (or that does not change due to encountering that which is "conditioned"). Thus, only essences or things like essences could be of "intrinsic value." When philosophers claim that a "rational being" is an "end-in-itself," it is precisely as Dewey states: philosophers have reached this conclusion because they have conflated different concepts and have forgotten the original and particular significance of these distinctions. Initially, an "end-in-itself" was understood in terms of a means/ends relationship. It makes no sense to call an object an "end-in-itself" if we only intend to denote that the object has intrinsic worth. The significance of the name no longer matches the reality. In the Kantian framework, an "end-in-itself" now does not mean anything in relationship to *actual* means and ends when we attribute the term "end-in-itself" to a particular object (i.e., the human *subject*). Although it might seem reasonable to use the terms inherent and intrinsic to describe certain objects, there is nothing "final" and "complete" about rational beings that would justify them being named "ends." The only way that Kant can rightly consider rational beings to be "ends-in-themselves," in the sense that they are the "ends" of a means-ends deliberation, is because the Kantian framework assumes that the rest of nature is merely of "nonintrinsic value." In this sense, all of nature becomes a *mere means* or is only of "instrumental worth" towards the "end" of nature, which is deemed to be "humanity." Because rational beings possess a (substance-like) one-way causal efficacy over nature and thus also have "intrinsic worth" due to this, the rest of nature is then merely of "instrumental value" to the beings that stand over and above mere conditioned relationships. Note that this is not really a temporal "end" within this framework. It is only a statement about whether a thing has intrinsic worth or not. Because rational beings exist in this place above nature, nature is then (*assumed to be*) a mere means for the purposes of humanity. All of these claims within the Kantian system are reducible to the idea of a "substance" exercising a one-way causal influence. What the philosopher means when they make these claims is that a rational being has "intrinsic value" and not that they are "final" or "complete." An object maintains its value regardless of the relationships that are currently situating the object in question. This goes for humanity as a whole. It can only be considered an "end" in the sense that humanity transcends conditioned existence.

The next step in the Kantian formula is that, given that all rational beings are "ends-in-themselves," each rational being should make sure to never treat another "end-in-itself" as a mere means to their own ends.

It is here that Kant collapses two distinct notions of an "end-in-itself" to reach a conclusion that is not supported. If a person was thinking of how they wished to go about fulfilling their own desires, they would employ means to achieve their desired "ends." They would perceive many different things in their world that they might employ to achieve their desired "ends." Such an individual is thinking about means and ends in a temporal sense. If they were to encounter another "end-in-itself" (an *autonomous* persons) and use this person as a mere means to their own ends, they would then be using an object that is supposed to be "final" and "complete" in a way that only contributed to their own personal ends, but there is nothing "final" or "complete" about another rational being. A rational being, as able to *choose* their own ends, is a *potentiality*. Rational beings have a one-way causal influence over nature, and there is nothing "final" or "complete" about this capacity. The justification for this Kantian position is guilty of conflating two distinct metaphysical realities.

Although it is admittedly a *creative* misapplication of certain metaphysical distinctions, Kant falsely conflates two distinct concepts. There is an alternative way of framing why using another person as a "mere means" to one's own ends is problematic, but this way would not at all be grounded in the discourse of means, ends, and "ends-in-themselves." It would represent the other half of how Kant conflates two different notions in metaphysics. If a particular agent was to use another rational being as a mere means to their own ends, we could say that such conduct does not recognize or respect the "intrinsic value" of that particular object or, alternatively, that such conduct treats a rational being as a *mere* object and *not also as a subject*. This rational subject possesses "intrinsic value" because the subject is (*ontologically*) a special kind of object. They possess *autonomy* or an *unconditioned capacity* to choose their own ends. Their value stems from a non-natural metaphysical realm that exerts a one-way causal influence on nature. This "intrinsic value," a value that is not actually possible to value, is only a particular object that can be recognized or comprehended. It is a nonnatural, conceptual object that must be projected on to experience by a rational being. That object is what is called *dignity*, which is really only an object possessed by all such rational agents. To recognize that another being has *dignity* is not at all to value that being. In fact, this is exactly what Kantians want in their system. The kind of value that transcends all other values and that cannot be evaluated alongside other values is what is denoted by "intrinsic value" or, in the case of it being attributed to a rational being, *dignity*. In recognizing another being as possessing dignity, one is only attributing a metaphysical object to the being in question. It is a nonnatural, transcendent kind of object that possesses a one-way causal capacity (again, just like an "essence"). The dignity of people is then due to their possession of a capacity or force that is unconditional and ultimately comes from a nonnatural or transcendent source. They are then true subjects and not mere objects in the world. As subjects with autonomy, the value they possess is really only due to them being "essences" because only an "essence" (unconditioned) can possess the kind of value that is free of conditions.

What should be clear now is that we actually cannot value anything that has "intrinsic value." I can *acknowledge* that certain objects have "intrinsic worth," but there is no actual way to value that object which is supposed to be of "intrinsic worth." All the Kantian formula says is that all things that are essences should treat all other things that are essences as essences. Put another way, all beings that have a "one-way causal efficacy" should recognize all other beings with a "one-way causal efficacy" as having a "one-way causal efficacy." If we behaved in such a way that we treated an "end-in-itself" as a mere means to an end, then we would be interacting with that rational being in a way that only acknowledged their instrumental worth. It is my capacity to *choose* my ends (none of those ends can ever be of "unconditional value") that makes me a thing that *has* "unconditional value." "Intrinsic value" in this system is then not an actual kind of "value." It is merely a metaphysical, nonnatural object *attributed* to nature. Furthermore, for Kant, if my "ends" are in accordance with the "moral law," then it is *my willing of the good* that can be considered to have "intrinsic value" (what Kant calls the "good will"). This, again, has nothing to do with *actually valuing anything*. It is merely an issue of recognition, the recognition of possessing a metaphysical object. In recognizing all other "ends-in-themselves" as subjects and in never treating them as mere means to one's own ends, a person is then in accord with the "moral law." Being in accord with the "moral law" would only mean that a person recognizes they too are a particular kind of object (an object that transcends nature, i.e., a subject with autonomy). By acting in accord with the moral law, a person projects onto experience the framework that holds that rational beings are metaphysical substances. People that are guided by inclinations (*like compassion*) cannot really be considered to be acting in a way that is of moral worth. At times, Kant even belittles these kinds of inclinations and persons that might be motivated by them.[42] What is clear under this metaphysics is that you cannot value something that is "unconditionally valuable." You can *be* a thing that is "unconditionally valuable," but any relationship you bear to them (i.e., *other* rational beings) is necessarily going to be a *conditioned* relationship. All objects associated with the Kantian "moral metaphysics" are nonnatural and nonempirical. As such, they are supersensible and only *attributable* to nature by a "rational being."

"Intrinsic Value" and the Metaphysics of (Racial) Oppression

For most philosophers, there is nothing problematic about the above metaphysical assumptions. These are good and "rational" beliefs. For them, it is this kind of philosophical system that is the only thing standing in the way of terrible cultural movements like racism and antisemitism. Such arguments by the Kantian and liberal metaphysicians are highly dubious and uncritical as they clearly have not spent any effort in trying to understand morally problematic ideological systems and the way they function. Underlying both the moral metaphysics of the Kantian and the anti-Semite is one and the same cognitive process of applying nonnatural and nonempirical objects to different features of nature. Ultimately, both systems attribute objects to nature in a way that bifurcates nature into two different realms; that which is equal in so far as they have a kind of value that cannot be adjusted based on conditions or relationships ("intrinsic value") and that which does not ("instrumental value"). That which does not have "intrinsic value" can never be elevated to a higher status than those particular objects that are the correct kind of things. Both metaphysical systems insist that objective values are metaphysical realities and thus fail to discuss *real* values or the actual *process of valuing*. They assume that there are metaphysical objects and then *reduplicate* them on to the realm of values (that is, as above, assume the existence of an "intrinsic object" and then insist that said object must also have "intrinsic value"). In light of the above account of metaphysics, we must be apprehensive of the relationship that our metaphysical assumptions have to the epistemological framework that shapes how we interpret situations. In *Metaphysics and Oppression*, McCumber presents a critique of "substance" (Greek; *ousia*) and explains how these metaphysical assumptions help to inform human conduct. McCumber claims that this metaphysics does not necessarily lead to the cultivation of oppressive conduct but, "Rather, ousia seems to function generally as a kind of recipe; it suggests how people should deal with the world. [. . .] Ousia does not create practices of oppression but clarifies and legitimates them *to their practitioners*. And it has done so, paradoxically, without its own functioning being either clarified or legitimated. It has guided us from behind our backs, and all the more surely for that."[43] For McCumber, metaphysics arguably functions as a kind of "final vocabulary" (Rorty) or provides a "horizon of relevance" (Gadamer) and has helped to structure and legitimize the oppressive practices and institutions of Western civilization. In light of the Daoist critique of "knowledge," we can say much the same thing. Nonempirically grounded "knowledge" and "desire" play a role in, as I discussed in chapter 3, predisposing us to danger. It is precisely when our "knowledge" posits that things are independent that we run into problems.

As with Kantian moral metaphysics, the logic behind the anti-Semite's understanding of value involves making nonnatural, nonempirical assumptions and *projecting* them onto nature and experience. As Sartre explains, in *Anti-Semite and Jew*, in order to understand the anti-Semite's "indignation we must recognize that he had adopted in advance a certain idea of the Jew, of his nature and of his role in society. [. . .] Far from experience producing his idea of the Jew, it was the latter [i.e., the "idea"] which explained his experience."[44] For the anti-Semite, as well as with other forms of racism, it is a metaphysical framework that provides a "horizon of relevance" where perceived differences (or, as in the case of anti-Semitism, there are no actual empirical differences[45]) can be *interpreted* as having a particular significance. The practice of interpreting "other people" as possessing a special kind of object cannot simply be equated to a "fear of difference" or as a natural offshoot of human biology. This metaphysical *interpretation* of difference is unempirical (and even considered *virtuously* unempirical) as it involves the reification and further ossification of conceptual distinctions in experience that produces an epistemological framework (one indebted to a "substance ontology").

Sartre further claims that "the principle underlying anti-Semitism is that the concrete possession of a particular object gives as if by magic the meaning of that object."[46] With anti-Semitism, peoples in the world are interpreted as possessing a particular property, an object, that determines their meaning in a way that could never be adjusted by history, growth, or relationships. In light of this behavior, we can also consider the anti-Semite as someone in "bad faith" in the sense that he "regards values—including the value that constitutes himself—as transcendent, independent 'givens' and desirability, including his own desirability, as a material feature of objects instead of a contingent feature of their relation to human reality. He is therefore Manichaean in spirit, treating good and evil as material features of the world that can be encouraged or eliminated like bacteria in water."[47] The process of reducing persons to distinct substances that cannot be changed lends itself to the Manichean spirit of the moralist. As soon as relationships are ignored and devalued, people treat moral problems as having simple solutions like simply removing the problematic substances from society. Instead of seeing social disharmony as institutional and systematic, the person of "bad faith" reduces the history of causal relationships to substances that need to be either destroyed or protected from the substances that need to be destroyed.

With antiblack racism, an identical structure occurs within human consciousness. As Gordon has described it, antiblack racism is also indebted to the tendency to be in "bad faith" or the desire to evade reality. For Gordon, "bad faith is the effort to hide from human reality, [and] the effort to hide from ourselves. From the standpoint of bad faith, racism is the ossification of human reality into a monadic entity identical with any one aspect of an assumed duality."[48] Antiblack racism, as a form of "bad faith," bi-furcates the natural world into the realms of light/purity and darkness/impurity. It is not just a "fear of difference." Antiblack racism involves the process of attributing or projecting metaphysical objects onto the natural world. As Gordon claims, "blackness and whiteness are projections."[49] They are not features of reality. Antiblack racism attributes objects and "characteristics" to certain peoples in spite of all the evidence to the contrary. They make these "peoples" into either nonpersons or "mere property" (mere "means" to the ends of transcendent "humanity"). Ironically, the characteristics that are projected onto the natural world cannot be explained by natural, causal relationships (i.e., they are metaphysical objects just like a "nonnatural quality" of the kind that Moore believes the "good" to be). Although there may be differences in physical appearances between peoples, the metaphysical objects projected onto these differences bear no actual relationship to reality (in the sense that the *conceptual constructs* "whiteness" and "blackness" do not bear nor even need to bear a relationship to concrete reality. This metaphysical object, with its perceived "value," is prior to empirical reality and held as sacrosanct). In this way, the value of a "Jew" (for the anti-Semite) and the "black" (for the antiblack racist) is fully determined (i.e., *virtuously* determined) prior to empirical experience. Contrary to empirical experience, the racist interprets another person as possessing or being an "intrinsic object." As Sartre describes, from the perspective of the anti-Semite, "by treating the Jew as an inferior and pernicious being, I affirm at the same time that I belong to the elite. This elite, in contrast to those of modern times which are based on merit or labor, closely resembles an aristocracy of birth. There is nothing I have to do to merit my superiority, and neither can I lose it. It is given once and for all. It is a *thing*."[50] In defining the "Jew" in this way, the anti-Semite then interprets themselves as being a special kind of object (one that *lacks* all "badness," for example). The same goes for antiblack racism as rooted in "bad faith." "Whites" possess a kind of value that cannot be adjusted based on history of contingent relationships. It makes them into a kind of substance that possesses what Gordon calls "license" or specifically "white license." This kind of license finds its metaphysical parallel in Kant's proclamation that everything in nature is a *mere means* to the end of humanity. Gordon juxtaposes "license" with "privilege" to stress that an important problem of white supremacy and antiblack racism was not simply that one group is given systematic political "privilege" over others. What "license" does is permit people to behave like "substances" in the sense that they are "free" to exert their causal influence on the world without being limited or punished. Although we might theoretically agree that "one never has the privilege to murder, pillage, and rape [. . .] there are people throughout history who have been granted a license for such activities. Sometimes they were called 'soldiers' during times of war. In practice, given the systemic protection of whites who have conducted such activities as lynching, pillaging, rape, and many other technologies of violence and theft against non-whites or those they deemed not white enough, the status of whiteness is historically a license."[51] It is not a mere "privilege" but is a kind of "license" that is systematically justified through a nonnatural metaphysics that bifurcates the world into distinct kinds of objects (those that are like "substances" and those that are not). When we distinguish between "inherent" or "intrinsic values" in this Kantian way and map said values onto reality (and *in spite* of empirical reality), value becomes reduced to ontology.

The "intrinsic values" of both the Kantian and the anti-Semite are not actual values. Nothing has been merited, there has been no growth, and the status of this value cannot change. This way of interpreting values is simply the reduplication of "substances." As Sartre further states, "now the anti-Semite flees from responsibility for his own consciousness, and choosing for his personality the permanence of rock, he chooses for his morality a scale of petrified values. Whatever he does, he knows that he will remain at the top of the ladder; whatever the Jew does, he will never get any higher than the first rung."[52] Regardless of one's conduct, both systems insist that only those who are certain kinds of things are of real "objective value." These values transcend any relationships that can be possessed. Philosophers might still try to insist that one case is a misapplication of certain concepts and values while the other presents an accurate account of reality. The anti-Semite is in error because they are not a Kantian. What they will not want to admit is that the same process by both is unempirical, employs nonnatural metaphysical assumptions, and further does not actually provide us with a real system of values. The whole cognitive process is merely one of recognition; of recognizing that there are certain objects in the world and that these objects are the only ones that can possess another object that, as if by magical force, determines the value of the being in question.

In adopting the Daoist processual account of values, we could just abandon all of these metaphysical assumptions and actually discuss the nature of values and what it means to value in a way that is empirical. From the Daoist account of values, there are also constraints that can be placed on forms of value as well. Considering that all the Kantian account of "intrinsic value" actually contributes is that it sets up constraints on forms of conduct (relevant only to beings that are "rational"), there is not much we are missing if we abandon this metaphysics. The Kantian, liberal individualist framework still must explain why their metaphysical system (the great chain of being)[53] does not actually function like the racist humanism the West historically has been responsible for.

An "End-in-Itself" in Coordinating Means and Ends Is Oppressive

In the context of regulating means and ends, "intrinsic value" is also problematic when attributed to a desired end. "Intrinsic value" structurally involves the disregard and devaluation of "instrumental value" or anything else that is not of "intrinsic value." Since "intrinsic value," as sui generis, transcends "instrumental value" in the sense that "instrumental value" can never change the value of "intrinsic value," the achieving of "intrinsic value" legitimizes "any means necessary." The structure of an "end-in-itself" (apart from being a metaphysical fiction) is structurally oppressive in the sense that there can only be a one-way causal influence working *from* the "intrinsic value" towards that which is of less value (i.e., traditionally "nature," or "lesser, nonrational beings"). "Intrinsic value" attached to the notion of an "end-in-itself" in relationship to the potential aims and goals of persons provides a formula for oppression. Dewey makes this point regarding an "end-in-itself" brilliantly in his *Theory of Valuation*. "The conception involved in the maxim that 'the end justifies the means' is basically the same as that in the notion of ends-in-themselves; indeed, from a historical point of view, it is the fruit of the latter, for only the conception that certain things are ends-in-themselves can warrant the belief that the relation of ends-means is unilateral, proceeding exclusively from ends to means."[54] The relation of ends-means is unilateral because and "end-in-itself" cannot be adjusted or changed due to the means being employed. As such, it functions just like an essence in being able to adjust and determine relationships and yet cannot be adjusted or determined by these relationships. Dewey then claims that there are two "rationalizations" that can be used to defend the logic behind the notion of an "end-in-itself."

> One of the views is that only the specially selected "end" held in view will actually be brought into existence by the means used, [. . .]; the other (and more probable) view is that, [. . . an] arbitrary selection of some one part of the attained consequences as *the* end and hence as the warrant of means used (no matter how objectionable are the *other* consequences) [. . .], and hence possessed of "value" irrespective of all its existential relations.[55]

Contrary to the traditional account by philosophers, an "end-in-itself" as a temporal "end" (i.e., *not* in the Kantian sense of being applied to a "substance") is related to both 1) the means that can be utilized to achieve the desired end and 2) the "possessor" of such valued "ends." A "good-in-itself" or *eudemonia* is an example of an "end" in the temporal sense. It is an "end" in the sense of finality and completeness of a process. No other "value" exists higher than the "highest end." The "intrinsicness" of a temporal "end-in-itself" is attributed to its "finality." It is complete, and when it is complete, it is unchanged by any further "accidental relations." One problem here is that, depending on the means being used to achieve a desired end, there is no reason to believe that the means used to reach a desired end produce only one "simply located" quality or object. The means used could be such that, even though some good or favorable "ends" were brought about, there are also other destructive side effects. Yet an "end-in-itself" would be of a kind of value that these other side effects could not diminish the value of an "end-in-itself." Another problem is that philosophers make the fallacious leap when taking an "end" as "final" to assuming that it was also *ahistorical*. Their (fallacious) logic runs like this: a "final" end is assumed to have "intrinsic" and thus objective value (i.e., unconditional in the sense that it would be uninfluenced by relations/conditions). As "final," all future relations would then be mere "accidents" (a tautology). Therefore (fallaciously), all previous relations (*means utilized*) must also be mere "accidents." If not, then the definition of the "highest end" as "intrinsically good" could be intellectually suspect. When an "end" is taken to be "intrinsically good," to maintain this position the philosopher takes the next fallacious step in negating the history that was required for such a "good" to be achieved. An "end-in-itself," by definition, is of more value than anything that is "instrumentally" or "accidentally" valuable. The value of an "intrinsically valuable end," being of a kind that transcends "instrumental value," has the power to negate the value (or dis-value) of the means that are utilized to achieve such an "end." The other "ends" that are brought about, simply by virtue of being merely "accidental" and not "intrinsically valuable," would never adulterate the "intrinsic value" of such a self-defined "end-in-itself." When "intrinsic value" is identified with a particular "end" that one desires (and thus becomes an "end-in-itself"), we have the necessary formula for justifying war, carelessness, and domination all in one.

Committing the nonnaturalistic fallacy bifurcates the world into sets of values. It can be further said that "intrinsic value," unalterable due to historically contingent relationships, provides the justification for separating means and ends into a dualism where means and end form a unilateral relationship. This itself provides the foundation for justifying "any-means-necessary" conduct. With this processual and naturalistic account of values, the values of means and ends are always interdependent. Violent and oppressive conduct like war is never a viable means to a valued end. Scholars familiar with the *Daodejing* would have already recognized an important theme in the work: its "antiwar" position. It helps to make sense of the Daoist's "antiwar" position when "intrinsic value" is recognized as necessary for justifying war as a means to a "valued end." For the Daoist, war is never a means to a valued end.[56] As *Daodejing* 31 claims, "Military weapons are inauspicious instruments, and so when you have no choice but to use them, it is best to do so coolly and without enthusiasm. Do not glorify weapons, for to do so is to delight in killing people, and anyone that delights in killing people will come up short in the world. [. . .] When the casualties are high, inspect the battleground with grief and remorse; When the war is won, treat it as you would a funeral."[57] Though the Daoist is against war, they do not argue for complete pacifism. If another state is attempting to take human life, self-defense and the preservation of life can still help to minimize suffering. Although there are possible situations where there is no choice but to use military weapons, war undertaken in any form is never of *positive* moral value. This is why the *Daodejing* suggests that even in victory should we still treat such victory like a funeral. If we were to properly understand the social reality of war, we would see that there are no real victors. When two societies resort to war, they have already reached the lowest of calamities.

When the population is taught to "value" or find certain war like behaviors "virtuous," this then normalizes and helps to enable the worst of human behaviors towards each other. War always involves a ruling class using the vast majority of an alienated population towards the ruling class's desires (which are in turn also indebted to alienation). A "thick" moral vocabulary and a "moral metaphysics" are simply two of the best tools for normalizing the culture of imperialism. Properly understanding the implications of war requires understanding how even self-defense and the preserving of one's own life do not make up for the value loss due to war. What is left after war is, furthermore, an environment that only helps to foster resentment where we can expect similar behavior and attitudes (violence, aggression, resentment) to emerge in the populace. It is for this reason that the Daoist would never defend the idea that victory in war could be celebrated. War never solves human problems because the effects of war do not end when the war is over, win or lose. The dispositions of people are drastically altered such that we need to expect the same (if not more) levels of resentment, anger, and political scapegoating from the ruling class. Real value only comes about through the creation of valuable relationships. This requires communities become free of coercive, metaphysical ideologies. The idea that war could be a means to a "greater good" is, for the Daoist, metaphysics justifying oppression par excellence.[58] The idea that war can lead to a "greater good" is just an example of how metaphysical beliefs can be appropriated to justify great levels of violence and suffering. Imperialism (as is still the case with modern American imperialism), always needs to convince its populace that war and conquest can bring about a greater good. This metaphysics that sees the means used as merely accidental (i.e., the ideology of "American exceptionalism") presents a whole population with a rationale where the means used are arbitrary or play no role in the "final cause" of the civilizing project. Though the vast majority of those of us "used" to make conquest a possibility will never see any real benefit from it, we are convinced usually by means of a moral myth or nonnatural metaphysical reality. Assuming the existence of "intrinsic value" helps to justify the idea that war (or other forms of violence) can produce value.

Conclusion

With this account of values and valuing, there are better and worse ways of valuing and interrelating with the world. Regardless of how the world might end up being constituted (chaotic or peaceful), maintaining attention to the qualitative dimensions of our existence is the best way of dealing with it. The worry in Daoist philosophy is that we must not allow certain beliefs to ossify because this can potentially lead to error. Reified habits of desire (*yu*) and knowledge (*zhi*) obstruct our attention of the concrete valuing we do in everyday existence. The natural process of valuing will anarchically play itself out if we do not allow problematic metaphysical beliefs to inform or determine human conduct. Regardless of the context, there are always more valuable ways that experience can be undergone such that more holistic interrelationship can occur. If we are mindful of this, then the amount of extraneous suffering introduced into human society due to certain nonnatural and metaphysical beliefs will be lessened. As the previous chapters have shown, what regulates the Daoist understanding of values are the natural limits of things themselves rather than something that transcends nature. "Eye desires" and the "knowledge" that accompanies them thus involve neglecting the way "value" is a cocreative process. Conduct that is shaped *merely* by the secondary and cognitive dimensions of experience, ipso facto, neglects the noncognitive context that gives the cognitive aspects of experience their meaning. It is for this reason that the Daoist insists we forget the "knowledge" that structures the problematic epistemology that informs our "human" conduct. In doing this, we can be said to have cultivated dispositions such that the perception of situations and things no longer commits the nonnaturalistic fallacy.

With the Kantian metaphysical framework, we are left with "rational beings" that do not actually value that which was supposed to be "intrinsically valuable." This cognitive process of attributing nonnatural, nonempirical "substances" to reality presents a similar metaphysical framework to the metaphysics that informs anti-Semitism and antiblack racism. In showing how the metaphysics of both the moral philosopher and the racist are similar in structure, this was not meant to suggest that the Daoist, over two thousand years ago, was presenting a position that was explicitly critical of anti-Semitism or antiblack racism. This chapter presented reasons for why Daoists are critical of "moral philosophers" and their metaphysical system. The Daoist presents a functionally equivalent but different alternative to the "moral philosopher." In light of this analysis, it is actually on the moralist ideologues in philosophy departments to assure the rest of us that their moral metaphysics actually can address these key issues when it comes to the relationship between metaphysics and (racial) oppression. The Daoist alternative to moral metaphysicians is that we never needed their nonnatural metaphysics to begin with. In the Daoist view, these kinds of metaphysical beliefs are the root of our problems anyways.

As the next chapter will further explain, there are constraints on values in a processual framework. Philosophers have been caught basically "reduplicating" the same conceptual notion when they take on the Kantian account of "intrinsic value" as being attributable to particular objects. The Daoist understanding of nature and experience provides a naturalistic account of values. Experience and knowledge are both irreducibly cocreative for Daoist philosophers as well as for Dewey. Valuing is the way one aspect of experience is *internally* related to other aspects. When we do not recognize how our values are the quality of interaction between environment and organism, we can be said to commit the nonnaturalistic fallacy. We, by the very act of taking our values as independent of context and environment, neglect the immediate way that our values are a product of interrelationship. In our ignorance, we impose a foreign set of behaviors on other aspects of nature, thereby transgressing the natural, sustainable limits of things. Through forgetting (*wang*) the ossified desires and reified forms of propositional knowledge, we cultivate an attention once again to the natural interdependence that constitutes existence. We no longer act from alienated dispositions.

Chapter Five

Alienation and Attunement in the *Zhuangzi*

The *Zhuangzi* on the "Sages" and "Robbers"

In continuing the discussion from the previous chapters, this chapter returns to the theme of amorality and the Daoist critique of the moral discourses of their contemporaries. Although it is not uncommon for the Daoist to critique the morality of the Confucians and the Mohists, one of the chapters of the *Zhuangzi* where such a critique is explicit is the first chapter of the "Outer Chapters," chapter 8 of the *Zhuangzi*, "Webbed Toes." Although it uses a different vocabulary from the earlier *Zhuangzi* and was clearly written later than the "Inner Chapters," as it references the *Daodejing*, we should consider chapter 8 of the *Zhuangzi* to be elaborating on the themes found in the "Inner Chapters." The most unusual claim from chapter 8 is the accusation that the sages are just as responsible for social ills as the robbers. For example, it states, "Bo Yi [a Confucian paragon of virtue] died in pursuit of fame at the foot of Mt. Shouyang, while Robber Zhi died in pursuit of profit at the top of Mt. Dongling. They died for different things, but they were alike in damaging their lives and harming their inborn natures [*xing*, 性]."[1] The text criticizes the Mohists, Confucians, Egoists, and robbers as not truly rectified, and "that which is the utmost rectified does not lose the actuality of their endowed circumstances" (彼正{至}正者，不失其性命之情)[2]. The character *xing* (性) is not commonly used in the *Zhuangzi*, and it does not show up anywhere in the "Inner Chapters." In light of the analysis in the previous chapters on the Daoist understanding of things, *xingming* (性命) is translated here as "endowed circumstances" to avoid the implications of translating *xing* as "nature."[3]

While *xing* refers to what is natural, the Daoist does not consider *xing* to be like an essence. Translating *ming* as "fate" also carries connotations that are far too deterministic and teleological as well. The *xing* of all things is that they are *wu* (無) or indeterminate. All things are unique particulars that are constituted by their relationships to the rest of nature. Persons lose sight of the "actuality of endowed circumstances" due to how their dispositions have been shaped by certain cultural institutions.[4] This is not to say that culture per se is problematic. For the Daoist, the cultural institutions that are problematic are those that encourage people to depart from their naturally endowed particularity.

The distinction between alienation and attunement that has up to this point only been cursorily outlined is a useful way to understand the reasons behind the Daoist's critique. For the Daoist, certain cultural institutions promote our alienation from nature. A society informed by Daoist philosophy would still be a kind of culture but would be one that does not promote alienation from nature. It would help maintain its opposite or what has been called "attunement" and an attunement to nature.[5] When the cultural forms that produce alienation are absent, an attunement to nature is normal, and for the Daoist, it can be considered our original spontaneity (*ziran*, 自然). The distinction between alienation and attunement is also useful for clarifying different aspects of Daoist philosophy. For example, the "*wu*-forms" of the *Daodejing* can be understood as expressing how the Daoist can respond to situations such that they are attuned and responsive to nature. The *wuwei* or "nonegoistic action" of the Daoist sage is spontaneous and responsive because the Daoist sage is *not* alienated from nature. *Jing* (靜) or "tranquility" can also be understood as denoting an attunement to nature. Any form of experience where we cognitively foreground certain aspects of experience and ignore the context that such isolation was grounded in produces alienation from nature.[6] If persons achieve the Daoist ideal, they will recognize that they are fundamentally like an "uncarved block of wood" (*pu*, 樸). They would recognize that they are constituted by nature and are not determinate things that stand opposed to or above nature. As will be explained further below, this antirepresentational account of experience (what has also been called the "ontological relativism" thesis) informs the critique of both the sages and the robbers. The belief that any aspect of nature is like a metaphysical substance or exists in a way free of relationships is thus to suffer from alienation. In the context of human society, egoism, in both the hedonistic sense and the moralist sense, is to be abandoned because it is indebted to an epistemological framework that obscures our relationship to nature. Both sets of dispositions are a result of alienation.

The Daoist critique of the sages and robbers, as detailed in chapter 8 of the *Zhuangzi*, needs to be taken seriously. Both the (non-Daoist) sages and robbers are in fact equally responsible for society's ills because both are perceptually alienated from nature. This perceptual alienation involves the inability to perceive nature as fundamentally indeterminate (*wu*, 無). The Daoist alternative to the sages and robbers is to cultivate a dispositional sensitivity to our interdependence. This process involves maintaining an attunement to nature or, as chapter 8 describes it, to not depart from "the actuality of their endowed circumstances" (其性命之情). The end of chapter 8 of the *Zhuangzi* describes the Daoist alternative to being a sage and robber. It suggests that persons need to cultivate the ability to "see themselves" (自見) and to "see themselves when they see others/things" (自見而見彼). To "truly see oneself" is to maintain an attunement to nature and thus recognize the interdependence of all things with each other (which is also the source of their novelty)[7]. This, in contrast with Confucian ideas as found in the *Xunzi*,[8] helps the Daoist bind and fuse things together in a noncoercive way or "to bind things without needing cords" (約束不以纆索). If persons are alienated from nature when addressing societal ills, then they are predisposed to act coercively as if cutting the "webbed toes" of others. Although chapter 8 of the *Zhuangzi* might at times sound like it is espousing individualism, the position is consistent with the Daoist notion of the "true person" or *zhenren* that was described in chapter 3 of this book. Contrary to first appearances (and this is also the reason why I focus on chapter 8 here) even the "Primitivist" *Zhuangzi* is ascribing to the view that persons exist in a state of interdependence. We can make sense of the Daoist critique in chapter 8 when we see the sages and the robbers as guilty of neglecting the underlying continuity and interdependence of all things. Both reduce persons to independent things and are thus alienated from nature.

Ontological Relativism and the "Muddy Confusion" (*Hundun*)

The Daoist critique of the sages and robbers is grounded in their account of nature as fundamentally indeterminate. In this sense, the Daoist position blurs the lines between what we would traditionally label as "metaphysics" and "ethics" in the sense that their critique of morality is inseparable from their critique of a reified account of nature.⁹ Immediately before chapter 8 begins, the "Inner Chapters" ends with a story that arguably alludes to the themes of chapter 8 in making the explicit connection between the inability to perceive nature as fundamentally indeterminate and the negative implications that result from this ignorance. The last story of the "Inner Chapters" of the *Zhuangzi* explicitly warns against imposing rigid metaphysical assumptions onto a world that is inexhaustibly novel and indeterminate (*wu*). On my reading of the *Zhuangzi*, the "Hundun" (渾沌) story is the logical conclusion to the "Inner Chapters."

> The emperor of the southern sea was called Swoosh. The emperor of the northern-sea was called Oblivion. The emperor of the middle was called ["Muddy Confusion," "Hundun"]. Swoosh and Oblivion would sometimes meet in the territory of ["Hundun"], who always attended to them quite well. They decided to repay ["Hundun"] for his virtue. "All men have seven holes in them, by means of which they see, hear, eat, breathe," they said. "But this one alone has none. Let's drill him some."
> So each day they drilled another hole. After seven days, [Hundun] was dead.¹⁰

For those unfamiliar with Chinese cosmology, "Hundun" (literally meaning "muddy confusion") is not an actual person. "Hundun" is the primordial, undifferentiated natural world before there are distinctions and divisions. With the Daoist understanding of nature, "muddy confusion" is not an event that takes place in a distant past. Each moment of experience can involve disclosing the world without clinging to conceptual distinctions as these are merely provisional, secondary aspects of experience as a whole. For the Daoist, cognitive habits (*zhi*) can inhibit perception such that we no longer bring our attention to our noncognitive, qualitative relations with the world. "Hundun" refers to this all-embracing, lived context of experience where all possible distinctions are drawn. Guo Xiang's own commentary on this *Zhuangzi* passage references the *Daodejing* passages 29 and 64; "those who deliberately act ruin it"¹¹ (為者敗之). The emperors of the northern and southern seas impose a reified account of "things" onto nature as if the provisional way they "carve up" distinctions corresponded to a reality "in-itself." With the Daoist understanding of nature, undesirable suffering is created not because people lack an understanding of a transcendent moral order or rational principles. We ignorantly create undesired suffering because we fail to perceive the world as an "uncarved block of wood" (*pu*). We do not recognize that the world is fundamentally indeterminate (*wu*) because human experience is obstructed by the ossification of conceptual distinctions (*zhi*).

If persons fail to recognize how the ontological distinctions drawn in experience are relative and provisional, they become predisposed to behave like the emperors of the southern and northern seas in the Hundun story. They might have good intentions, but they simply end up creating more suffering. Conduct grounded in a perceptual alienation from nature is inevitably going to obstruct the ability to understand and respond to situations in a way that is sensitive to the situation's qualitative particularity. Following the final story of chapter 7, this is thematically how *Zhuangzi* chapter 8 begins. Chapter 8 starts by drawing from *Daodejing* passage 12 and interprets it in a way similar to the Hundun story.[12] Passage 12 of the *Daodejing* (as outlined in chapter 3 of this book) does not merely argue for people to have fewer desires. The divide between the desires of the "eye" and those of the "stomach" is not arbitrary. Passage 12 critiques a reified account of nature. It then critiques certain kinds of desire: those that can be rightfully called "objectified" forms of desiring in the sense that they make nature into distinct objects. As chapter 3 illustrated, these desires go beyond mere animal needs. Furthermore, these desires are not truly valuable because they are shaped by alienation from nature. Problems emerge when desires go beyond the fundamental way we are related to the world (*via*, the stomach, 腹). Desires based on alienation from nature lead to undesirable suffering.

With the Daoist account of experience, each interaction with the world simultaneously structures the way the world is disclosed. The ability to group experiences into the "five colors" or "five tones" (into "sameness" and "difference") is only a provisional way of disclosing the world. The *Zhuangzi* describes how we have the capacity to highlight particular aspects of experience such that we *provisionally* foreground similarities or differences. As I previously explained in chapter 1, "ontological relativism" claims that the way we conceptually individuate things is relative to the purposes we might have.[13] A key passage from the *Zhuangzi* describes this as such, "Observed from the perspective of its differences, the liver and gall bladder are [like the kingdoms of] Chu and Yue; Observed from the perspective of its sameness, ten-thousand things are all one. Assuming this is so, moreover [a sage] does not know [*zhi*, 知] of that which suits the ears and the eye, and the heart/mind wanders in the harmony of virtuosity [*de*, 德]."[14] This passage suggests that we can observe things from different perspectives (sameness and/or difference). With an antirepresentational understanding of mind and experience, it is a normal process of consciousness to highlight particular aspects and relations in the field of experience and bring them to the foreground. Daoists do not merely passively absorb "given" data about the world. In this passage, the *Zhuangzi* is also describing interdependence and the way each particular thing depends on and is related to "what it is not," that is, how any posited aspect of experience depends on the context it emerges from to be intelligible.[15] The view of "seeing all things as one" is both the recognition of "ontological relativism" and the capacity to perceive the indeterminate and all-encompassing context of all possible experience. If each thing is related to and dependent on the context it was isolated from, then each thing is uniquely dependent on everything else "that it is not," that is, each thing is *uniquely caused* by the rest of nature. This is what it means to be *ziran* or "self-so" for the Daoist.

The experience of alienation rooted in "knowledge" is a nonessential byproduct of the cognitive process of making conceptual distinctions in experience. When conceptual distinctions (*zhi*) become ossified, the world is then disclosed *as if* things exist ontologically independent of relations. Although other scholars have also highlighted how the Daoist critiques political authority as coercive,[16] the coerciveness of these political practices is, in reality, due to an epistemological framework (discussed in the previous chapter). An inability to perceive the interdependence of all things is tantamount to perceptual alienation.[17] By the end of *Zhuangzi*, chapter 8, it is suggested that our problems are rooted in our habitual failure to "see ourselves" (*zijian*, 自见) when we engage with the world. This is why both the sages and robbers share responsibility for "casting the world into confusion." They are equally alienated from nature in the sense that they "depart from the actuality of their endowed circumstances." In other words, they are alienated from how "things" are constituted by their relationships and, as such, novel focal point of nature's constant fluctuations.

Carving Up Nature: "Webbed Toes" and "Extra Fingers"

The Daoist understanding of nature as primordially indeterminate informs the critique of both the sages and robbers in the *Zhuangzi*. Although a critique of the sages might first suggest that the Daoist argues for amorality, this critique must also be understood in light of their critique of "knowledge" and "carving up" nature (making this a critique of metaphysics as well). After alluding to *Daodejing* passage 12, the *Zhuangzi* chapter 8 continues with an account of nature like that of the "Hundun" story. Nature forms an indeterminate continuum. "Carving up" nature into categories of "types" adulterates its particularity. As chapter 8 states,

> That which is the utmost rectified [正{至}正者] is to not lose the actuality of its endowed circumstances [其性命之情]. Thus, that which is combined together does not act as if forcibly joined, and that which branches does not act as an "extra toe"; that which is long does not act excessive; that which is short does not act as insufficient. Therefore, the wild duck's legs, although they are short, extending them would cause it misery. The crane's legs, although they are long, severing them would cause it sorrow.[18]

Although at first it might seem like the *Zhuangzi* is describing different things as each having an essence, each aspect of nature is actually radically novel and unique insofar as they become what they are in relationship to the changing environment that produces them.[19] The "actuality of endowed circumstances" (其性命之情) describes nature in a way comparable to *ziran* (自然) or as being "self-so" as found throughout the Daoist texts. This is not a claim that essences underly the existence of things. "Objecthood" is a derivative and provisional aspect of experience. Each aspect of nature is a unique coalescence of relationships and subject to constant transformation. Building on this, chapter 8 of the *Zhuangzi* then claims that both the sages and robbers suffer from going beyond the "actuality of their endowed circumstances." As chapter 8 continues, "Now the 'benevolent' men of today are anxious about the calamities in the world, whereas the nonbenevolent people have broken away from the actuality of their endowed circumstances and gluttonously and covetously value riches and honors. This is why I think Humanity and Responsibility are not the actuality of people! [故意仁義其非人情乎!]."[20] There are a few ways that this passage can be understood. One way to read this is that Humanity (仁) and Responsibility (義)—the *institutions* of morality—are only remedial and contingent. With a functional understanding of morality, there is no value to morality "in and of itself."[21] Moral discourse is only useful and valuable in relationship to the chaotic social order it is meant to help remedy. In both the *Daodejing* and the *Zhuangzi* there are passages that suggest that the institutions of the Confucians are secondary, derivative, and merely signs that human society has already departed from Dao. *Daodejing* passage 18, for example, claims that when the great Dao has departed/declines, *then* the Confucian institutions and virtues emerge (大道廢, 有仁義). It does not explicitly claim that these institutions are the cause, but only that they are secondary and remedial. The Confucian ideas do not necessarily help us get back to the "great way."[22] The *Zhuangzi* chapter 6 story of the fishes gathering together on the shore of the river can likewise be understood as a critique of moral discourse when it becomes ossified. The story states that "When the springs dry up, the fish have to cluster together on the shore, gasping on each other to keep damp and spitting on each other to stay wet. But that is no match for forgetting all about one another in the rivers and lakes. Rather than praising Yao and condemning Jie, we'd be better off forgetting them both and transforming along our own courses."[23] The fishes spitting on each other is not a natural occurrence. Such behavior was only introduced due to the particular circumstance of the fish being removed from the river. Morality as remedial is only valuable in relationship to unfavorable conditions. Although an important aspect of these stories is that they critique moral discourses, the Daoist critique of morality is indebted to their critique of "carving up" nature (that is, the Daoist metaphysics). This theme is a pervasive one in many other Daoist stories. *Zhuangzi* chapter 5, for example, describes morality as an attempt to "bind things together" yet one that ignores how "all things are already bound and glued." Chapter 5 describes the sage as follows:

> The sage has his ways of wandering. For him, understanding is merely a bastard son, obligations and agreements like glue (約為膠), virtuosity a mere continuation of something received, skill merely salesmanship. The sage makes no plans, so what use would he have for understanding? He is unsplit, so what use would he have for glue (不斲, 惡用膠)? He loses nothing, so what use would he have for the attainment of virtuosity?[24]

The key to this passage is that the sage is "unsplit" or "does not cut up" (不斲). The Daoist sage recognizes that their conceptual distinctions are provisional and thus perceives the primordial continuity and interdependence of all nature. Their actuality (*qing*, 情) is of being "uncut" and of forming an interrelated continuum like the "uncarved block of wood" (*pu*). *Zhuangzi* chapter 6, for example, also claims that "we cannot release ourselves—being beings, we are always tied up by something."[25] The above story of the fishes trapped on the shore should be read in light of the Daoist understanding of nature as indeterminate. The fish, in their natural environment (the water), would be better off returning to the way of life that is a natural fit.[26] The fishes spitting on each other, symbolizing certain institutions of morality, is only obstructing their ability to simply "forget" (*wang*, 忘) and return to the river. The best way to understand this story is that, metaphorically speaking, "returning to the river" symbolizes that the fishes would no longer be alienated from nature.[27] The ossified moral discourses of the sages, that is, the fishes spitting on each other, ignorantly perpetuates alienation from nature. The *Zhuangzi* chapter 8 continues along these lines.

> Moreover, that which depends on hooks, ropes, compasses and squares to rectify things, this is to scrape and cut off its nature [是削其性]; that which depends on strings and fastenings, glues and varnish to make things firm, this is to invade their virtue/excellence [是侵其德也]. The bending and stopping in rituals and music, exhortations to "benevolence" and "righteousness" as the means to comfort the hearts of all under heaven, this is a loss of that which is constant in all things [此失其常然也]. All under heaven have what is constant [i.e., what makes them naturally "so"]. That which is constantly so; that which is crooked does not need the hook to make it so; that which is straight is not made so by means of ropes and cords; that which is round is not made so by means of a compass; that which is square is not made so by means of a square; [natural] adhesion is not so because of glues and varnish; being bound together is not so because of ropes.[28]

Depending on "hooks, ropes, etc. to set things straight" (待鉤繩規矩而正者) only *seems* to be a good idea when a person believes that nature is composed of independently existing objects. If all things are already bound together—continuous, overlapping, and interdependent—then attempts to "glue," "bind" and "carve" said things is misguided. To try to bind things together that are already bound necessarily involves an inability to understand and accurately perceive situations. Whether it be selfishly trying to amass wealth or the attempt to universalize human conduct (demanding vastly different "perspectives" to conform to the same abstract standard), each form of conduct transgresses the endowed circumstances of things because each involves the prior belief that things exist independently. Imposing an "external form" and determinate order on another perspective is like trying to cut their "webbed toes" to make them fit an ideal standard. The Daoist alternative is to "join things without using glue" (附離不以膠漆) and "bind things without using cords" (約束不以纆索), which requires an attunement to how nature forms an interdependent continuum. It is not that binding things together is necessarily bad for the Daoist. The problem is that we are already bound together. An inability to recognize this is due to the ossification of cultural "knowledge" that makes us consciously alienated from each other and the rest of nature. To bind things together in a noncoercive way (i.e., "without cords") requires that persons cultivate an ability to undermine and subvert the ignorant habits of thinking (*zhi*) that "carve up" reality, thus creating the alienated condition where they are, metaphorically speaking, carving up Hundun or end up like the fish stranded on the river shore.

The *Zhuangzi* on the Capacity for "Self-Seeing" (自見)

The final feature of chapter 8 that helps to clarify how both sages and robbers suffer from the same epistemological error is to look at how the Daoist understands the ability to perceive nature as indeterminate. For the Daoist, the egoist's selfish desire, in the sense that such desire is structured and informed by the belief in an independent self, can be considered a form of desire that is rooted in alienation from nature. Selfish desire transgresses the "actuality of the endowed circumstances" of "things" in the sense that this desire is rooted in a misinterpretation of the natural world (i.e., literally grounded in the belief that there is a self that is independent of others). The *Zhuangzi* chapter 8 claims that the sages suffer from the same epistemological error. The (ironically named) sages are, if the Daoist is correct, equally alienated from nature and their fellow communities because they misinterpret situations.

Humans are born into communities and families. For better or worse, these communities will inevitably shape the next generation of people. This aspect of human existence is, as care ethicists have stressed, inescapably universal.[29] Although it might sound strange to consider the (ironically

Alienation and Attunement in the *Zhuangzi* | 151

named) sages to be responsible for "cutting up" nature and then trying to "glue and bind" things together, this is precisely how one Confucian philosopher describes the process of bringing the human community into harmony. The *Xunzi* makes exactly these kinds of arguments about the nature of human community and social relations that the *Zhuangzi* chapter 8 criticizes. For Xunzi, humans are different from animals because they have the ability to form communities based on their ability to first make divisions. He asks:

> How are humans able to form communities? I say: it is [social] divisions [*fen*]. How can [social] divisions be carried out? I say by means of "right conduct" [*yi*]. Thus if "right conduct" is used to make [social] divisions, then you have harmony; once you have harmony, then you have unity; once you have unity, you have greater strength; once you have greater strength, then you have determination; once you have determination, then you surpass [other] animals. Thus, humans can obtain palaces and rooms and inhabit them. Thus, the four seasons can be ordered, the ten-thousand things cultivated, and benefit brought to all under heaven. There is no other reason for this than obtaining [social] divisions and "right conduct." Thus, human life is not possible without community.[30]

For Xunzi, it is because of the human capacity to make divisions (*fen*, 分), that we can then use "right conduct" (*yi*, 義) to bring people into harmony (*he*, 和) and unity (*yi*, 一). Then, because of this unity, we have the collective power (*li*, 力) to overcome other animals and survive. For a Confucian like Xunzi, the human community does not exist naturally or fundamentally in a state of harmony. Although Xunzi would agree that persons are relationally constituted, they would not think that the human community is naturally in a state of harmony. Cultural forms[31] are needed to shape human dispositions such that human communities can be brought into harmony. For the Daoist, the fact that the Confucian believes there are "humans" that need to be shaped (regardless of whether their nature is good or bad) is already to miss the point. The means that the Confucians are using are coercive and do not respect the uniqueness of all things because such practices are informed by "knowledge." The Daoist agrees that communities need to be brought into harmony. The difference is that the Daoist critiques the very idea of "human" nature and "human" community. There is no "human" underlying the person. Each being is a radically novel convergence of relationships. The Daoist, contrary to the *Xunzi*, would argue that you cannot bring different things into harmony if you do not first understand how such beings are constituted by their world and are thus always novel. Before you have even tried to bring the community into harmony, you have falsely *made* them into humans (a *type* of "thing") with characteristics they simply do not have.

The Daoist understanding of the "actuality of endowed circumstances" involves seeing how all things are already bound together in interdependence. A key example of a claim like this comes from chapter 4 of the *Zhuangzi*. As *Confucius (as mouthpiece for Zhuangzi) states, "there are two great constraining obligations in the world. One is what is [given], one's mandated limitations, and the other is responsibility, doing what is called for by position. A child's love for his parents is [endowed]—it cannot be removed from his heart."[32] In this passage, it is better to translate *ming* (命) as "endowed" in the sense that this endowment is ontological in character. The child's love for its parents is a function of its dependence on the parent's care. The child cannot live out its allotment without the care of its parents and is in this sense endowed in a state of dependence. Guo Xiang's comments on this passage state that the child is "self-so connected firmly, not capable of unfastening" (自然結固，不可解也). Persons are initially bound and tied to their family and community. In the context of human relationships, "webbed toes" are cut when social institutions break up familial and communal relationships. When the Daoist describes the "actuality of endowed circumstances," it is this irreducibly relational self that they are referring to. Contrary to the *Xunzi*, *Zhuangzi* chapter 8 argues that it is precisely the fact that we make divisions (*fen*) and forget the original continuity of all things that leads to ignorance and confusion. This is why the Daoist critiques such moral beliefs and institutions as oppressive and coercive. Xunzi's plan is like the story of the fishes trapped on the river shore. The story of the fish stranded on the shore expresses how their situation is already one where they are alienated from nature and each other. Trying to stay on the shore (through participating in cultural institutions) ignores how the fish are not naturally attuned to (i.e., do not "fit") that environment. Cultural institutions that begin with a false diagnosis of problems perpetuate the coercive status quo. Making assumptions about the "type" of thing we are and how to organize us into a harmonized unity ipso facto ignores our novelty and particularity.

The Daoist critique of sages and robbers involves a more complicated understanding of the relationship between culture and nature. For the Daoist, society runs into problems when culture encourages the people of a community to become alienated from each other. Language and other cultural institutions have both liberating and inhibiting functions. Although the majority of *Zhuangzi* chapter 8 critiques the sages and robbers, the end of the chapter provides a solution for overcoming alienation and returning to a spontaneous attunement with nature. What the Daoists call it is the capacity for "self-seeing" (自見). The *Zhuangzi* states:

> What I call sharp hearing is not hearing others, but rather truly hearing yourself, nothing more. What I call sharp vision is not seeing others, but rather truly seeing yourself, nothing more. For to see others without seeing yourself, to gain some external *thing* without finding yourself, is to attain the success of others not in your own comfort. In taking their comfort [*shi*, 適] in something external to themselves, Robber Zhi and Bo Yi are alike. Both perverted and distorted themselves.[33]

In the context of chapter 8, the most important feature of being able to "see yourself" is that this involves understanding the "actuality of endowed circumstances" (其性命之情). Although "seeing yourself" might sound individualistic, what this involves is actually the realization that one is embedded in nature as indeterminate (*wu*), that is, that there are no individual persons that can be isolated from the rest of nature. Although the text is explicitly critical of Robber Zhi and coercive conduct, there is a sense that (ironically) it is in the Daoist's self-interest to recognize that the self is not independent. Robber Zhi can be understood as not "seeing himself when he sees things" (不自見而見彼). His conduct is one that, when he obtains things (both in the physical and abstract), this process perceptually alienates him from himself *as* nature *as* an "uncarved block of wood." If the Daoist is right, Robber Zhi (alienated due to "knowledge") is perpetually pursuing pleasures of the "eye" (as *Daodejing* 12 states). He is endlessly pursuing such things because he believes they can bring about success or comfort (*shi*, 適). For the Daoist, forms of life indebted to alienation cannot truly bring satisfaction or comfort. Maintaining attunement with nature requires that we do not depart from the "actuality of endowed circumstances." Xunzi's attempt at ameliorating society is likewise as ignorant as Robber Zhi. In not recognizing the primordial continuity of all things, both depart from the "actuality of endowed circumstances" and are unable to "see themselves when they see things." They both "carve up" different beings just as chapter 8 warns us. When we carve persons up and isolate them from their communities and the rest of nature, it is tantamount to "cutting webbed toes."

Conclusion: Alienation as Ignorance

As this chapter has attempted to show, the *Zhuangzi* provides a critique of why certain cultural beliefs and social institutions become coercive and oppressive. It is not that all forms of culture are inevitably morally and epistemologically dubious. The Daoist is critical of those practices and beliefs that are ignorant of how all persons and things exist in an interdependent web of relationships and form an indeterminate continuum (*wu*). An inability to perceive this is tantamount to being perceptually alienated from nature *as* an "uncarved block of wood." Though persons can never be isolated and removed from nature in an absolute sense, the inability to disclose situations in their primordial and indeterminate character does predispose us to creating suffering and further prevents us from understanding the nature of such suffering and coercion. The Daoist does not reject all forms of (metaphorically) "binding and blending" things together. To do this in a noncoercive way requires that we are attentive to how all things are unique because they are embedded in a web of interrelationships. Contrary to Xunzi, the Daoist does not "carve up" nature and forget the indeterminate and concrete context of experience. To harmonize the relations of persons and nature, we need to be perceptive to how things are radically novel convergences of relationships (and thus, novel focal points of nature). The Daoist avoids "cutting the webbed toes" and can bring about success or comfort (*shi*) in a noncoercive way that is respectful of the particularity of things and situations.

In drawing the distinction between alienation and attunement, the goal was to outline a new way of thinking about how people can be considered ignorant about their world. This form of ignorance is not necessarily reducible to proposition meaning and abstract thinking. It is not about possessing or reflecting upon the right concepts, principles, or ideas. What it involves is the inability to perceive the fundamentally indeterminate and primordially interdependent world that underlies conceptual thinking. When we can maintain attention to the qualitative aspects of experience, this elucidates how we and all other aspects of nature participate in an underlying oneness. This oneness does not collapse all differences into sameness but, like the story from chapter 2 of the *Zhuangzi* (quoted earlier in this book), instead allows each of the distinct things to emerge in their own distinct locations. The wind runs through each pipe, thus allowing them all to spring forth as if only from themselves. Each "self-so" aspect of nature is naturally endowed as unique. Any political and cultural institutions that do not acknowledge this particularity are bound to become coercive in how they shape social relationships. Both the moralist project and the bureaucracy of the state can function like they are cutting the "webbed toes" of people. Most important is that the Daoist believes that both the (Confucian and Mohist) moralist and the egoists are equally guilty of this same epistemological error. Both are guilty of a form of egoism in either trying to make the world like themselves (in their own self-image) or trying to use the world in a self-serving and selfish way. The very process of imposing a moral homogeneity onto the natural world is one that is ultimately narcissistic in the sense that the (non-Daoist) sages cannot appreciate the particularity of things in their uncoerced states (i.e., they cannot appreciate differences). The robbers likewise fail to appreciate their own naturalness in pursuing "eye desires." They end up making themselves into things. They might believe they are a special kind of thing that should or can exert their will or power over other things. In this alienation, they can even be considered to suffer from a kind of *pathology*. They do not recognize that they themselves are parts of nature and thus, like a numbness in the arm, cannot actively feel the relationships that are underlying their egoistic conceptual framework.

This is ultimately why the distinction between alienation and attunement was drawn in this way. Attunement, at some level, should be viewed as the norm or what would have been normal if not for the introduction of certain cultural and political institutions. Alienation, on the other hand, is pathological in the sense that those who suffer from it cannot rightfully be said to be acting willfully or wisely. They act on the objects of their epistemological framework and are not in accord with the natural dispositions of things. In this way, they are like persons cutting another's "webbed toes" (and also their own). They do this ignorantly and without any ability to see these behaviors in the larger context of relationships. They harm their own lives and the lives of others. If they were able to stay in accord with their naturally endowed spontaneity, then they would be like the *zhenren* or "true person" that was spoken about in earlier chapters of this book. In both the earlier chapters of the *Zhuangzi* and the primitivist chapters (and many other Daoist sources), the Daoist view of the self is one that is always situated and interdependent. It is this realization of the indeterminacy and underlying continuity of all things that functions as an alternative to both the moral Manicheanism of the sages and the egoism of the robbers. In the following and final chapter, I present one more important reason why the Daoist is correct to abandon a substance metaphysics; a substance metaphysics helps to promote moral bigotry.

Chapter Six

The Daoist Critique of Moral Bigotry
Amorality and Compassion
in the *Daodejing* and the *Zhuangzi*

The Daoist Sage: "Without Heart/Mind"

In this chapter, I present one final account of why the Daoist sage's conduct is compassionate, impartial, and nurturing due to how the Daoist is free of egoism and the belief that persons are independent selves. As *Daodejing* passage 49 states, the Daoist sage cultivates a capacity to see the world as one "chaotic muddle" through being "without heart/mind" (*wuxin*, 無心). When people are "with a constant heart/mind" and perceive the world through "knowledge," they interpret situations through the framework of "Moral Manicheanism." Such behavior is ignorant for a few reasons. One reason is that it attributes a level of agency and freedom to people that they do not possess. All people are conditioned by their environment and are thus limited in their perspective. Another reason is that, because persons are conditioned by their environment, the Daoist sage takes the cultural and political institutions to be the real causes of social ills. As long as the same cultural and political institutions are present, the same dispositions to act will continue to be produced and reproduced in the population. If a society's cultural institutions promote alienation, such alienation further produces resentment and negative emotions that reinforce social disharmony. When the Daoist sage is "without heart/mind" they can respond to situations with compassionate and nurturing behavior.

Being "without heart/mind" is likewise to be of the dispositions that do not suffer from alienation.

In order to clarify how the Daoists understood being "without heart/mind," this chapter proceeds as follows. First, the Daoist account of nature entails a heteronomous or conditioned understanding of human agency and cultivation. Second, the Daoist has a more nuanced and critical understanding of criminals and the causes behind any kind of deviant and bad behavior. There are two main causes behind social chaos. The first, minor cause is that political and social organization is responsible for the crime that is occurring. Corrupt leadership and political organization promote criminal conduct in the masses of society. Humans are fundamentally communal animals that depend on each other to increase our ability to survive. Although certain political and cultural institutions may have been created initially to help mitigate potential social problems, such as potential food scarcity, these institutions can also be used in ways that help to control and coerce the population into working more for less or to encourage work of the kind that helps to support the violent institutions of the state (like soldiers and law enforcement). The second, and more fundamental, reason is that the miseducation of persons with certain cultural forms promotes alienation. When humans are alienated from each other and the rest of nature, this promotes negative emotions such as resentment and generally encourages the population to interpret different peoples as beyond the bounds of moral relevance. Without seeing the wider context of relationships, the population and the rulers do not have the ability to understand their social conditions and the nature of social ills. Although there are many examples of how the Daoist describes the dispositions of the Daoist sage, this chapter focuses on the description that comes from *Daodejing* 49. It is because the Daoist sage is "without heart-mind" that they can noncoercively fuse or meld the heart-minds of persons into "one muddled mind."

Daoism and the Interdependent Self

As the previous chapters have already outlined, the Daoist position entails a conditioned and heteronomous understanding of human conduct. An independent capacity to adjust human behavior (i.e., the metaphysical sense of "autonomy") is and always will be a fiction. As Flanagan has previously described it, "libertarian free will is a myth," but there are still greater and lesser degrees of freedom that can be cultivated.[1] From this Daoist perspective, the usual way society attributes "merit" and "blame" to people is misguided because it mischaracterizes the nature of social ills. As with other nonnatural metaphysical objects, the assumptions behind moral merit and responsiblity have also played a huge role in legitimizing coercive and hierarchical social practices and political institutions. A philosophical position that accurately diagnoses how the cultural institutions are the causes of social ills presents a more accurate account of social life than a metaphysics that tries to attribute the source of social ills to "simply-located" realities like individuals wills or "evil natures." As *Daodejing* passage 5 claims, "heaven and earth are not humane, they treat people like straw dogs." There is no external, nonnatural reality that plays a causal role in rewarding and punishing good and bad behavior. The Daoist sage views the world without an independent sense of self, and they recognize that other peoples are also not independent things (i.e., *not libertarian selves* freely choosing or desiring to create or cause suffering). It is for this reason that the Daoist sage treats those that are suffering from alienation as a mother would treat *innocent children*. Those who create suffering are doing so out of ignorance. This compassion is the result of the Daoist understanding of nature as constituted by "non-simply located" processes. With this in mind, we can see why the Daoist account of compassion is extended *even to criminals*.

Although freedom as an unconditioned capacity or power does not exist for the Daoist (and is also a fiction in light of modern science), there are still greater and lesser degrees of being conditioned by nature and culture.[2] Freedom is not an inborn capacity but instead emerges from cultivation. Each "perspective" is formed by their environment regardless of the values they possess. Some of us are lucky (for example, those that are culturally valued sages). Some of us are unlucky (those of us not born into loving families, those that are unable to secure the basic means of survival, etc.). Without taking into consideration that all persons are products of their environment, we will not be able to adequately address the causes of social disharmony. One account of a heteronomous self in the *Zhuangzi* is described in the "Inner Chapters" with a series of questions.

> The hundred bones, the nine openings, the six internal organs are all present here as my body. Which one is most dear to me? Do you delight in all equally, or do you have some favorite among them? Or are they all mere servants and concubines?

Are these servants and concubines unable to govern each other? Or do they take turns as master and servant? If there exists a genuine ruler among them, then whether we could find out the facts about him or not would neither add to nor subtract from that genuineness.[3]

In this passage, there is no "organ that is most dear"; the way one delights in any one organ is unique/particular to that organ (i.e., each organ is valuable in relation to each other organ); and no organ should be favored more than the others. If a thing depends on "what it is not" to sustain its existence, then the very hierarchy of ruled versus ruler is thrown into question. At any given moment, the aspect of experience that is most manifest or dominant can easily change as well. *What* is guiding conduct is easily reversible.[4] For Sonya Özbey, this "passage is clearly arguing against thinking about the heterogeneous and pluralistic psycho-physiological makeup of one's person along reductive lines by primarily focusing on the heart and exalting it."[5] The Daoist account of nature holds that each aspect of nature depends on something else just as the Penumbra depends on the Shadow, the Shadow on another thing—as the story goes in the *Zhuangzi*.[6] The point is not simply one of rejecting the existence of ontologically separate and distinct objects. The belief that there exists something like agency or an agent, especially in the robust Kantian sense of *autonomy*, is simply a fiction. Although rejected by modern science, the assumption of an independent and autonomous self is still present in both the Kantian and Rawlsian accounts of Deontology. Although Kant admits that freedom is a presupposition needed for the possibility of ethics, there is more to his presuppositions. Indeed, we find in Kant's *Groundwork* the usual definition of substance, an "in-itself," prior to its relations where said relationships must be external to the substance and do not constitute it.[7]

As chapter 4 of this book already summarized, a rational being was assumed to have "intrinsic value," that is, value independent of historical conditions and relationships. This was because only substances could have the kind of value that would not change due to the influence of external, conditioned realities. As Sandel is right to point out, the later deontology of Rawls also presupposes an independent, antecedent subject prior to experience and prior to the relationships that they *merely possess* and are *not constituted by*.[8] The Daoist would agree with Sandel's critique of Rawls when he claims: "The assertion that a man deserves the inferior character that prevents him from overcoming his liabilities is equally problematic; for his character depends in large part upon unfortunate family and social circumstances for which he cannot be blamed."[9] For the Daoist, all dispositions are environmentally and contextually embedded.[10] Regardless of whatever level of freedom and spontaneity one can potentially cultivate, the ability to act and react to the environment inevitably takes a heteronomous form.[11] For the Daoist, a real sage would recognize that criminals cannot be said to be "guilty" of their transgressions in a robust sense. Likewise, exemplars are not solely responsible for their "merit" and their virtues. Every instance of purported "merit" is ultimately an issue of chance and contingency. Even the Daoist sage is a product of contingency. The difference between their virtue and the morality of non-Daoist exemplars is that they recognize the contingency of their "perspective" and that they were shaped by their environments. Without this insight to contextualize our judgments, morality will inevitably become a self-undermining and hypocritical endeavor. It will devolve into 1) "virtuous people" or (non-Daoist) sages continuing to insist on their superiority because they believe they have tapped into some "power" independent of nature and change. They will believe that they are the sole cause or author of their deserved "merit" and virtue. In other words, they become moral egoists. These same "exemplars" will then 2) continue to condemn those that are *also the mere products of their environments*. Actual compassion involves an understanding of the social conditions that others suffer under. Nonegoistic humility involves an understanding that one's "merits" are because of those chance encounters with the right situations and teachers. The belief that there are free individuals that gain merit, especially "moral merit" is exactly what undermines the moral attitude.

The Daoist account of the ethical life is not straightforward. Their position can best be understood as taking a "diagnostic perspective."[12] They do not simply offer a theory of morality that can easily be juxtaposed with alternative accounts. Their perspective, as diagnostic, involves a metaethical critique of certain ways of theorizing about moral behavior. If the metaphysical assumptions that ethical theory is grounded in are mistaken, then the capacity of such theory to help guide conduct and alleviate social ills will be suspect as well. Such theory might even be encouraging and legitimizing the same ignorant behavior it was meant to ameliorate. Daoism takes a diagnostic perspective because Daoists are more critical of the causes and conditions that give rise to deviant behavior than typically found with other theoretical frameworks. Moral discourse can, *as a tool*, contribute to perpetuating the same problematic behaviors that such theory was meant to address.[13] It is the epistemological framework that the entire population is enculturated with that is responsible for producing and reproducing social disharmony.

Criminals and the Daoist Critique of the "Moralists"

Central to understanding the Daoist account of compassion is their critique of the moral or moralist attitude. The Daoist is often critical of the moral theories and social practices of the Confucians and Mohists because their moral discourses have been guilty of justifying and normalizing both oppression and suffering (which is, paradoxically, precisely what morality was supposed to be remedying). As the *Daodejing* states, "those who act [*wei*] ruin it." There is no greater example of this than the way moral beliefs can end up de-sensitizing us to the suffering of others, which discourages us from empathizing with the people who might deserve it the most. For the Daoist, this means that we must cultivate the capacity to be attuned to all situations, even to the point of empathizing with criminals and their circumstances as well. The causes and conditions that give rise to criminal behavior need to be understood, and it is precisely the typical moralist attitude that discourages us from doing this properly. As the Daoist understands it, *criminals are equally victims of society's institutions*. They are, ultimately, the *biproducts of an already criminally structured society*. The stories in the *Zhuangzi* that discuss criminals must be viewed in this light.

The *Zhuangzi* contains quite a few stories about criminals and crime in human society. Some of the criminals in these stories end up being portrayed as sages and even of higher virtue and understanding than Confucius. To make sense of these stories and the Daoist understanding of criminal behavior, it is important to distinguish between the crimes of the common people and the crimes of a ruler that are, arguably, never actually labeled as crimes. As chapter 10 of the *Zhuangzi* highlights, there are the "small thieves" and the "great thieves." "Small thieves" are those who might steal a chest of someone else's material possessions. The "great thieves" are those who might, like a military general or foreign power, steal an entire state. A "small thief" is guilty of crime *within* the context of the social and political institutions of a given society. They function as a part of a social system, and their crime should be viewed as a biproduct of the system itself. Given the way the cultural and social norms emerge at the given time, there are certain incentives or pressures on the population that can either encourage them or discourage them to act in favor of or against the social and political systems they live under. The "great thieves," on the other hand, are thieves in another sense. Stealing a state does not get one punished. In a way, we can consider this kind of theft *outside* the limits of the social system. There are two points the *Zhuangzi* makes with such a distinction. The first is that, although the social, cultural and political institutions might have been produced to serve the population in a specific way, all it takes is a change of leadership (a "great thief") to adjust the institutions in a way that benefits the ruling class most (for example, overextracting resources and overworking the population limits their freedom because more work is required to sustain the worker's basic sustenance). The second reason is that, in calling the rulers "thieves," it points out what should be a blatant double standard in the moral and political institutions that shape our lives ("white-collar" versus "blue-collar" crime, for example). Both features are what is involved with the notion of a "criminal society." In introducing this notion that there can be a "criminal society," what it suggests is that we ultimately need to adopt a different understanding of responsibility. We need to learn to critique political institutions differently by viewing them as taking precedence to individual persons. For example, the freedom of the ruling class is made possible due to how society is economically stratified where those social institutions are themselves legitimized by "knowledge" and physical force; moral discourse is often useful for normalizing physical coercion. Only after society has been hierarchically structured with social classes is "stealing a state" even possible. Those people who possess this kind of power can then set up political institutions that permit murder (as I illustrate below) or punish anyone else who stands against this political system by labeling them as moral transgressors. Generally, we can consider a "criminal society" to be one that operates through certain contradictions that are (in my view) often legitimized by a moral discourse.

The stories in the *Zhuangzi* that discuss criminals and convicts are (ironically) passed over by many Western commentators. It is ironic (or *fitting*) because the commentators who fail to grasp the meaning of these stories possess the very attitudes that these stories aim to critique. Before reading and trying to understand *any* of the stories in the *Zhuangzi* that involve criminals as characters, there are two important but brief passages that can help to contextualize each of them. The first comes from chapter

4. The story is of Yan He, who, after being appointed tutor to the crown prince of Wei, asks Qu Boyu for advice. This is how Yan He describes his problem (which will be called "Yan He's problem" for reference later): "Here is a man who is just naturally no good. If I find no way to contain him, he will endanger my state, but if I try to contain him, he will endanger my life. His cleverness allows him to understand the crimes people commit, but not why they were driven to commit these crimes."[14]

It is subtle, but, as Guo Xiang and other commentators suggest, it is the rules and regulations of the tyrant ruler that are the source of crime in the state. As Guo Xiang states, the ruler "does not realize that the faults of the people are all due to him. Therefore, he blames his people for crimes but does nothing to reform himself."[15] When the ruling class overexploits the common people such that they cannot maintain sustenance without great effort, this creates the conditions where "clever" behavior (as the Daoist calls it) is encouraged. Because overexploitation is inherently undesirable, a cultural ideology and/or physical force is needed to help maintain this undesirable political arrangement. Usually a mythic or moral ideology (i.e., nonnaturalist metaphysics) is employed to help legitimize to the population such stratification of wealth in society (*merit*, for example, is a common moral excuse). The larger problem is that this creates a vicious cycle that does not bode well for the common people. What is important is that, if we were to follow the Daoist reasoning in "Yan He's problem," we are actually shifting the attribution of "blame" in this situation. Criminals are *driven*, given their circumstances, to commit crimes, and they are not doing so merely because of free choice (even the sages do not exercise "autonomous free choice"). This shouldn't be a controversial claim. For the Daoist, the problem is that this is not the principal or initial way that we interpret situations where crime is committed. Because of the way we have been conditioned by society (the myths that society tells us), we usually do not think of criminals as having been *forced* into their circumstances. For example, if a person is starving and has no means of obtaining food reliably, they might steal food or other material goods to feed themselves.

What is most important to take note of is that these thought experiments are precisely what the *Zhuangzi* is inviting us to do when it discusses the virtues of ex-cons. When scholars usually read these stories, it is the moralist attitude that inhibits their ability to imaginatively empathize with the experience of other people (i.e., "Those who act ruin it," 為者敗之). For the Daoist, there is an absolutism and moral bigotry that is inherent with the Manichean moral attitude. One good example of this, and one I will remention throughout this chapter, are some of the moral arguments made by the Mohists. For reference, this story will be referred to as the "Mohist argument." As the *Zhuangzi* chapter 14 points out, "Yu ordered the world by causing the people's hearts and minds to focus on making changes, so that leaders had definite intentions and armies obeyed whatever order there were given, saying that 'to kill a thief is not really murdering a person'" (which is a claim defended by Mohists).[16] Key to understanding why an argument like this one by the Mohists is so problematic is that criminal behavior cannot be understood as simply a "choice" that people make. Daoists see criminal conduct as a biproduct of a society that produces social incentives to act in deviant ways. With the moralist attitude and the belief that persons are free to choose good and bad courses of action, the whole context of feudalism and its corruption is ignored. Whenever we think about criminals and their criminality, when we fail to see their behavior in light of "Yan He's problem" (that the society is a *criminal society* and produces criminals as a biproduct), and we interpret criminals in light of the "Mohist argument" (a naïve, Manichean account of morality and moral behavior,) we are then literally guilty of precisely what the Daoist is critiquing. Moral Manicheanism and the moralist attitude place the "bad" outside the bounds of moral consideration and thus, by reducing social reality to a substance like source, the moralist attitude legitimizes violence.

Keeping these two previous stories in mind, the dialogue of the virtuous criminal in chapter 5 of the *Zhuangzi* can be understood as making this exact point about the moralist attitude. We are guilty of moral Manicheanism when we interpret the criminals as mere "wrong doers" in a moral sense. The story states:

> There was this ex-con in Lu, whose feet had been mutilated as a punishment, named Toeless of Unk Mountain. He heeled his way over to see Confucius, who said to him, "You were careless in your past behavior and thus ended up in this condition. Isn't it a little late to come to me now?"
>
> Toeless said, "I just didn't understand where to direct my labors and undervalued my own body, and so I am lacking a foot; but as I come to you now I still have retained something more than a foot, which I am trying to keep whole. Heaven covers all things. Earth supports all things. I used to think that

you, sir, were just like heaven and earth—I never imagined you would instead say something like this!" [. . .]

Toeless said to Lao Dan, "Confucius is certainly far from being an Utmost Person, isn't he? Why does he go around imitating you so subserviently? He must be seeking some bizarre, deceptive, illusory, freakish think like a good name, not realizing that the Utmost person views such things as handcuffs and leg chains."[17] (The story then concludes with a statement about how it is *ming* or "fate" that put Confucius in this position).

Setting aside the interpretive issue of whether this story accurately represents the Confucian position for a moment (as I don't believe it completely does), what the Daoist is critical of is the moral obtuseness and narrow mindedness that come from moral Manicheanism. Regardless of historical context, what the Daoist would suggest is that, if you were to tell an ex-con that it is "too late" to get moral or scholarly teaching or advice, then you are *literally a moral bigot*. At minimum, what this story is trying to portray is the uncritical way that the moralist attitude inhibits the capacity to understand the nature of criminal conduct and the social situation that we are currently inhabiting. With such an attitude towards this ex-con, it illustrates an ignorance about the nature of suffering and the ways that society is structured in an unequal and criminal fashion. Although the "Mohist argument" is a more extreme example of how a moral discourse can be used to justify an oppressive status quo, Confucius as portrayed in this story is also guilty of the same attitude. It does not take much imagination to understand how problematic Confucius's attitude is with regard to this ex-con. As with "Yan He's problem," the situation could be that this ex-con was desperate and starving. This is due to the corrupt political structure of society. His crime is then a biproduct of an inegalitarian society. A society structured such that the greed of the ruling class restricts the ability for everyday people to maintain their own livelihood and survive will inevitably produce this kind of criminal behavior. Yet this is not the only reason why someone might end up being punished in a criminal society. As the last story of chapter 4 of the *Zhuangzi* states, from the perspective of a "madman" singing as they walk past Confucius, "When the Course [Dao] is present in the world, the sage perfects himself with it. When the Course is lacking in the world, he just lives his own life with it. But in the present age, avoiding execution is the best he can do with it."[18]

In a criminal society, is there much reason to believe that those being punished for crimes are merely "bad people"? In this previous passage, especially in light of the fact that this singing is taking place *near* Confucius, the story suggests that those persons who are *truly* virtuous are simply doing their best to avoid being killed by tyrants and their henchmen. Those who are not so virtuous, in the sense that they are trying to get political power or wealth/privilege, might be capable of getting an audience with the ruling tyrants (as the story of the ex-con from Lu suggests when it claims Confucius is trying to get a "good name"). Because of the political incentives, a scholar might even be thinking of logical arguments that help to legitimize the idea that "killing a thief is not really killing a person." If the situation that the *Zhuangzi* is presenting is an accurate one, then there is no reason to believe that true sages or virtuous persons can survive long given the political situation suggested in the story of the "madman." Getting an audience with a corrupt ruler might involve defending the violent and corrupt policies of their tyrant rule. The *Zhuangzi* also suggests that it is incredibly difficult to effect social change for the benefit of society. Both "Yan He's problem" and other stories of the *Zhuangzi* suggest that dealing with a tyrant is a difficult task that is likely to get you killed.[19] Given the many examples above, we need to resist the equation that "criminals" are equal to "bad" or immoral people. The moralist attitude usually interprets the ex-con story to suggest that the ex-con was *initially* a bad person. On that reading, the *Zhuangzi* is then suggesting that *even* an ex-con can *become* a person of virtue. In reality, the story is even more problematic because, as the "madman" story tells us, there is not much reason to think that persons of real virtue are able to get an audience with the rulers. The real sages are simply doing their best not to be killed by the might of the state. The ex-con story presents Confucius as highly unaware of the nature of crime and the oppressive nature of the political institutions of his time. The ex-con in that story could be innocent, could have been starving, or could have been practicing "civil disobedience" with the hope of dealing with corruption or standing against violence. Social reality is far more complicated than the moral Manicheanism of the typical moralist attitude. When the social and political systems are to blame, it is highly problematic to attribute the source of social ills to a single "will" or "bad agent." It is the political institutions that permit one to "steal a state" and benefit from these class divisions. When the moral philosopher misses this, it is clear that they are doing the work to either normalize or defend the ruling class and their "noncrimes" such as "stealing a state," justifying murder, or overexploiting the common people.

The Daoist Solution: Seeing the Oneness of All Things

Although there might be Daoist scholars who take issue with the idea that the Daoist's position espouses care and nurture, part of the confusion is perhaps because of the ironic nature of the Daoist's care. As has been highlighted repeatedly throughout this book, the Daoist is most interested in getting rid of a separate sense of self and the egoistic attitude. Their position is not straightforward because they deal with the more fundamental issue of egoism and the subtle way that even a moral discourse can become guilty of narcissistic tendencies. Their project is one of *not* "ruining things," while the other (non-Daoist) sages around them *act and ruin things*. When the Daoist sage is "without heart/mind" (*wuxin*), "without self-interest," or like a "true person" (*zhenren*), they are nonpurposive in their conduct. It is this *spontaneous* capacity to be without egoistic tendencies that the Daoist's dispositions realize. Purposelessness thus plays a crucial role in the Daoist sage's care and compassion. If scholars are not careful when they read the Daoist stories that describe how the Daoist sage is without purpose, they might read them to be espousing noninterference or as a retreat from society. A good illustration of how the Daoist understood care can be seen in a story from *Zhuangzi* chapter 4. The story introduces the reader to a carpenter who comes upon an enormous tree. It is subtle, but the story makes this exact point: purposivelessness and being "without merit" correspond to the kind of care that others respond to and gravitate towards. The story begins with a carpenter and his apprentice hiking through the woods. When they come upon a gigantic tree, the apprentice wonders to the master why he is not interested in chopping this tree down to use in his craft. The master explains that such a tree must be useless and of no value. That is why it has not been cut down yet. Later that night, the carpenter has a dream in which the tree visits him and teaches him about what it means to be a Daoist. The tree explains:

> What do you want to compare me to, one of those cultivated trees? The hawthorn, the pear, the orange, the rest of those

fructiferous trees and shrubs—when their fruit is ripe they get plucked, and that is an insult. [. . .] They batter themselves with the vulgar conventions of the world, as do all the other things of the world. As for me, I've been working on being useless for a long time. It almost killed me, but I've finally managed it—and it was of great use to me! If I were useful, do you think I could have grown to be so great?

Moreover, you and I are both things, objects—how then should we objectify each other? We are members of the same class, namely, things—is either of us in a position to classify and evaluate the other?[20]

In this context, we can consider the criticism of being cultivated to be specifically about *purposive* cultivation towards the end of being useful for others. It is the clinging to fixed evaluations that is problematic. As is the case with the many other stories in the *Zhuangzi* that discuss the virtues of being useless, this story suggests that those who are willing to become useful will end up cutting their lives short. They become entrapped in the workings of value and "merit" (i.e., become *alienated*). In doing so, they become things within a system of other things. As was analyzed in chapters 4 and 5 of this book, the tendency to reify values and make "things" out of nature by classifying them as "types" of things is like "cutting the webbed toes of people" in order to make them fit an antecedent or ideal model. The key to this story and why the story is connected to ideas from the *Daodejing* that speak about being "without self-interest" and "without heart/mind" is the apprentice's subtle comments in reply to his teacher. Ironically, this is the part of the story that is probably glossed over by scholars hoping to read Western individualism into Daoist philosophy. When the man awakens and tells his apprentice about his dream, he gets this reply:

"If it's trying to be useless, what's it doing with a shrine around it?"

[The carpenter replies:] "Hush! Don't talk like that! Those people came to it for refuge on their own initiative. In fact, the tree considers it a great disgrace to be surrounded by this uncomprehending crowd. If they hadn't made it a shrine, they could easily have gone the other way and started carving away at it. What it protects, what protects it, is not this crowd, but something totally different. To praise it for fulfilling its responsibility in the role it happens to play—that would really be missing the point!"[21]

In being useless and without egoistic purpose, the Daoist sage becomes a focal point that other people in the community gravitate towards. The common people, on their own accord, value and resonate with the "useless" tree. This is because real virtue is spontaneously nonimposing and nonegoistic. This story is expressing the same point that the Daoist of the *Daodejing* wants to convey; the noncoerced and spontaneous capacity to lead people through care. The Daoist capacity to preserve their own life is not because they have completely retreated from society. As passage 7 of the *Daodejing* stresses, it is through being "without self-interest" (*wusi*) that the Daoist sage is able to preserve their own life. It is specifically the nonpurposive, nondesiring attitude that enables the Daoist sage to bring about the kind of harmony that the Mohists and Confucian sages were not able to bring about. In preserving the empty center like a *zhenren*, the Daoist thus achieves the dispositions that are both most epistemologically sensitive to situations and that are in accord with how both they and others are naturally endowed.

The Daoist alternative to moral Manicheanism is described as an ability to see moralist ideologies from a larger context or from the perspective of the larger whole of nature. When we can view these forms of cultural ideology with a larger context of relationships, this grants us a greater understanding of the nature of social ills. In getting rid of the desire for "merit" and the like, the Daoist is not simply relativizing values. Their abandonment or forgetting of (ossified) values is actually (ironically) the real way to achieve valuable interrelationships. Chapter 2 of the *Zhuangzi* has many stories that describe this capacity. For example, it states:

> For courses have never had any sealed boundaries between them, and words have never had any constant range. It is by establishing definitions of what is "this," what is "right," that boundaries are made. [. . .] Wherever debate shows one of two alternatives to be right, something remains undistinguished and unshown. What is it? The sage hides it in his embrace, while the masses of people debate it, trying to demonstrate it to one another. Thus I say that demonstration by debate always leaves something unshown.[22]

A passage like this one might at first suggest relativism, but in reality, the Daoist is arguing that those like the Confucians and the Mohists are both wrong. In abandoning the fixed moral interpretations of the Confucians and Mohists, the Daoist recognizes how it is the very tendency to reduce complex relations to mere objects to be either promoted or extricated that produces the same kinds of behavior that were initially deemed to be "bad." The moralist does not recognize that their "horizon of relevance" is making them complicit in exactly what they insist they are against (為者敗之). In maintaining attention to what "remains undistinguished and unshown" (i.e., the context of relationships), persons would perceive the social and political institutions as the real sources of social ills.

When moral philosophers hear the term "amorality," the last thing that they might ever associate with it is the practice of compassion or conduct akin to "motherly loving care." As mentioned in the introduction to this study, the *Daodejing* and *Zhuangzi* at times espouse many (*seemingly*) different positions about what is considered moral conduct. What *Daodejing* passage 49 presents is another instance of different ideas being associated together that, at first, might seem to be in contradiction. In my view, *Daodejing* passage 49 presents the best account of the Daoist sage's understanding of compassion:

> The sage is constantly without a heart/mind [*wuxin*, 無心];
> he takes the heart/mind of the common people as their own heart/mind.
>
> Those who are good he treats good. Those who are not good he also treats good. Thus, he attains goodness. Those who are trustworthy he trusts. Those who are untrustworthy he also trusts. Thus, he attains trustworthiness.
>
> When the sage resides in the world, he fuses himself with it. For the world he merges hearts. All the people fix ears and eyes on him, and the sage regards them as smiling children.
> [*with minor changes*][23]

Although this passage is possibly a critique of the Confucian claims from the *Analects* 14.34 (or the *Analects* 14.34 is a response to the *Daodejing* claims here and *Daodejing* passage 63),[24] it is not too much a stretch to think that this *Daodejing* passage runs contrary to *most* systems of morality, both East and West. What is most important are the three interrelated ideas that are each rooted in the Daoist's understanding of nature as primordially indeterminate (*wu*). The Daoist sage is "without heart/mind" when they recognize that they are without an independent sense of self. This passage then connects being "without heart/mind" with an understanding of persons that might at first look like amorality. "Those who are good" and "those who are bad" are both to be treated as good. Those who are trustworthy and those that are untrustworthy are to be treated as trustworthy. Finally, the passage concludes with the idea that the sage fuses themselves with the world and merges the hearts of the community. This is compared to a mother caring for *innocent children*. What passage 49 describes is an account of compassion and care that is grounded in their understanding persons as heteronomous selves and of how care and virtue are learned from particular environments. From the Daoist perspective, those persons that are "not good" (不善) have not been treated with virtue or as "good" (*shan*, 善).

If all perspectives are conditioned, then learning to care for others is not something one can learn through mere self-reflection. Care and nurture are particular kinds of environments. The lack of exposure to these environments leads to alienation or the inability to feel fused with the world (this lack of exposure would also promote "criminal behavior"). Care for others, for the Daoist, amounts to "fusing with the world" or "melding the hearts and minds of the people." This form of care is beyond the usual way of dividing up "good" and "bad." It is one that is purposive-less just as the Daoist tree in the above story. The Daoist sage's care, impartial towards the way persons and things have been determined to be either "good" or "bad" by society, sees all persons as a product of chance and circumstance. They are not agents that are the sole causes behind their fortune and/or misfortune. In fact, if we really wanted to ameliorate the ills of society, the last thing we should do is approach problems from the moralist perspective. The attitude that seeks to punish or extricate "the bad substances" of society is the best example of an attitude that undermines itself. (*Those who act ruin it.*) The only way to truly deal with social ills is to address the environments themselves. Those that are "not good" lack the feeling of being fused with the world either due to the general processes of cultural education that promote alienation (e.g., teaching people they are "individuals") or due to how they lack the experience of others fusing with them through care and virtue. Without the experience of "becoming one muddled mind" through care, neither the rulers nor the common people can learn to appreciate the value of such relationships. In light of the above criminal stories, we can see how a "criminal society" promotes the opposite of a caring environment. The whole system of power is set up to steal and has a lack of empathy for those whom it systemically disempowers. The Daoist, like the useless tree above, can help to adjust society for the better only because they are spontaneously without an egoistic attitude. It is through their lack of clinging to reified things and values that they are enabled to *not ruin things*.

Conclusion

The belief in nonnatural assumptions such as an autonomous self is itself grounded in the belief that nature is constituted by ontologically distinct objects. We fail to recognize that all peoples are *heteronomous selves* because of "knowledge." The moralist attitude is problematic because it falsely places people beyond the bounds of moral consideration. This particular way of creating divisions is not only inaccurate; these borders and boundaries then are such that, by definition, that which is beyond the boundary is extinguishable. A metaphysics that involves seeing people as independent and not embedded in their environments undermines its supposed efficacy.

The Daoist position is not then a kind of "fatalism." Humans are shaped by our cultural and political environments. If we do not acknowledge our environmental and cultural embeddedness, if we do not find methods for dealing with the limited (heteronomous) nature of the human perspective, then there is little hope for dealing with the human condition. The more human society begins to see all peoples as the product of their environments, the more we can adjust the cultural and political institutions that contribute to suffering and the formation of certain dispositions to act (both the non-Daoist sages and the robbers). From the Daoist perspective, when such institutions are informed by ignorant beliefs that rely on nonnaturalist assumptions (especially with the nonnaturalist account of human agency), such institutions are "cutting the webbed toes" of people for the sake of manufacturing conformity, docility, and the sameness of things. The Daoist is happy to suggest that most deviant behavior is tied to either the inability to maintain basic sustenance and/or the feeling of alienation from being "one muddled mind" with the community. For the

Daoist, certain cultural assumptions and habits of belief alienate us from each other and nature. If persons can become attuned to our interdependence, then those who have cultivated some level of freedom will have a better sense of how to teach and educate others. This will, in an anarchical spread outward from the potency and sensitivity of the Daoist sage, help to liberate others from the fetters of "knowledge."

Conclusion

A Daoist Alternative to the "Sages"

Challenging Western Moral Metaphysics

When looking at Daoism, philosophers biased with Western ideas must work to charitably understand foreign philosophical traditions. Unless a philosophical tradition explicitly announces that it supports "anything goes" moral relativism, such claims should perhaps only be taken as ad hominem arguments. The Daoist tradition is first and foremost diagnosing the sources behind concrete instances of suffering and social unrest. This book has classified this problem as further rooted in the problematic epistemological framework that produces perceptual alienation. Such an epistemology is informed by what is called a "substance ontology" or the belief that "things" and their individuation take precedence over relationships. What the Daoist can further conclude is that ethical non-naturalism, as a *misinterpretation* of the natural world, is creating the very dispositions in people that the "moralist" was hoping to remedy. As the *Daodejing* states perfectly, "Those who act ruin it." If the Daoist was truly okay with any particular set of values or beliefs, there would be nothing to "ruin." The epistemology of the sui generis moral attitude undermines its own intentions and aims. As long as philosophers cling to the same metaphysical assumptions they will continue to misunderstand social problems. They will continue to "ruin things," although they believe they are ameliorating society.

If we continue to insist that only *Western* ideas are worth valuing and that Western culture is the only source of values, then there is no reason to do comparative philosophy or engage with non-Western philosophical traditions. The reality, though, is that the West has arrived at its purported superiority and universality through the physical erasure of philosophical and cultural differences. The West's "first encounter with significantly different people [. . .] led to the decimation of 95 percent of the native Amerindian population, [. . .] the rise of the trans-atlantic slave trade, which according to demographers' estimates, may have halved Africa's population through deaths on the continent and exportation of its population, [. . .] and the founding of new settler-colonial nations via] the extermination, displacement, or herding onto reservations of aboriginal population"[1]. Indeed, the West has achieved its cultural preeminence primarily, if not solely, through physical domination. It is precisely this attitude that Franz Fanon describes in his critique of western universal values. In actuality, western values have been proven under the barrel of a gun. As Fanon states, "But it so happens that when the native hears a speech about Western culture he pulls out his knife—or at least he makes sure it is within reach. The violence with which the supremacy of white values is affirmed and the aggressiveness which has permeated the victory of these values over the ways of life and of thought of the native mean that, in revenge, the native laughs in mockery when Western values are mentioned in front of him."[2] To a great extent, the thesis of this book helps to explain how this kind of behavior could have become normalized and made to look "reasonable" to the population. It is a particular kind of moral discourse that provides a "horizon of relevance" such that people commit mass murder under the guise that they are ameliorating the world. Philosophers who uncritically believe that it is only through the discovery of "moral facts" that we can condemn these practices are arguing from bad faith insofar as they do not understand their own violent history. The Daoist tradition provides us with resources that help us to ameliorate society, yet in a way that also explains how the usual moral project might become corrupt or self-undermining.

My task in this book was not merely to argue for an alternative understanding of human life. Admittedly, this book makes the stronger claim that this new understanding of experience and nature can help shed some light on why this discipline of philosophy and what it holds as indubitably sacred is, in fact, misguided. James Baldwin, in the profoundly humanist way that he writes, offers these reflections about the Western world in his works *No Name in the Street* and *The Fire Next Time*. In *No Name in the Street*, he claims that "all the western nations are caught in a lie, the lie of their pretended humanism: this means that their history has no moral justification, and that the West has no moral authority."³ In *The Fire Next Time*, he similarly claims that white Americans believe themselves to be in the possession of an "intrinsic value" that they believe black people must necessarily want. On the contrary, Baldwin suggests that there is little in the lives of white people that anyone should desire to emulate. He continues:

> How can one respect, let alone adopt, the values of a people who do not, on any level whatever, live the way they say they do, or the ways they say they should? I cannot accept the proposition that the four-hundred-year travail of the American Negro should result merely in his attainment of the present level of the American civilization. I am far from convinced that being released from the African witch doctor was worthwhile if I am now—in order to support the moral contradictions and the spiritual aridity of my life—expected to become dependent on the American psychiatrist. It is a bargain I refuse.⁴

Indeed, certain aspects of Western culture and civilization come off as incredibly schizophrenic. Far from believing that Western values express universal facts about the moral order of the universe or even that they are *functionally better* than other alternatives, from the Daoist perspective, morality that takes a nonnaturalistic form is just another symptom of social decline. The metaphysical beliefs that we cling to are making us alienated from the natural world and each other. The Daoist understanding of experience recognizes how certain metaphysical assumptions are simply post facto justifications that help to legitimize and normalize oppression and domination. In fact, two modern examples of the unholy marriage between metaphysics and ethics come from "American exceptionalism" and Western radical individualism. The idea that the means used to achieve a "valued end" were merely contingent or accidental in relation to such an end is an obvious case of totalitarian behavior justified with ethical theory. As chapter 4 showed, the idea that particular objects had "intrinsic value" bears a similar oppressive structure. "Intrinsic value" is an idea we would be better off forgetting.

What is more troubling is that, even now in the twenty-first century, the discipline of philosophy is still stuck using Greek metaphysical assumptions that should have been abandoned long ago. Related to that problem is how philosophers still take seriously the highly unrealistic distinction between "moral objectivism" and "moral relativism." Critics of Daoism, as well as Buddhism, can't continue to cling to their question-begging assumptions while ignoring empirical reality. The tendency to do this, and of even considering themselves to be *virtuous* for doing so, makes the discipline of philosophy into something irrelevant and decadent. Similar to Baldwin's claims above are those from the modern philosopher Lewis Gordon who has written on the decadence of philosophy departments and academia generally. Philosophers that cling to those old-school myths of the West need to seriously consider whether the work they do bears any relationship to social reality. As Gordon describes it, reality is much larger than the scope of any single academic discipline. Scholars of all fields need to have a bit more humility than they usually practice. An inability to appreciate how our perspective is limited is tantamount to a failure to appreciate reality in all of its complexity.

> Failure to appreciate reality sometimes takes the form of recoiling from it. An inward path of disciplinary solitude eventually leads to what I call *disciplinary decadence*. This is the phenomenon of turning away from living thought, which engages reality and recognises its own limitations, to a deontologised or absolute conception of disciplinary life. The discipline becomes, in solipsistic fashion, *the world*. And in that world, the main concern is the proper administering of its rules, regulations, or, as Fanon argued, (self-devouring) methods. Becoming "right" is simply a matter of applying, as fetish, the method correctly. This is a form of decadence because of the set of considerations that fall to the wayside as the discipline turns into itself and eventually implodes.[5]

Many of the debates in anglophone philosophy departments are in reality a kind of decadent, fetishization of certain question-begging assumptions. The debates about how "moral facts" function, for example, are highly dubious when done without any sense of how provincial and chauvinistic such debates have become. We have arrived at a point where philosophers in these departments, philosophers doing philosophy in the heart of the world's most powerful empire and the world's most *unstudied empire*, preach that they are the only ones standing in the way of all of the worse forms of oppression and human suffering imaginable. The fetishization of their philosophical discourses keeps them irrelevant with respect to the concrete social and political problems of our times. One of the best ways to get out of this decadence and provincialism is to engage more with non-Western philosophical traditions such that these philosophers learn to question their own metaphysical assumptions. Until this can happen, the discipline of philosophy will continue to function like an elitist "club." Philosophers must give up their narcissistic self-image and engage with the concrete problems of human society. Doing so may release them from the cage that is their own question-begging epistemology.

Those Who Act Ruin It

In the introduction to this book, it was stressed that the many different (seemingly) conflicting positions of the *Daodejing* could be viewed as consistent if we were to see them all as indebted to a metaphysics of interdependence that understood that all things ultimately formed an underlying continuity. In this way, the Daoist position is not one that is merely critical of or parasitic upon other philosophical positions that attempt to put forth a picture of the "good life" and moral or political doctrines. The Daoist's own position is one that simply recognizes that all things are interdependent. Daoist conduct is likened to empty mountain valleys, unworked/raw wood, or chaotic muddles and muddy mixtures. The Daoist believes that emulating the fundamental continuity of nature can bring about lasting peace and solidarity.

In the previous chapters, the different characteristics of the Daoist sage's dispositions were outlined. Because the Daoist sage is "without knowledge," they no longer cling to the problematic epistemological framework indebted to a reified account of things. Relatedly, the Daoist sage is "without desire" because they no longer see themselves as independent persons and thus no longer cling to an "objectified" account of nature and the attendant desires. They see themselves as parts of the larger whole of nature and their community. Being both "without desire" and "without knowledge" can then be understood as two features that help enable the Daoist sage to respond to situations with "nonegoistic conduct" (*wuwei*). Although the Daoist would reject the idea that that there are sui generis moral facts, their account of persons as empty centers provides a functional substitute in the sense that the mitigation of selfish desires and the spontaneous care for others are both behaviors of the Daoist when they are in accord with nature as indeterminate (*wu*).

With the Daoist account of ethical naturalism, values are created through interaction. Values are not "properties" of subjects or individual persons, nor are they "objective realities" that exist independent of the human mind. "Values" are not "simply located" in the sense that they must involve establishing and maintaining *internal relationships* to other aspects of nature. Merely operating through external relationships is not of real value. An inability to feel grounded in a network of internal relationships is tantamount to alienation and is the main cause of social calamity. If nature is constituted by internal relationships where all things are overlapping and interdependent, there are important constraints that can be placed on certain cultural beliefs that can possibly be said to be of real value. Ignorance about the nature of values and the way that all things exist promotes the epistemological framework that encourages coercive and oppressive behavior. If the ethicist wants more than this, they might be asking for just another system of totalitarianism and oppression. The Daoist position of cultivating the ability to perceive nature as fundamentally indeterminate is more than enough to adequately address the social ills of human society.

Philosophers might wonder, after all of this, why the Daoist philosopher couldn't provide a more straightforward and less esoteric solution to our problems. Such sentiments are guilty of exactly the point that Gordon makes in the above passage. Reality is just much bigger than our "knowledge" of it, and human society is far more complicated. The moralist attitude can end up being as guilty of egoistic behavior as the egoist. The Daoist does not need moral facts because they provide a different framework for diagnosing moral problems, but the reason why their works employ a kind of philosophical irony is that they have witnessed the way that the "serious man," "sage," and "moral philosopher" end up becoming co-opted by power and their own narcissism. This is why "those who act (*wei*) ruin it." Egoistic and narcissistic attitudes are what corrupt and undermine the moral attitude.

The Daoist position provides a different account of the forms of life that we can consider to be indebted to ignorance. Conceptual thinking and language, although important for human society and communal flourishing, can be used in ways that are no longer merely liberating. Insofar as certain habits of experience can play a role in inhibiting our perception of situations, we must cultivate other human potentials such that we undermine the negative existential effects of being fixed on the provisional way we have individuated nature into things. By grounding all forms of "knowledge" in the context of nature as fundamentally indeterminate, people would no longer be alienated from nature and each other. They would return to their naturally endowed capacity to form greater coherence with the world or what this book has called "attunement." By returning to our naturally endowed spontaneity, we become free of self-interest and a separate sense of self. It is this capacity that is more fundamental and more important to cultivate than those features of experience that the "moralist" would have us realize. The Daoist sage, unlike those other sages that "ruin things," acts spontaneously and nonegoistically and thus *does not ruin it*.

Notes

Introduction

1. For accounts of the *Zhuangzi* and the *Daodejing* that try to argue there is thematic consistency, see Moeller, *The Moral Fool*, and Ziporyn, *Ironies of Oneness and Difference*.

2. This is my translation of passage 2. For the original Chinese, please see "Chinese Text Project: A Dynamic Digital Library of Premodern Chinese."

3. Moeller, *Daodejing* (hard copy), 15.

4. Moeller, *Daodejing* (kindle), 12.

5. This is my translation of *Daodejing* 7. For the original Chinese, please see "Chinese Text Project: A Dynamic Digital Library of Premodern Chinese."

6. Lynn, *The Classic of the Way and Virtue*, 63.

7. Moeller, *Daodejing* (hard copy), 23.

8. Perkins, "What Is a Thing (wu 物)?," 68.

9. For a useful account on the difference between a "doctrine of internal relations" versus a "doctrine of external relationships," please see Kasulis, "The Mosaic and the Jigsaw Puzzle." Generally, when the relationships between things constitute the things in question, this means that the things are internally related.

10. Previously, Lewis Gordon has critiqued the tendencies of academic disciplines to retreat into themselves and behave in solipsistic and narcissistic ways insofar as they treat their own discipline as complete and final. This way of thinking about our academic disciplines is related to a substance metaphysics in the sense that the discipline itself is treated like a substance. Interdisciplinary work, for example, is then treated as inferior. For an analysis of decedent behavior in academia, see Gordon, *Disciplinary Decadence*.

11. Ma and Van Brakel, *Beyond the Troubled Water of Shifei*, 2.

12. See Ma and Van Brakel, *Beyond the Troubled Water of Shifei*, 133. Generally, they suggest that by adopting the idea of "stances," they can get beyond the relativism/objectivism distinction and the usual hangup, by sinologists, that Zhuangzi is either a "skeptic" or "relativist."

13. Wong, *Natural Moralities*, 106.

14. Wong, *Natural Moralities*, 93.

15. In Richard Bernstein's book, *Beyond Objectivism and Relativism*, he argues that all forms of knowledge (both scientific and moral) operate in a way similar to Aristotle's *phronesis*. In drawing on the works of Rorty, Arendt, Habermas, and Gadamer, he argues for the importance of *phronesis* as a form of understanding. His method of getting philosophers beyond "objectivism and relativism" thus argues that all people should be encouraged and permitted to realize the capacity to effectively choose and judge situations. It is this capacity to cultivate *phronesis* that he believes presents a viable alternative to the traditional distinction. A greater ability to exercise *phronesis* is what all human beings should be able to realize. In *Morality for Humans*, Mark Johnson draws on modern science and the works of John Dewey when outlining his account of a naturalistic morality. Ultimately, the nonnaturalistic account of morality is not possible in light of modern science. We need to cultivate a context dependent sensitivity to situations instead of insisting on reflecting on "rational" principles or abstract meaning if we want to be moral persons. Likewise, the work presenting an account of embodied cognition by George Lakoff and Mark Johnson argues that *both "objectivism" and "subjectivism" are myths*. See Lakoff and Johnson, *Metaphors We Live By*, for their account of both "the myth of objectivism" (186) and the "myth of subjectivism" (188).

16. Scholars that have previously argued that the Daoist sage is attuned to the *Dao* or "way" have used the term "attunement" to suggest a nonnatural or religious account of attunement where attunement functions like a form of knowledge or insight derived from a transcendent source. For one such book, which I will reference in a later chapter, see Jung Lee's *The Ethical Foundations of Early Daoism*.

17. Lai, "*Ziran* and *Wuwei* in the *Daodejing*," 325.

18. Lai, *Learning from Chinese Philosophies*, 105.

19. Johnson, *Morality for Humans*, xi.

20. Johnson, *Morality for Humans*, 15–16.

21. Wang, *Yinyang*, 53.

22. Wang, *Yinyang*, 54.

23. Grondin, *Introduction to Metaphysics*, 25.

24. Perkins, "Metaphysics and Methodology in a Cross-Cultural Context," makes this point as well. If we maintain a narrow understanding of something like "metaphysics," then it is easy to conclude that "only western philosophy has metaphysics." This goes for any subfield of study.

25. Ontology specifically is the study and analysis of *Being* in the West. For this study, I stick with the very specific account of ontology being the study of Being as opposed to becoming. Ontology implies discreet, independent, and self-enclosed "things."

Chapter 1

1. This is my translation of passage 1. For the original Chinese, please see Sturgeon, "Chinese Text Project."

2. There is an alternative translation of this opening passage as well (but it would express the same basic meaning). Instead of translating *wuming* (無名) and *youming* (有名) as denoting "nameless" and the "named," the passage could alternatively be translated as "nonbeing (*wu*) names (*ming*) the beginning of heaven and earth, being (*you*) names (*ming*) the mother of the ten-thousand things." In terms of what the sentence is trying to express, the metaphysics in both cases is essentially the same. As will be explained more throughout this study, being or being a "thing" is a secondary and provisional aspect of nature. Nature, the world, is an interconnected continuum. The isolation of things from their environment is merely a mental and provisional exercise. Desire still plays a key role, *somehow*, in the nature of observation. Following Wang Bi, I stick with the reading of this passage as being "without name" or the "nameless."

3. Ames and Hall, *Dao De Jing: Making This Life Significant*, 135. The Chinese version of their translation comes from the *Mawangdui* B, paragraph 32. See https://ctext.org/mawangdui/lao-zi-jia-dao-jing for the older Chinese version of this passage of the *Daodejing*. The modern versions of the *Daodejing* replace *wuming* (無名) with *wuwei* (無為) or "without action." These particular changes are in part, thanks to the comments by Randy LaPolla. As he claims, in a private conversation, "In terms of the grammar, 欲 is the topic and 作 is the comment, the predication."

4. Wang, *Yinyang*, 47.

5. Hansen, *A Daoist Theory of Chinese Thought*, 4.

6. For example, see *A Daoist Theory*, 3. Hansen thinks his account of classical Chinese philosophy "reveals a unified philosophical point of view that develops and matures in an interesting way until banned, buried, and burned by political authority. The only cost of this new perspective is that Confucianism does not come out on top philosophically. In fact it ends up near the bottom. The same political authority that stifled further philosophical development also awarded Confucianism its high position in history. One of my Daoist biases is against argument from authority—especially political authority." In agreement with Hall and Ames, *Thinking from the Han*, 171–80, Confucianism and philosophical Daoism need to be understood as far more similar than how they are assumed to be by Western scholars like Hansen. They claim: "The principal point is that Confucianism and Daoism may be thought to exist on a continuum, or a set of continua really, with respect to any number of variables." *Thinking from the Han*, 180.

7. Hansen's account of both Confucianism and Indian/Chinese Buddhism should be read as highly intellectually suspect. In my view, Hansen

grossly mischaracterizes both traditions as well as the later development of neo-Confucianism. I also depart from Hansen's account of the *Daodejing* as something philosophically distinct and antithetical to the *Zhuangzi*. I take the two texts as far more philosophically consistent than Hansen's account of the *Daodejing* as "anti-language" and Zhuangzi as being a "philosopher of language."

8. Hansen, *A Daoist Theory of Chinese Thought*, 22.

9. Ziporyn summarizes Hansen's view using this terminology as well. Ziporyn claims Hansen "notes in particular the circumvention of both Platonic ideas and mentalist ideas in Classical Chinese thinking. The mind is not a representational faculty that entertains ideas or perceives the intelligible realm of ideas. There are no universals, just stuff-kinds. The mind is a faculty of actively *distinguishing* among real kinds." Ziporyn, *Ironies of Oneness and Difference*, 50–51.

10. Although Hansen believes that his work presents a radical and unique account of Chinese philosophy and he praises "analytic philosophy" as his main resource, only a small minority of "analytic philosophers" have ever accepted an antirepresentational account of mind. The writings of the later Wittgenstein, Quine, Putnam and *especially* Rorty are all marginalized and not taken seriously by modern Anglophone analytic philosophy. There are many different schools of Western philosophy that provide what can be called an "antirepresentational" account of mind and language. Dewey, on whom I draw in this study, is one. The phenomenology of both Heidegger and Merleau-Ponty also present something similar. No philosopher should believe that "analytic philosophy" is what uniquely provides an account of mind and language that is "antirepresentational." For Rorty's account of antirepresentationalism and his account of the history of philosophy, please see Rorty, *Philosophy and the Mirror of Nature*.

11. A better way of thinking about the *Zhuangzi* is perhaps, as Wang claims in *Linguistic Strategies in Daoist Zhuangzi and Chan Buddhism* (33) that "Zhuangzi's philosophy of change involves a theory of language, but it does not confine itself to such a theory."

12. For scholars who wish to reject this important dimension of John Dewey's later works, please read both *Experience and Nature* (where Dewey develops an account of aesthetic meaning in the latter half of the work) and his follow-up *Art as Experience* (which is dedicated to clarifying his account of aesthetic experience). Although I quote numerous passages from these works in this book, there are also secondary sources on Dewey's understanding of aesthetic experience as well. For those, please see Mark Johnson's *Meaning of the Body* or his chapter on Dewey's aesthetics in the *Cambridge Companion to Dewey*, Richard Shusterman's *Thinking through the Body: Essays in Somaesthetics*, chapter 6, and Thomas Alexander's *John Dewey's Theory of Art, Experience & Nature*.

13. Dewey, *Experience and Nature*, 65, makes a similar argument as Hansen does here.

14. Hansen, *A Daoist Theory of Chinese Thought*, 16.

15. Hansen, *A Daoist Theory of Chinese Thought*, 50.
16. Lakoff and Johnson, *Metaphors We Live By*, 203.
17. See Keskinen, "Quine on Objects: Realism or Anti-Realism?," for a more nuanced account of how Quine's philosophy maintains a form of realism but not a "metaphysical realism."
18. Quine, *Ontological Relativity*, 26–27.
19. Dewey, *Experience and Nature*, 179.
20. Dewey, *Experience and Nature*, 339.
21. Dewey, *Experience and Nature*, 338.
22. Another useful way to think about this difference, though not something explicitly claimed by Dewey, is to think of "noncognitive" or aesthetic meaning primarily (if not solely) as involving "knowing-how," while "cognitive" or conceptual meaning is a kind of "knowing-that," especially in light of the first few pages of Dewey's *Experience and Nature*, chapter 9.
23. Dewey, *Logic, The Theory of Inquiry*, 111.
24. See, for just one example, Eames, S. Morris. "The Cognitive and the Non-Cognitive in Dewey's Theory of Valuation." The study highlights how Dewey's position is ambiguous with respect to this issue.
25. This particular way of framing this claim is indebted to my private conversations with Brook Ziporyn.
26. See Idhe, *Listening and Voice*, chapters 4, 5 and 6.
27. Johnson, *Meaning of the Body*, 9–10 (Kindle).
28. Alexander, *John Dewey's Theory of Art, Experience & Nature*, 28.
29. Johnson, *Meaning and the Body*, 7 (Kindle).
30. Johnson, *Meaning and the Body*, 8 (Kindle).
31. See Hansen, *A Daoist Theory of Chinese Thought*, chapter 6. He also claims that "Laozi was, like Mencius, a mystic in one key sense: he was antilanguage," 203.
32. Meaning is a quality of interrelationship. The "sense" of any given experience is then the relationship between the human and the environment. It would be more accurate to say that "meaning" was simultaneously the property of the biological organism and the natural environment.
33. Ames and Hall, *Dao De Jing: Making This Life Significant*, 142–43, significantly modified.
34. See Wang, *Linguistic Strategies in Daoist Zhuangzi and Chan Buddhism*, 50. In discussing the passage from chapter 2 of the *Zhuangzi*, Wang states: "In this sense Zhuangzi talks about the relation among one, two and three. It seems like a direct commentary on the first line of chapter 42 in the *Dao De Jing*."
35. Ziporyn, *Zhuangzi: The Essential Writings*, 16.
36. Dewey, *Experience and Nature*, 85.
37. Johnson, *Meaning of the Body*, 66.
38. Ames and Hall, *Dao De Jing: Making This Life Significant*, 120.
39. Wang, *Yinyang*, 59.

40. Ames and Hall, *Dao De Jing: Making This Life Significant*, 42.
41. Hansen, *A Daoist Theory of Chinese Thought*, 20.
42. Dewey, *Experience and Nature*, 21. In the last part of this block quote, what Dewey means is that concrete values naturally emerge from our relationships with nature and other persons.
43. Here I am alluding to the title of a book by Joan Stambaugh, *The Real Is Not the Rational*. The book outlines how Western philosophers like Schopenhauer and Heidegger do not identify the "rational" aspects of human experience as being the most fundamental aspects of reality.
44. See Wang, *Linguistic Strategies in Daoist Zhuangzi and Chan Buddhism*, 11.
45. Ames and Hall, *Dao De Jing: Making This Life Significant*, 82.
46. Ziporyn, *Ironies of Oneness and Difference*, 158.
47. Arguably Nietzsche, Heidegger, Merleau-Ponty, Beauvoir, and their predecessors provide an account of experience that is embodied and somatic. For example, Hamrick and Van der Veken describe Merleau-Ponty's work in a similar way to how Dewey's work has been described in this book. As they state, for Merleau-Ponty, "the meaningfulness of the world is neither fully formed, waiting to be discovered by consciousness, even a bodily one, nor produced within consciousness to be applied to an inherently meaningless world. Rather, through bodily motility, meaning is developed." Hamrick and J. Van der Veken, *Nature and Logos*, 23.
48. How we understand the nature of experience and the nature of the self are both culturally contingent and provisional beliefs. There is nothing about concrete experience that lends itself to Western metaphysical assumptions about the self. Phenomenologically, there is not much reason to assume that there is a self that is independent of context or that exists prior to experience. Yet, for Dewey, if a culture does set up these beliefs and forms habits of attention and thinking around these sets of beliefs, then these beliefs, in the sense that they structure a different interpretation of reality, do concretely shape human nature (which for Dewey, is *not* a "nature" but a vast potential that can be formed in various different ways).
49. For those unfamiliar with Dewey's works, this is often the case for most of his books. If the title of his work involves two things, like "Freedom and Culture" or "The Public and Its Problems," the main thesis of the work is usually that the two are one and the same thing. If the title is "X and Y," then the thesis usually is "X is Y," where the project is to show why this is the case. For Dewey, experience (something that is usually understood as private and individual) *is* nature in the sense that there is no divide or separation between the world and subjectivity, nature and experience.
50. Dewey, *Experience and Nature*, 86.
51. Dewey, *Experience and Nature*, 259.

52. See Lakoff and Johnson, *Metaphors We Live By*, 186, for their account of "the myth of objectivism." For the "myth of subjectivism," see page 188.

53. Dewey, *Experience and Nature*, 23.

54. For an account of the aesthetic dimensions of James's work and its relationship to other pragmatists, see Shusterman, "The Pragmatist Aesthetics of William James." In particular see the passages on page 359.

55. Ziporyn, *Ironies of Oneness and Difference*, 183.

Chapter 2

1. For example, think of the term "virtue" (*de*, 德) when he states, "The Daoist use of terms that traditionally signify coherence is always, I claim, ironic, in the specific sense of indicating the impossibility of coherence in the literal sense, and yet, ironically, indicating that *this impossibility* is a *higher form of coherence*, in the sense that it fulfils the original promise of coherence more successfully than the original, non-ironic coherence did." Ziporyn, *Ironies of Oneness and Difference*, 140–41. In other words, the "impossibility of virtue" is itself the "real/true virtue" and *fulfills the original promises* "virtue" was supposed to bring about.

2. This is my translation of *Daodejing* 38. For the original Chinese, please see Sturgeon, "Chinese Text Project."

3. Both of these terms are borrowed from Richard Rorty and Hans Georg Gadamer, respectively. For Rorty, different cultures develop a vocabulary of terms that help to describe their deeply held values and beliefs. This is a "final vocabulary" or a set of terms that generally is self-referential and cannot be explained without recourse to the vocabulary itself. Rorty also uses Gadamer's term "horizon of relevance" at times. For thinkers in the hermeneutic tradition, persons are situated in such a way that their beliefs and language help to shape how they interpret their world. There is no "pure" empirical experience. Instead, our habits, both cognitive and noncognitive, help to shape how experience of the world is constituted by consciousness. A "final vocabulary" can then be further understood as shaping the "horizon of relevance" of persons within a community. They learn to perceive and interpret situations in a way indebted to their own assumptions and languages.

4. This is my translation of *Daodejing* 38. For the original Chinese, please see Sturgeon, "Chinese Text Project."

5. See Xiang, Shuchen, *A Philosophical Defense of Culture: Perspectives from Confucianism and Cassirer*, for an account of Confucian ritual as giving form to emotions. In particular, both chapters 3 and 5 address this theme.

6. Considering that the *Zhuangzi* presents many different stories about death and the response to death is never one single "prescription" for how to

best handle death and dying, we need to avoid the hasty generalization that the Daoist is merely a stoic in response to death. For example, chapter 6 of the *Zhuangzi* has many stories that talk about how one needs to recognize that death is an inevitable part of life. We are fated to die, and the transformation of things is not necessarily a bad thing. Chapter 18 of the *Zhuangzi* has the story of the death of Zhuangzi's wife. Amy Olberding's analysis of this story connects it to the earlier story in chapter 5 of the *Zhuangzi* of the piglets that still cling to their mother even after she has died. As she argues, "the pigs exhibit a pre-reflective impulse, a response to pain that is untutored and immediate. Zhuangzi's sorrow is similarly immediate, his response prior to any reflective evaluation of his loss and its larger meaning and significance." Olberding, "Sorrow of the Sage," 342. Another story, in chapter 24 of the *Zhuangzi*, tells us of the death of Huizi. I have analyzed this story in a previous publication. What the story tries to convey is that the relationships we bear with the environment are always particular and context dependent in the sense that we cultivate dispositions sensitive *to those particular* environments. See Bender, "Justice as the Practice of Non-Coercive Action," especially pages 8–10. Considering that there is no single "prescription" that the *Zhuangzi* offers, it is best to see this as just another expression of the Daoist critique of formulaic and "fixed" responses to situations. If persons recognize that all things are in constant transformation, then this insight will contextualize our experience of death. It will not make us stoic and unfeeling in the face of it. Olberding's essay presents the complexity of the Daoist view on death. Although she does not explicitly describe it like this, we could say that her account shows how even Zhuangzi's account of death is similar to the *Daodejing* notion of *rouruo* (柔弱). See Olberding, "Sorrow of the Sage," for her analysis, which also relates the *Zhuangzi* to Nussbaum's work.

    7. Ziporyn, *Zhuangzi: The Complete Writings*, 72.

    8. See Graham, A. C. *Chuang-Tzŭ*, 195–217. Although I significantly disagree with Graham's account of the "Primitivist" Chapters, I borrow the name he gives chapters 8–10 of the "Outer Chapters" of the *Zhuangzi*. It is also important to note that some scholars would include other chapters of the "Outer Chapters" under the category of the "Primitivists." Although I do not have the time to do this here, I would argue that it actually might be best to abandon the distinction considering these chapters are still very much philosophically consistent with many Daoist ideas.

    9. Ziporyn, *Zhuangzi: The Essential Writings*, 24.

    10. Here I am alluding to the previous quoted story in the *Zhuangzi*. Please see Ziporyn, *Zhuangzi: The Essential Writings*, 16.

    11. Ziporyn, *Zhuangzi: The Essential Writings*, 24.

    12. Ziporyn, *Zhuangzi: The Essential Writings*, 26–27.

    13. Ziporyn, *Zhuangzi: The Essential Writings*, 28.

14. Although Slote may also agree that there is more to the distinction between mere prudence and morality, from the virtue ethicist's perspective, he describes different virtues as capable of being considered either "other regarding" or "self-regarding." See Slote, *From Morality to Virtue*, chapter 1, for his general introduction to this distinction.

15. Although there are other ways of making this distinction, generally I follow Flanagan's account of altruistic behavior from Flanagan, *The Really Hard Problem: Meaning in a Material World*.

16. Ziporyn, *Zhuangzi: The Complete Writings*, 5.

17. Ziporyn, *Zhuangzi: The Complete Writings*, 11.

18. Ziporyn, *Zhuangzi: The Complete Writings*, 11.

19. Van Norden, "Zhuangzi's Ironic Detachment and Political Commitment," 4.

20. Rorty, *Contingency, Irony, and Solidarity*, 73.

21. For this kind of analysis, please see Nietzsche's work on ascetic ideals. In particular, see chapter 3 of *The Genealogy of Morality*. Two further accounts (arguably influence by Nietzsche's work) on how certain cultural movements have clung to metaphysical realities at the expense of actually achieving real values, desires, or the capacity to maintain basic sustenance can be seen in Jean Paul Sartre's *Anti-Semite and Jew* and Hannah Arendt's *Eichmann in Jerusalem*.

22. For an account of how, in Western philosophy, the moral life involves the domination of the desires and passions by "reason," please see McCumber, *Metaphysics and Oppression*, 61. In particular, he discusses Aristotle, who shares this in common with Plato, Christianity, and the later Christian philosopher Kant. Since the philosophy of Socrates and Plato, the assumption has been that some sort of "external order" must be imposed on the natural world of becoming. Without it, we would only have the "city of pigs" and morally dubious, self-interested fulfillment of bodily desires. A person that does not let reason lead and suppress bodily desires is the "incontinent man." As McCumber claims, the incontinent man is led by his desires (which are merely natural, conditioned processes). If people are led by their desires, then they cannot be said to be realizing their true sense of independence, that is, realizing their identity as "animals with reason," McCumber, *Metaphysics and Oppression*, 61.

23. Both Van Norden, "Zhuangzi's Ironic Detachment and Political Commitment," and Moeller and D'Ambrosio, *Genuine Pretending*, consider Zhuangzi to be similar to Rorty's "ironist." Van Norden considers the ironist a "morally dubious" position while Moeller and D'Ambrosio see the ironist in a positive light.

24. For this quote in Nietzsche, please see Nietzsche, *Beyond Good and Evil*, 89.

25. Rorty, *Contingency, Irony, and Solidarity*, 73.

26. Rorty, *Contingency, Irony, and Solidarity*, xvi.

27. Shusterman, "Thought in the Strenuous Mood," 451.
28. Shusterman, "Thought in the Strenuous Mood," 444.
29. Shusterman, "The Pragmatist Aesthetics of William James," 354.
30. For Rorty's own particular way of describing this, see Rorty, *Contingency, Irony, and Solidarity*, 93.
31. Shusterman, "Thought in the Strenuous Mood," 447.
32. Alexander, "John Dewey and the Moral Imagination," 193.
33. Dewey, *Art as Experience*, 77.
34. Johnson, *The Meaning of the Body*, 70.
35. Hall, *Eros and Irony*, 23.
36. Hall, *Eros and Irony*, 26.
37. Rorty, *Contingency, Irony, and Solidarity*, 88.
38. Another example of Rorty saying just this occurs in Rorty, *Contingency, Irony, and Solidarity*, 92.
39. Rorty, *Contingency, Irony, and Solidarity*, 94.
40. For Rorty's specific language claiming just this, please see Rorty, *Contingency, Irony, and Solidarity*, 5.
41. I am alluding to Stambaugh, *The Real Is not The Rational*, here. The small book provides a brief account of the history of Western philosophy and of how Schopenhauer, Heidegger, and Buddhism do not assume, as it is traditionally assumed in the West, that the "real is what is rational."
42. For an entire study dedicated to Dewey's understanding of mind, nature, and experience, and of how Dewey's philosophy overcomes the realist/antirealist dualism, please see Hildebrand, *Beyond Realism and Anti-Realism*.
43. Dewey, *Experience and Nature*, 39.
44. This is a reference to the first story of chapter 5 of the *Zhuangzi*. The "ex-con" story, a story I refer to later in this study, describes the person of Daoist insight as viewing the chopping off of their own leg as "nothing more than the casting away of a clump of soil," see Ziporyn, *Zhuangzi: The Complete Writings*, 46.

Chapter 3

1. Another useful way to think about the issue can be read in Behuniak, "John Dewey and the Virtue of Cook Ding's Dao," in his discussion comparing Dewey's account of method with Zhuangzi's philosophy. As I understand his work, both Dewey and Zhuangzi can be understood as warning us against the negative and harmful forms of education and method that obstruct our capacity to be sensitive to situations.

2. In particular, the traditional distinction between "moral objectivism" and "moral relativism" or extreme "moral subjectivism" is incredibly problematic as it relies on "question-begging" assumptions. Johnson, in *Morality for Humans*,

systematically argues that the traditional view of morality and moral theory are incompatible with what modern neuroscience tells us about how humans experience the world. See Johnson, *Morality for Humans*, for his critique of what he calls "moral fundamentalism."

3. Coutinho, *An Introduction to Daoist Philosophies*, 69.

4. This is my translation of passage 1. For the original Chinese, please see Sturgeon, "Chinese Text Project."

5. Another scholar who has argued that the *Daodejing* passage 1 suggests there are two different ways of "knowing" or perceiving the world is Wong Kwok Kui. He suggests that passage 1 "seems to be putting forward two methods of knowing them respectively: without desire/with desire (無欲/有欲). There are, therefore, two ways of contemplating, appropriate to their respective objects of knowledge." Kui, "Hegel's Criticism of Laozi and Its Implication," 61. In the essay, he also suggests that there are two different ways to think about or perceive "meaning." Kui has also highlighted that the Daoist is critical of desire and how desire shapes perception.

6. As I do in my article, "On Being 'Without-Desire' in Lao-Zhuang Daoism," I criticize Curie Virag's work on desire in Daoist philosophy. In chapter 3 of her book, *The Emotions in Early Chinese Philosophy*, she argues that it is desire that guides the Daoist sage. Another recent argument about desire as guiding human conduct in the *Zhuangzi* is in Jenny Hung's "Is Zhuangzi a Wanton? Observation and Transformation of Desires in the Zhuangzi." Hung's study attempts to fit Zhuangzi's philosophy into the work of Harry Frankfurt. In particular, she attempts to argue that, for Zhuangzi, "our first-order desires transform, and our unnatural first-order desires fade away so long as we practice being observers." Hung, "Is Zhuangzi a Wanton?" 293. Again, both the *Daodejing* and the *Zhuangzi* are critical of desires, so such arguments are not grounded in the text.

7. See Bender, "On Being 'Without-Desire' in Lao-Zhuang Daoism," for a more textual account of why the Daoist is critical of desire.

8. Liu Xiaogan has described this aspect of Daoist philosophy as well. He states that "as with *wuwei*, no-desire does not mean the negation of all desires, but only the ordinary desires of common rulers and people. In the *Laozi*, no-desire appears five times, in chapters 1, 3, 34, 37, and 57." Liu, *Dao Companion to Daoist Philosophy*, 88. "The precondition to practicing *wuwei* is its agent's internal *wuwei*, namely, the exclusion of personal desires for such as merit, fame, victory, etc.; otherwise, no one can practice the principle of *wuwei*, or the external *wuwei*." Liu, *Dao Companion to Daoist Philosophy*, 89.

9. Hansen, drawing on Quine, claims that for classical Chinese thinkers, "reality is not a multitude of independent, fixed objects, but a ground out of which a linguistic community *carves* distinctions and marks them with names. Each part-whole assignment is relative to some presupposed standard and purpose. A part, in turn, has parts. Any whole can be a part of some larger whole."

Hansen, *A Daoist Theory*, 50. Hansen is not the only scholar to make this point in light of Daoist philosophy. Of the other scholars this study quotes, Lai, Ames and Hall, and Ziporyn also follow Hansen in holding that Chinese philosophy of mind was generally antirepresentational.

10. This is my translation of passage 12. For the original Chinese, please see Sturgeon, "Chinese Text Project."

11. Scholars have previously argued that Daoist philosophy aspires to be nonanthropocentric. Irving Goh has even suggested that we can consider the *Zhuangzi* a kind of "animal philosophy." See Goh, "Chuang Tzu's Becoming-Animal."

12. See Ziporyn, *Ironies of Oneness and Difference*, pages 148–50, for his description of the distinction between "stomach" and "eye" desires. This distinction generally takes place within the context of describing the Daoist account of nature as the "unhewn" (*pu*).

13. Previously, Coutinho has suggested this as well. In light of the *Daodejing*, "the cultivation of naturalness thus becomes the deconstruction of desires for such goods, *wuyu* 無欲: the cultivation of satisfaction with natural simplicity. And this is achieved by curtailing our tendency to use evaluative labels *ming* 名 to distinguish some objects as more desirable than others." Coutinho, *An Introduction to Daoist Philosophies*, 70.

14. For a modern account arguing that a processual framework provides a better classificatory framework when it comes to analysis of biological reality, see Dupré and Nicolson, *Everything Flows: Towards a Process Philosophy of Biology*. Dupré and Nicolson believe that "it is possible to see the processual character of biological entities as providing a deep explanation of why a multiplicity of ways of classifying such entities is precisely what we should expect to find. Promiscuous realism, as one of us has denominated this pluralism of classifications (Dupré 1993), thus finds a metaphysical justification in process ontology." *Everything Flows*, 23.

15. Although I do not agree with everything Chad Hansen argues for in *A Daoist Theory of Chinese Thought*, and in particular his characterization of the *Daodejing* and the *Zhuangzi* as significantly departing from each other, Hansen's reading of the *Daodejing* does make this connection. Hansen correctly describes the Daoist account of *pu* as "nameless, it is uncarved, undivided. Freedom from names and distinctions is freedom from desire. As soon as it is cut—as soon as there are distinctions—there are names." Hansen, *A Daoist Theory of Chinese Thought*, 213.

16. Ziporyn, *Zhuangzi: The Complete Writings*, 16.

17. This account of the two kinds of desires is, again, indebted to Ziporyn's account in *Ironies of Oneness and Difference*.

18. Recently, Bryan Van Norden, in "Zhuangzi's Ironic Detachment and Political Commitment," has criticized the *Zhuangzi* for this. He argues that Daoist irony, because it lacks a "final vocabulary," is "easily prone to certain kinds of wrongdoing. Specifically, whether one has any deep values or not, one can see

the force of satisfying immediate and superficial desires, such as desires for food, sex, wealth, prestige, and power." see "Zhuangzi's Ironic Detachment and Political Commitment," 4. Considering that the *Zhuangzi*, like the *Daodejing*, is critical of desires, such claims are "straw-man" arguments.

19. Not all scholars believe that the *Daodejing* and the *Zhuangzi* depart from each other with respect to their understanding of desire. For example, see Coutinho, *An Introduction to Daoist Philosophies*, 101–2, for his account of how the *Zhuangzi* is also critical of desires.

20. This particular way of describing *ziran* and the Daoist understanding of things is similar to how Hall and Ames do it in their work *Making This Life Significant*.

21. Please see Ziporyn, *Ironies of Oneness and Difference*, chapters 2 and 4, for a philosophical analysis of how the Chinese philosophers, and especially Daoist philosophers, understood the nature of "things" as "centers" of nature. In particular, Ziporyn describes "centers" as forming a coherence (either ironically or nonironically) and thus made intelligible as coherences.

22. For two earlier accounts of perspectivism in the *Zhuangzi*, see Tim Connolly's "Perspectivism as a Way of Knowing in the Zhuangzi" and Karyn Lai's "Philosophy and Philosophical Reasoning in the 'Zhuangzi': Dealing with Plurality."

23. Valmisa, *Adapting*, 29. Please also see pages 25–28 for her introduction leading up to these ideas.

24. Lee, *The Ethical Foundations of Early Daoism*, 49.

25. Ziporyn, *Zhuangzi: The Complete Writings*, 54.

26. Ziporyn, *Zhuangzi: The Complete Writings*, 29.

27. For a study on the limits of language (liminology) in Daoist philosophy, see Youru Wang's *Linguistic Strategies in Daoist Zhuangzi and Chan Buddhism: The Other Way of Speaking*. In particular, see chapter 5 where he discusses the *Zhuangzi* and the limits of language.

28. Ziporyn, *Zhuangzi: The Complete Writings*, 31.

29. I will elaborate more on this point in chapter 5 of this book. In his discussion of the *zhenren* in the *Zhuangzi*, Kim-chong Chong also argues, like the primitivist Zhuangzi, the spontaneous human community would live without the coercive ideas the Daoist labels as "knowledge." Chong states that "left alone in their natural state, they do not form separate parties. They would have lived in harmony with other animals and been unaware of the distinctions between being noble and ignoble. Thus, they would have been without desires and remained in a simple, unadorned state," Chong, "The Concept of 'Zhen' 真 in the 'Zhuangzi,'" 328.

30. Ziporyn, *Zhuangzi: The Complete Writings*, 30.

31. Ziporyn, *Zhuangzi: The Complete Writings*, 53.

32. Ziporyn, *Zhuangzi: The Complete Writings*, 30.

33. Andersen, *The Paradox of Being*, 69.

34. Wang, *Yinyang*, 135.
35. Ziporyn, *Zhuangzi: The Complete Writings*, 55.
36. Ziporyn, *Zhuangzi: The Complete Writings*, 139.
37. Ziporyn, *Zhuangzi: The Complete Writings*, 53.
38. Ames and Hall, *Dao De Jing: Making This Life Significant*, 135. The Chinese version of their translation comes from the *Mawangdui* B, paragraph 32. See https://ctext.org/mawangdui/lao-zi-jia-dao-jing for the older Chinese version of this passage of the *Daodejing*. The modern versions replace *wuming* (無名) with *wuwei* (無為) or "without action."
39. Another scholar that makes a similar argument is Chong. In light of his analysis of the *zhenren*, Chong argues that the "social and political system involving the rites must have developed to a complex state governing all forms of human relations. We can imagine that at the same time, these relations and their associated practices gave rise to more desires of all kinds and hypocritical and corrupt behavior at various levels. Thus, while the Mohists criticized the expansion of ritual practices as luxurious and economically wasteful, some writers of the Outer Chapter, on the other hand, emphasized their corrupting nature." Chong, "The Concept of 'Zhen' 真 in the 'Zhuangzi,'" 328.
40. This is my translation of passage 3. For the original Chinese, please see Sturgeon, "Chinese Text Project."
41. Ames and Hall, *Dao De Jing: Making This Life Significant*, 194.
42. This is a reference to the story of *Zhuangzi*, chapter 9. The story makes the distinction between "small thieves" and "great thieves." I elaborate on this further in chapter 6 of this book.
43. Ames and Hall, *Dao De Jing: Making This Life Significant*, 126–27, with slight modifications.
44. This is my translation *Daodejing* 7. For the original Chinese, please see Sturgeon, "Chinese Text Project."
45. Moeller, *Daodejing*, 117.

Chapter 4

1. For example, the idea of "intrinsic value" was used as a justification for both racism and sexism/patriarchy in the West. Only "white men" had intrinsic value. At best, women and nonwhites could be of "instrumental value," similar to animals and nature. This chapter is arguing that "intrinsic value," as an assumption, is 1) formulaically oppressive and 2) not necessary anyways. There has, fortunately, been terrific work already spelling out some of these implications. Shuchen Xiang argues in her paper, "Chinese Processual Holism and Its Attitude Towards 'Barbarians' and Non-Humans," the processual nature of Chinese metaphysics has implications for the epistemological taxonomizing of the natural world. Things are not understood

to have discrete boundaries, and this has the moral implication that there are no "subpersons" who are beyond the boundaries of moral concern. An idea like "race," as understood in the West, is really not a possibility in a processual framework.

2. For this study, I primarily draw on Mark Johnson's account of naturalism in *Morality for Humans* when I use the term "naturalism." Johnson's account draws from the works of John Dewey. In another account of naturalism in Chinese philosophy, Jeeloo Liu differentiates her understanding of naturalism from what is called "scientific naturalism." Liu's account of "naturalism adopts a humanistic perspective, and argues that the scope and significance of our ontology should be related to creatures like us. It is termed 'Humanistic Naturalism,' and it centers on humans and their values, capacities and conceptions in the way it defines Nature. This view takes nature and humans' attitudes toward nature as essentially intertwined." See Liu, "In Defense of Chinese Qi-Naturalism," 37. Although the two works are not identical, they do share a desire to see naturalism in respect to the human subject. In concluding, Liu takes it that a kind of "neutral monism" is the metaphysics required for grounding the naturalism of Qi-cosmology. I take Chinese cosmology to be radically processual and pluralistic in ways similar to Ames and Hall who draw on Dewey and Whitehead.

3. Youru Wang, in *Linguistic Strategies in Daoist Zhuangzi and Chan Buddhism*, describes a similar position. He argues that Zhuangzi is interested in "Liminology," or the study of the limits of language, and by extension, knowledge and experience. Although Daoist philosophy is in many ways different from Kantian philosophy, Zhuangzi's project is Kantian in the sense that it is concerned with the limits of language or the "bounds of possible experience." The *Zhuangzi* is not simply espousing "skepticism." It takes issue with the nature of experience and what lies within and beyond the bounds of possible experience. The account I provide below is one that draws on Dewey's account of aesthetic meaning.

4. Pappas, *John Dewey's Ethics*, 26.

5. See Pappas, *John Dewey's Ethics*, chapter 1, for a nice summary of the different ways the "philosophical fallacy" has been framed and named throughout Dewey's works.

6. Dewey, *Experience and Nature*, 32.

7. Pappas, *John Dewey's Ethics*, 26.

8. Putnam, *Ethics without Ontology*, generally see pages 17–19.

9. Moore, *Principia Ethica*, 9–10. Originally, this particular quote was retrieved from Mark Johnson's *Morality for Humans*, 19. Both citations are put here for reference.

10. Putnam, *Ethics without Ontology*, 18.

11. Johnson, *Morality for Humans*, 19.

12. Johnson, *Morality for Humans*, 173.

13. See Hansen, *A Daoist Theory of Chinese Thought*, for his account of Zhuangzi and ontological relativism.

14. For an account of the fallacy of the "simple location" and the fallacy of "misplaced concreteness," see Whitehead, *Science and the Modern World*, 48–49, 51.

15. Ames and Hall, *Dao De Jing: Making This Life Significant*, 158. The Ames and Hall translation uses the character *xi*, 襲, in the last line. This character is in the older, *Mawangdui*, version of the *Daodejing*. The more recent version uses the character *xi*, 習, instead.

16. For other accounts of Daoist philosophy as describing an "interdependent self," see Ziporyn, *Ironies of Oneness and Difference*; Lai, *Learning from Chinese Philosophies*; and Hall and Ames, *Thinking from the Han*.

17. This particular insight is, in part, indebted to comments by one of my blind reviewers at PEW.

18. This is my translation of passage 2. For the original Chinese, please see Sturgeon, "Chinese Text Project."

19. Ames and Hall, *Dao De Jing: Making This Life Significant*, 139.

20. For example, Ziporyn and Hansen have both argued that the *Zhuangzi* presents a form of relativism. See both Ziporyn's "How Many Are the Ten Thousand Things and I?" and Hansen's "Guru or Skeptic? Relativistic Skepticism in the *Zhuangzi*," in *Hiding the World in the World*.

21. Traditional "relativism" would hold that for whatever is "relative," it is a property of a single object; that is, what was "relative" was merely a "secondary property" and also "simply locatable." If we take relationships as "primary properties," then the relationships say as much about the particular contexts as they do about the other provisionally isolated things. Quality is produced by the interactions between various aspects of nature. There are, in other words, particular objective conditions that must be brought about for an interaction to even take place. We can empirically study what sorts of qualities emerge from concrete interactions. Value emerges from a "cocreative" process. They do not derive from "single sources." In other words, both moral objectivism and moral subjectivism are myths. The Daoist position is beyond both of these question-begging frameworks.

22. Ziporyn, *Zhuangzi: The Essential Writings*, 12.

23. Although there have been numerous accounts of the "perspectivism" of Zhuangzi, see Lai, "Philosophy and Philosophical Reasoning in the *Zhuangzi*." Her account also draws the distinction between "great wisdom" (*dazhi*) and "little wisdom" (*xiaozhi*) in the *Zhuangzi*. I take this distinction to claim that although there are different perspectives and that all perspectives are "embedded" in historical interdependence, we can still say that some perspectives are better. "Great wisdom" means that one properly understands the nature of "values." Alternatively, please also see Chen Guying's "Zhuang Zi and Nietzsche: Plays of Perspective."

24. Ziporyn, *Zhuangzi: The Essential Writings*, 18.

25. For the full story, please see Ziporyn, *Zhuangzi: The Essential Writings*, 76.

26. Ames, "'Knowing' as the 'Realizing of Happiness' Here, on the Bridge, over the River Hao," 283.

27. For example, if you eat one kind of healthy food "x" and only eat this kind of food, there is a good chance that you will become ill. Its value is always related to the other foods that play a role in one's diet. The quantity of food that the biological organism is eating also plays a role as well. "Health" and "good health" are not "simply located."

28. Ames and Hall, *Dao De Jing: Making This Life Significant*, 91.

29. Although there are many scholars that have discussed the religious aspect of Daoism and the Daoist religion's meditation practices, see Kohn, *Early Chinese Mysticism*, for her work on the Daoist religious practices and their understanding of religious/mystical experience.

30. This is a point that passage 29 of the *Daodejing* makes. It states, "If someone wants to rule the world, and goes about trying to do so, I foresee that they will simply not succeed. The world is a sacred vessel, and is not something that can be ruled. Those who would rule it ruin it; Those who would control it lose it," Ames and Hall, *Dao De Jing: Making This Life Significant*, 122.

31. See Behuniak's article "John Dewey and the Virtue of Cook Ding's Dao." In reference to both Mencius and Zhuangzi, he claims, "Each thinker agrees that the strict imposition of 'external' (*wai*) ends on activity does 'positive harm.' Dewey would not hesitate to call such harm 'evil.' " Although clarifying this more would go far beyond the scope of this chapter, I take it that there would be much agreement between this account of Daoist naturalism that I have provided and Behuniak's work juxtaposing Dewey and Zhuangzi.

32. For the phenomenologists, persons become habituated in how they perceive the world. These habits must be broken down so they can view the world in a new way. This process is what we can call "desedimentation" in the sense that, like a river becoming sedimented, people build up tendencies. Breaking these tendencies down involves getting rid of "sedimentation."

33. Ames and Hall, *Dao De Jing: Making This Life Significant*, 177–78.

34. Ames and Hall, *Dao De Jing: Making This Life Significant*, 178.

35. Ziporyn, *Zhuangzi: The Essential Writings*, 27.

36. Dewey, *Theory of Valuation*, 216.

37. Gordon, *Bad Faith and Anti-Black Racism*, 23.

38. As Christine Tan describes it, the traditional, Western account of "free-will" is not consistent with Chinese metaphysics as "one cannot expect [to find] this image of an inner will that must be protected from external threats and interference [to be found] in Chinese philosophy and metaphysics—there is simply no metaphysical equivalent to it." Tan, "Freedom In," 263. Likewise, Tan suggests that "if causation applies to everything, no one thing can be uncaused; yet, if everything is linked, then causality must therefore not be linear, so no one thing is caused by another one, and everything is caused by everything." Tan, "Freedom In," 267.

39. McCumber, *Metaphysics and Oppression*, 22.

40. Dewey, *Later Works*, "Theory of Valuation," 214.

41. For Kant's account of how all rational persons are "ends-in-themselves," see *Groundwork of the Metaphysics of Morals*, 41 (with my rewording of the literal quote). In particular, see pages 37 to around 43 for the main account of this formula.

42. For Kant's account of how "compassion is a beautiful thing" that means nothing in terms of morality, see Kant's "Observations on the Feeling of the Beautiful and Sublime," translated by Patrick Frierson. For example, Kant characterizes the person that is compassionate as a person who has no "principles" and is not reliable. Frierson, "Observations on the Feeling of the Beautiful and Sublime," 29. This person's emotional responses might be considered "beautiful" but not reliable and not guided by "laws." Alternatively, in the *Groundwork of the Metaphysics of Morals*, Kant claims, "To be beneficent where one can is a duty, and besides there are many souls so sympathetically attuned that, without any other motive of vanity or self-interest they find an inner satisfaction in spreading joy around them and can take delight in the satisfaction of others so far as it is their own work. But I assert that in such a case an action of this kind, however it may conform with duty and however amiable it may be, has nevertheless no true moral worth." Kant, *Groundwork of the Metaphysics of Morals*, 11. In other words, inclinations like compassion, for Kant, have no moral worth because they are conditioned existences.

43. McCumber, *Metaphysics and Oppression*, 183.

44. Sartre, Jean Paul, *Anti-Semite and Jew*, 13.

45. For this analysis of anti-Semitism, please see Xiang, "The Ghostly Other: Understanding Racism from Confucian and Enlightenment Models of Subjectivity." As Xiang highlights, one feature of European anti-Semitism that made it so much more intense for the anti-Semite is that the Jewish population was assimilating into European population. Although for the anti-Semite, the "Jew" was to be feared and removed from society, because the Jewish population was so assimilated, it was harder, if not empirically impossible, to recognize and distinguish the "Jew" from the "non-Jew." This made the fear of the "Jew" by the anti-Semite all the more intense.

46. Sartre, Jean Paul, *Anti-Semite and Jew*, 24.

47. Gordon, *Bad Faith and Anti-Black Racism*, 23.

48. Gordon, *Bad Faith and Anti-Black Racism*, 94.

49. Gordon, *Bad Faith and Anti-Black Racism*, 95.

50. Sartre, Jean Paul, *Anti-Semite and Jew*, 27.

51. Gordon, *Freedom, Justice, and Decolonization*, 20.

52. Sartre, Jean Paul, *Anti-Semite and Jew*, 27.

53. See Xiang's account of how the dominant world picture of Greco-Christian metaphysics has been a hierarchy of substances ranked in ascending order of perfection such that the more perfect legitimately dominates the lower in a "great chain of being." See Xiang, *Chinese Cosmopolitanism*, 113–27.

54. Dewey, *Later Works*, "Theory of Valuation," 228.
55. Dewey, *Later Works*, "Theory of Valuation," 228.
56. In Dewey's *The Public and Its Problems*, Dewey makes a similar claim in the introduction to the work.
57. Ames and Hall, *Dao De Jing: Making This Life Significant*, 125.
58. See also Moeller's *The Moral Fool*, chapter 11, "Masters of War," for his take on how Daoism is antiwar.

Chapter 5

1. Ziporyn, *Zhuangzi: The Complete Writings*, 79–80.
2. My translation. For the original Chinese, please see Sturgeon, "Chinese Text Project."
3. Although chapter 8 of the *Zhuangzi* uses the term *xing* (性) to describe what is natural to "things," this chapter of the *Zhuangzi* is also explicitly rejecting what the Confucians would describe as human *xing* (*renxing*, 人性). As this study will make clear, the phrase 其性命之情 in chapter 8 is meant to signify that the Daoist rejects the Confucian interpretation of human nature in favor of an understanding of all things as novel focal points in a continuum of interrelationships.
4. For example, the Daoist claims that the "distorted application of benevolence and "right conduct" [仁義], the "flashiness of the blue and yellow embroideries," and the soundings of instruments in ritual music are promoting the loss of "the actuality of endowed circumstances." Generally, I borrow the translation of Ziporyn, *Zhuangzi: The Complete Writings*, 77–78.
5. Alternatively, Ma and Brakel, in *Beyond the Troubled Waters of Shifei*, have described what they take to be the Zhuangzian account of "rightness" as "fitting." Although "attunement" may sound too cultivated and not *wuwei* (無為), I understand "attunement" in a way similar to how Ma and Brakel describe "fitting" in the *Zhuangzi*. They also compare their account of "fitting" to Ziporyn's work on *li* (理) as coherence. As they state, Ziporyn's account of *li* as coherence "may be seen as a possible theoretical background for *yi*/fitting because "coherence" can be considered as a kind of (appropriate) fitting." *Beyond the Troubled Waters of Shifei*, 65.
6. The previous chapter of this book was originally an article. This chapter is building on that argument. For the original article, see Bender, "The 'Non-Naturalistic Fallacy," in *Lao-Zhuang Daoism*."
7. Another scholar who has argued convincingly that the Daoist understanding of selves is an interdependent one is Karyn Lai. For example, see "Understanding Change: The Interdependent Self in Its Environment," where she argues that "Daoist philosophy likewise holds a concept of self whose life is integrated with that of others, and whose actions and intentions are understood

within a broader contextual environment. However, it is critical of the humanistic focus of Confucianism." 87. Likewise, see "Ziran and Wuwei in the Daodejing: An Ethical Assessment," where she argues that the Daoist "concept of selfhood is built upon the relations of the self to others, within the context of the whole. This conception of the realization of individuals in a relational and environmental context has important implications for moral theory." 328.

8. In particular, the Daoist would critique the idea that there is a human nature. Each aspect of nature is a unique and particular focal point. The *Xunzi* tries to harmonize "humans" when they should be trying to harmonize unique "things."

9. Perkins, "What Is a thing (wu物)?," makes this point in his discussion of what a "thing" is in the Daoist tradition. I would further add that the traditional distinctions between metaphysics, epistemology, and axiology are also blurred for the Daoist.

10. Ziporyn, *Zhuangzi: The Essential Writings*, 54.

11. For Guo Xiang's commentary, see Sturgeon, "Chinese Text Project." See https://ctext.org/wiki.pl?if=gb&chapter=898238 for this passage.

12. Chapter 8 of the *Zhuangzi* twice references the ideas in *Daodejing* passage 12.

13. Hansen, drawing on Quine, for example, claims that for classical Chinese thinkers, "Reality is not a multitude of independent, fixed objects, but a ground out of which a linguistic community *carves* distinctions and marks them with names. Each part-whole assignment is relative to some presupposed standard and purpose. A part, in turn, has parts. Any whole can be a part of some larger whole." Hansen, *A Daoist Theory*, 50. Although Hansen's work has been criticized by many, this connection he draws between Quine's "ontological relativism" and the *Zhuangzi* I take to be a useful and accurate comparison.

14. My translation. For the original Chinese, please see Sturgeon, "Chinese Text Project."

15. See Ziporyn, *Ironies of Oneness and Difference*, chapter 4, for an account of "ironic coherence" in the *Zhuangzi* and the *Daodejing*. For a more specific location, see Ziporyn, *Ironies of Oneness and Difference*, 182.

16. For recent examples, see Özbey, "Undermining the Person, Undermining the Establishment in the Zhuangzi"; Moeller, "The King's Slaughterer—or, The Royal Way of Nourishing Life"; and Goh, "Chuang Tzu's Becoming-Animal." Although I am sympathetic to these arguments, where I depart from them is with respect to why certain political practices and institutions are coercive. As this study hopes to clarify, when political institutions are based on ignorance of our interdependence, then such institutions become coercive and limiting to human flourishing and freedom.

17. Ma and Van Brakel, *Beyond the Troubled Water of Shifei*, 130, also claim that "Zhuangzi values Hundun's original state. He values a deep trust in life in its

wholeness." What I would further add is that an inability to see life in its wholeness is both to be alienated from nature and to be alienated from what is *actually* of value.

18. My translation. For the original Chinese, please see Sturgeon, "Chinese Text Project."

19. Lai, in "Ziran and Wuwei in the Daodejing: An Ethical Assessment," has also argued that for the Daoist, "the idea of ziran as "self-so" is not a philosophy promoting complete self-determination. Ziran as spontaneity refers to the expression of individuals in their webs of interdependence and environing contexts," 335.

20. My translation. For the original Chinese, please see Sturgeon, "Chinese Text Project."

21. Moeller, in *The Moral Fool*, has made a similar point in the introduction to his book.

22. See *Daodejing* passage 18 for the description and critique just described.

23. Ziporyn, *Zhuangzi: The Essential Writings*, 43.

24. Ziporyn, *Zhuangzi: The Essential Writings*, 38.

25. Ziporyn, *Zhuangzi: The Essential Writings*, 45. The larger context of this line is that things inevitably transform. Things die and their parts are scattered. All things are "bound" or "embedded" to this process of transformation.

26. Ma and Van Brakel, in *Beyond the Troubled Water of Shifei*, chapter 6, suggest and develop the idea that we can think of the *Zhuangzi* as putting forth a broader understanding of "rightness" as "fitting. They also consider their position as one similar to Ziporyn's account of *Li* (理) as "coherence" in *Ironies of Oneness and Difference*.

27. A similar reading of this passage is made by Chai. The fish, in returning to the water, forget themselves in their dependence on the water, and, for Chai, this also involves forgetting "all that is partial and selfishly motivated" and hence, recognizing our oneness with nature. Chai, "The Temporal Experience of Fish: Zhuangzi on Perfection in Time," 138.

28. My translation. For the original Chinese, please see Sturgeon, "Chinese Text Project." For an alternative translation of this passage, see Ziporyn, *Zhuangzi: The Essential Writings*, 58.

29. See Held, *The Ethics of Care*, for an introduction to care ethics. As Held describes it, a care ethics is built on and informed by the universal experience of care and being animals dependent on the nurture of care givers.

30. My translation. For the original Chinese please see Sturgeon, "Chinese Text Project."

31. I borrow this term "cultural forms" in relation to Confucianism from the recent work of Shuchen Xiang, who has argued that the "culture" (文) is central to the philosophy of Confucianism. Please see Xiang, *A Philosophical Defense of Culture*.

32. Ziporyn, *Zhuangzi: The Complete Writings*, 38.

33. Ziporyn, *Zhuangzi: The Essential Writings*, 60.

Chapter 6

1. See Flanagan, *The Really Hard Problem*, for his account of how a "libertarian" understanding of freedom is a fiction and how an Aristotelean and Deweyan understanding of agency is actually scientifically possible.

2. See Connolly, "Perspectivism as a Way of Knowing in the *Zhuangzi*," for another account of the philosophy of the *Zhuangzi* as "perspectivism." As Connolly argues, although we can consider the *Zhuangzi* to be describing a kind of "perspectivism," some perspectives (*da zhi*, 大知) are in fact better than others.

3. Ziporyn, *Zhuangzi: The Essential Writings*, 10–11.

4. This insight is indebted to my conversation with Brook Ziporyn.

5. Özbey, "Undermining the Person, Undermining the Establishment in the Zhuangzi," 127.

6. Ziporyn, *Zhuangzi: The Essential Writings*, 20–21.

7. For example, Kant states that "The essence of things is not changed by their external relations; and that which, without taking account of such relations, alone constitutes the worth of a human being is that in terms of which he must also be appraised by whoever does it, even by the supreme being." Kant, *Groundwork to the Metaphysics of Morals*, 46.

8. See Sandel, *Liberalism and the Limits of Justice*, chapter 1, for a systematic overview of Rawl's account of subjectivity, especially page 55.

9. Sandel, *Liberalism and the Limits of Justice*, 91.

10. For another account on the theme of interdependence in the *Zhuangzi*, see Lai "Understanding Change: The Interdependent Self in Its Environment." For example, Lai claims that an "awareness of the interdependent self, and of one's contextual environment, also impacts on how one lives life to the utmost, as a person with meaningful relationships, and who is able and willing to contribute to and participate in the life of society" (Lai, "Understanding Change," 82).

11. Ziporyn's account of the *Zhuangzi* (an account that also draws on the commentaries of Guo Xiang) has also made this point well. As he claims, the sage of the *Zhuangzi* is more fully responsive to situations insofar as they have cultivated a greater receptiveness to how they are completely dependent on their world. For Ziporyn, "one can become completely independent of things not by separating oneself from things, renouncing one's involvement with and responsiveness to them, but rather, ironically, through complete involvement with them, in a sense through complete dependence on (all of) them" (see Ziporyn, *Ironies of Oneness and Difference*, 164).

12. Nietzsche, arguably, is also best understood as taking on a diagnostic perspective as well. See Solomon, *Living with Nietzsche*, 60.

13. Moeller in the *Moral Fool* also describes moral discourse or moral ideology as a kind of "tool." It functions in a particular way and could be used for either helping to normalize murder or helping to organize society for the better.

14. Ziporyn, *Zhuangzi: The Complete Writings*, 40.
15. Lynn, *Zhuangzi*, 90.
16. Ziporyn, *Zhuangzi: The Complete Writings*, 125.
17. Ziporyn, *Zhuangzi: The Complete Writings*, 47–48.
18. Ziporyn, *Zhuangzi: The Complete Writings*, 42.
19. In chapter 4 of the *Zhuangzi*, the first two larger dialogues address this problem. In particular, each story stresses that in actually dealing with those people that hold much power, it is already an incredibly difficult task, let alone if you were hoping to encourage the tyrant ruler to be more benevolent and less violent and oppressive. Chances are, in feudal society, you will get yourself killed quickly.
20. Ziporyn, *Zhuangzi: The Complete Writings*, 41.
21. Ziporyn, *Zhuangzi: The Complete Writings*, 41.
22. Ziporyn, *Zhuangzi: The Complete Writings*, 17.
23. Moeller, Hans-Georg, and Laozi, *Daodejing*, 117.
24. Ames, *The Analects of Confucius*, 14.34.

Conclusion

1. Xiang, *Chinese Cosmopolitanism*, 1.
2. Fanon, Farrington, and Sartre, *The Wretched of the Earth*, 34.
3. Baldwin, *No Name in the Street*, 404.
4. Baldwin, *The Fire Next Time*, 95–98 (Kindle version)
5. Gordon, "Disciplinary Decadence and the Decolonisation of Knowledge," 86.

Works Cited

Alexander, Thomas. *John Dewey's Theory of Art, Experience & Nature: The Horizons of Feeling.* Albany: State University of New York Press, 1987.

Alexander, Thomas M. "John Dewey and the Moral Imagination: Beyond Putnam and Rorty toward a Postmodern Ethics." *Transactions of the Charles S. Peirce Society* 29, no. 3 (July 1, 1993): 369–400.

Ames, Roger. "'Knowing' as the 'Realizing of Happiness' Here, on the Bridge, over the River Hao." In *Zhuangzi and the Happy Fish*, edited by Takahiro Nakajima and Roger T. Ames. Honolulu: University of Hawai'i Press, 2015.

Ames, Roger T., and David Hall, trans. *Dao De Jing: Making This Life Significant.* New York: Ballantine Books, 2003.

Andersen, Poul. *The Paradox of Being: Truth Identity and Images in Daoism.* Cambridge Massachusetts: Harvard University Asia Center, 2019.

Arendt, Hannah. *Eichmann in Jerusalem: A Report on the Banality of Evil / Hannah Arendt; Introduction by Amos Elon.* New York: Penguin, 2006.

Baldwin, James. *The Fire Next Time.* 1st Vintage International edited by New York: Vintage International, 1993. (Kindle)

Baldwin, James. "No Name in the Street." In *James Baldwin: Collected Essays.* New York: Library Classics of the United States, 1998. 349–476.

Behuniak, James. "John Dewey and the Virtue of Cook Ding's Dao." *Dao* 9, no. 2 (June 2010): 161–74.

Bender, Jacob. "Alienation and Attunement in the *Zhuangzi.*" *Sophia* 62 (2023): 179–93. https://doi.org/10.1007/s11841-022-00931-2.

Bender, Jacob. "Justice as the Practice of Non-Coercive Action: A Study of John Dewey and Classical Daoism." *Asian Philosophy* 26, no. 1 (2016), 20–37. Doi: 10.1080/09552367.2015.1136200, 2016.

Bender, Jacob. "The 'Non-Naturalistic Fallacy' in Lao-Zhuang Daoism." *Philosophy East & West* 71, no. 2 (2021): 265–86.

Bender, Jacob. "On Being "without-Desire" in Lao-Zhuang Daoism," *Asian Philosophy* (2023). Doi: 10.1080/09552367.2023.2234202.

Bernstein, Richard J. *Beyond Objectivism and Relativism: Science, Hermeneutics, and Praxis*. Philadelphia: University of Pennsylvania Press, 1986.

Chai, David. "The Temporal Experience of Fish: Zhuangzi on Perfection in Time." In *Daoism and Time: Classical Philosophy*, edited by Livia Kohn. FL: Three Pines, 2021. 133–56.

Chan, Wing-tsit. *A Sourcebook in Chinese Philosophy*. Princeton: Princeton University Press, 1972.

Chen, Guying. "Zhuang Zi and Nietzsche: Plays of Perspective." In *Nietzsche and Asian Thought*, edited by Graham Parkes. Chicago: University of Chicago Press, 1991.

Chong, Kim-chong. "The Concept of 'Zhen' 真 in the 'Zhuangzi.'" *Philosophy East and West* 61, no. 2 (2011): 324–46.

Cochran, Molly. *The Cambridge Companion to Dewey*. Cambridge: Cambridge University Press, 2010.

Confucius, Roger T. Ames, and Henry Rosemont. *The Analects of Confucius: A Philosophical Translation*. New York: Ballantine Books, 1999.

Connolly, Tim. "Perspectivism as a Way of Knowing in the Zhuangzi." *Dao* 10, no. 4 (November 2011): 487–505.

Cook, Scott, editor. *Hiding the World in the World: Uneven Discourses on the Zhuangzi*. Albany: State University of New York Press, 2003.

Coutinho, Steve. *An Introduction to Daoist Philosophies*. New York: Columbia University Press, 2014. http://site.ebrary.com/id/10787755.

Dewey, John. *Art as Experience*. New York: Berkley, 1934 (or 1980).

Dewey, John. *Experience and Nature*. New York: Dover, 1958.

Dewey, John. "Theory of Valuation." In *The Later Works of John Dewey*, vol. 13, edited by Jo Ann Boydston. Carbondale: Southern Illinois University Press, 1984.

Dupré, J., and D. J. Nicolson. "A Manifesto for a Processual Philosophy of Biology." In *Everything Flows: Towards a Processual Philosophy of Biology*, edited by D. J. Nicolson and J. Dupré. Oxford: Oxford University Press, 2018. 3–45.

Eames, S. Morris. "The Cognitive and the Non-Cognitive in Dewey's Theory of Valuation." *The Journal of Philosophy* 58, no. 7 (March 30, 1961): 179–95.

Fanon, Frantz, Constance Farrington, and Jean-Paul Sartre. *The Wretched of the Earth*. London: Penguin, 1965.

Flanagan, Owen J. *The Really Hard Problem: Meaning in a Material World / Owen Flanagan*. Cambridge: MIT Press, 2007.

Frierson, Patrick. 2011. "Observations on the Feeling of the Beautiful and Sublime (1764)." In *Kant: Observations on the Feeling of the Beautiful and Sublime and Other Writings*, edited by Patrick Frierson and Paul Guyer. Cambridge Texts in the History of Philosophy. Cambridge: Cambridge University Press, 2011. 9–62. doi:10.1017/CBO9780511976018.006.

Goh, Irving. "Chuang Tzu's Becoming-Animal." *Philosophy East and West* 61, no. 1 (2011): 110–33. https://muse.jhu.edu/journals/philosophy_east_and_west/v061/61.1.goh.html.
Gordon, Lewis. *Bad Faith and Antiblack Racism*. Amherst, NY: Humanity Books, 1995.
Gordon, Lewis R. "Disciplinary Decadence and the Decolonisation of Knowledge." *Africa Development*, Volume XXXIX, no. 1, 2014: 81–92.
Gordon, Lewis R. *Disciplinary Decadence: Living Thought in Trying Times*. London: Routledge, 2016.
Gordon, Lewis R. *Freedom, Justice, and Decolonization*. New York: Routledge, 2021.
Grondin, Jean. *Introduction to Metaphysics: from Parmenides to Levinas* New York: Columbia University Press, 2012.
Hall, David. *Eros and Irony: A Prelude to Philosophical Anarchism*. Albany: State University of New York Press, 1982.
Hall, David L., and Roger T. Ames. *Thinking from the Han: Self, Truth, and Transcendence in Chinese and Western Culture*. Albany: State University of New York Press, 1998.
Hamrick, W. S., and J. Van der Veken. *Nature and Logos: A Whiteheadian Key to Merleau-Ponty's Fundamental Thought*. State University of New York Press, 2012.
Hansen, Chad. *A Daoist Theory of Chinese Thought: A Philosophical Interpretation*. New York: Oxford University Press, 1992.
Hansen, Chad. "Guru or Skeptic? Relativistic Skepticism in the *Zhuangzi*." In *Hiding the World in the World: Uneven Discourses on the Zhuangzi*, edited by Scott Cook. Albany: State University of New York Press, 2003.
Held, Virginia. *The Ethics of Care: Personal, Political, and Global*. Oxford: Oxford University Press, 2006.
Hildebrand, David L. *Beyond Realism & Anti-Realism: John Dewey and the Neo-pragmatists* Nashville: Vanderbilt University Press, 2003.
Hung, Jenny. "Is Zhuangzi a Wanton? Observation and Transformation of Desires in the *Zhuangzi*." *Dao: A Journal of Comparative Philosophy* 19, no. 2 (2020): 289–305. https://doi.org/10.1007/s11712-020-09723-2.
Hursthouse, Rosalind. *On Virtue Ethics*. Electronic resource. *Rosalind Hursthouse*. Oxford: Oxford University Press, 1999.
Ihde, Don. *Listening and Voice: Phenomenologies of Sound*. Albany: State University of New York Press, 2007.
Johnson, Mark. *The Meaning of the Body: Aesthetics of Human Understanding*. Chicago: Chicago University Press, 2008.
Johnson, Mark. *Morality for Humans: Ethical Understanding from the Perspective of Cognitive Science*. Chicago: University of Chicago Press, 2014.

Kant, Immanuel. *Groundwork of the Metaphysics of Morals*. Trans. Mary Gregor. Cambridge: Cambridge University Press, 1998.
Kasulis, Thomas P. "The Mosaic and the Jigsaw Puzzle: How It All Fits Together." In *Value and Values: Economics and Justice in an Age of Global Interdependence*, edited by Roger T. Ames and Peter D. Hershock. Honolulu: University of Hawaii Press, 2015. 27–48. doi:10.1515/9780824854522-003.
Keskinen, Antti. "Quine on Objects: Realism or Anti-Realism?" *Theoria* 78, no. 2 (May 2012): 128–45.
Kohn, Livia. *Early Chinese Mysticism: Philosophy and Soteriology in the Taoist Tradition*. Princeton: Princeton University Press, 1992.
Kui, Wong Kwok. "Hegel's Criticism of Laozi and Its Implication." *Philosophy East & West* 61, no. 1 (2011): 56–79.
Lai, Karyn. *Learning from Chinese Philosophies: Ethics of Interdependent and Contextualised Self*. Ashgate World Philosophies Series. Aldershot, England; Burlington, VT: Ashgate, 2006.
Lai, Karyn. "Philosophy and Philosophical Reasoning in the 'Zhuangzi': Dealing with Plurality." *Journal Of Chinese Philosophy* 33, no. 3 (2006): 365–74.
Lai, Karyn. "Understanding Change: The Interdependent Self in Its Environment." *Journal of Chinese Philosophy* 34, no. 1 (December 1, 2007): 81–99.
Lai, Karyn. "Ziran and Wuwei in the Daodejing: An Ethical Assessment." *Dao* 6, no. 4 (December 2007): 325–37.
Lakoff, George, and Mark Johnson. *Metaphors We Live By*. Chicago: University of Chicago Press, 2003.
Lakoff, George, and Mark Johnson. *Philosophy in the Flesh: The Embodied Mind and Its Challenge to Western Thought*. New York: Basic Books, 1999.
Lee, Jung H. *The Ethical Foundations of Early Daoism: Zhuangzi's Unique Moral Vision*. New York: Palgrave Macmillan, 2014.
Legge, James. *The Works of Mencius*. Oxford: Clarendon, 1985, accessed April 17, 2020. https://ctext.org/mengzi.
Liu, Jeeloo. "In Defense of Chinese Qi-Naturalism." In *Chinese Metaphysics and Its Problems*, 33–53. Cambridge: Cambridge University Press, 2015.
Liu, Xiaogan. *Dao Companion to Daoist Philosophy*. Springer Netherlands, 2014.
Lovejoy, A. O. *The Great Chain of Being: A Study of the History of an Idea*. Cambridge, MA, and London: Harvard University Press, 1964.
Lynn, Richard John. *The Classic of the Way and Virtue: A New Translation of the Tao-Te Ching of Laozi as Interpreted by Wang Bi*. New York: Columbia University Press, 1999.
Lynn, Richard John. *Zhuangzi: A New Translation of the Sayings of Master Zhuang as Interpreted by Guo Xiang*. New York: Columbia University Press, 2022. https://doi.org/10.7312/lynn12386.
Ma, Lin, and Jaap Van Brakel. *Beyond the Troubled Water of Shifei: From Disputation to Walking-Two-Roads in the Zhuangzi*. Albany: State University of New York Press, 2020.

McCumber, John. *Metaphysics and Oppression: Heidegger's Challenge to Western Philosophy* Bloomington: Indiana University Press, 1999.
Moeller, Hans-Georg. "The King's Slaughterer—or, The Royal Way of Nourishing Life." *Philosophy East & West* 70, no. 1 (2020): 155–73.
Moeller, Hans-Georg. *The Moral Fool: A Case for Amorality*. New York: Columbia University Press, 2009.
Moeller, Hans-Georg, and Laozi. *Daodejing (Laozi): A Complete Translation and Commentary*. Chicago: Open Court, 2007.
Moeller, Hans-Georg, and Paul J. D'Ambrosio. *Genuine Pretending: On the Philosophy of the Zhuangzi*. New York: Columbia University Press, 2017.
Moore, G. E. *Principia Ethica*. Cambridge: Cambridge University Press, 1903/1968.
Nietzsche, Friedrich Wilhelm, and Walter Arnold Kaufmann. *Beyond Good and Evil: Prelude to a Philosophy of the Future*. Translated, with Commentary, by Walter Kaufmann. New York: Vintage Books, 1989.
Nietzsche, Friedrich Wilhelm, and Walter Arnold Kaufmann. *On the Genealogy of Morals and Ecce Homo*. New York: Vintage Books, 1990.
Olberding, Amy. "Sorrow and the Sage: Grief in the *Zhuangzi*." *Dao* 6 (2007): 339–59. https://doi.org/10.1007/s11712-007-9020-2.
Özbey, Sonya. "Undermining the Person, Undermining the Establishment in the Zhuangzi." *Comparative and Continental Philosophy* 10, no. 2 (2018): 123–39.
Pappas, Gregory Fernando. *John Dewey's Ethics: Democracy as Experience*. Bloomington: Indiana University Press, 2008.
Perkins, Franklin. "Metaphysics and Methodology in a Cross-Cultural Context." In *The Bloomsbury Research Handbook of Chinese Philosophy Methodologies*, edited by Sor-Hoon Tan. London: Bloomsbury, 2016.
Perkins, Franklin. "What Is a Thing (wu 物)?" In *Chinese Metaphysics and Its Problems*. Cambridge: Cambridge University Press, 2015. 33–53.
Putman, Hilary. 2004. *Ethics without Ontology*. Cambridge: Harvard University Press.
Quine, W. V. *Ontological Relativity, and Other Essays*. New York: Columbia University Press, 1977.
Rorty, R. *Contingency, Irony, and Solidarity*. Electronic resource. Cambridge: Cambridge University Press, 1989.
Rorty, Richard. *Philosophy and the Mirror of Nature*. Princeton: Princeton University Press, 2009.
Sandel, M. J. *Liberalism and the Limits of Justice*. Electronic resource. Cambridge: Cambridge University Press, 1998.
Shusterman, Richard. "The Pragmatist Aesthetics of William James." *The British Journal of Aesthetics* 51, no. 4 (October 2011): 347–61.
Shusterman, Richard. "Thought in the Strenuous Mood: Pragmatism as a Philosophy of Feeling." *New Literary History* 43, no. 3 (2012): 433–54.
Shusterman, Richard. *Thinking through the Body: Essays in Somaesthetics*. New York: Cambridge University Press, 2012.

Slote, Michael A. *From Morality to Virtue*. Electronic resource. New York: Oxford University Press, 1992.

Solomon, Robert C. *Living with Nietzsche*. Electronic resource: *What the Great "Immoralist" Has to Teach Us*. Oxford: Oxford University Press, 2003.

Stambaugh, Joan. *The Real Is Not the Rational*. Albany: State University of New York Press, 1986.

Sturgeon, Donald. "Chinese Text Project: A Dynamic Digital Library of Premodern Chinese." *Digital Scholarship in the Humanities*, 2019, accessed April 17, 2020. https://ctext.org.

Tan, Christine Abigail L. " 'Freedom In': A Daoist Response to Isaiah Berlin." *Dao: A Journal of Comparative Philosophy* 22, no. 2 (2023): 255–75.

Valmisa, Mercedes. *Adapting: A Chinese Philosophy of Action*. Oxford: Oxford University Press, 2021. https://doi.org/10.1093/oso/9780197572962.001.0001.

Van Norden, B. W. "Zhuangzi's Ironic Detachment and Political Commitment." *Dao: A Journal of Comparative Philosophy* 15, no. 1 (2016): 1–17.

Virág, Curie. *The Emotions in Early Chinese Philosophy*. New York: Oxford University Press, 2017.

Wagner, Rudolf G. *A Chinese Reading of the Daodejing: Wang Bi's Commentary on the Laozi with Critical Text and Translation*. Albany: State University of New York Press, 2003.

Wang, Robin. *Yinyang: The Way of Heaven and Earth in Chinese Thought and Culture*. Cambridge: Cambridge University Press, 2012.

Wang, Youru. *Linguistic Strategies in Daoist Zhuangzi and Chan Buddhism: The Other Way of Speaking*. London, New York: RoutledgeCurzon, 2003.

Wang, Youru. "Philosophy of Change and the Deconstruction of Self in the Zhuangzi." *Journal of Chinese Philosophy* 27, no. 3 (2000), 345. *Academic Search Complete*, EBSCOhost, accessed June 7, 2018.

Wang, Youru. "The Strategies of 'Goblet Words': Indirect Communication in the Zhuangzi." *Journal of Chinese Philosophy* 31, no. 2 (2004): 195. *Complementary Index*, EBSCOhost, accessed June 7, 2018.

Whitehead, Alfred North. *Science and the Modern World*. New York: Macmillan, 1925.

Wong, David. *Natural Moralities: A Defense of Pluralistic Relativism*. Natural Moralities. New York: Oxford University Press, 2006.

Xiang, Shuchen. *Chinese Cosmopolitanism: The History and Philosophy of an Idea*. Princeton: Princeton University Press, 2023.

Xiang, Shuchen. "Chinese Processual Holism and Its Attitude towards "Barbarians" and Non-Humans." *Sophia* (2020). https://doi.org/10.1007/s11841-020-00781-w.

Xiang, Shuchen. "The Ghostly Other: Understanding Racism from Confucian and Enlightenment Models of Subjectivity." *Asian Philosophy* 25, no. 4 (2015): 205–22. https://doi.org/10.1080/09552367.2015.1105117.

Xiang, Shuchen. *A Philosophical Defense of Culture: Perspectives from Confucianism and Cassirer*. Albany: State University of New York Press, 2021.

Xiang, Shuchen. "Why the Confucians Had No Concept of Race (Part I): The Antiessentialist Cultural Understanding of Self." *Philosophy Compass* 14, no. 10 (October 2019).

Xiang, Shuchen. "Why the Confucians Had No Concept of Race (Part II): Cultural Difference, Environment, and Achievement." *Philosophy Compass* 14, no. 10 (October 2019).

Ziporyn, Brook. "How Many Are the Ten Thousand Things and I?" In *Hiding the World in the World: Uneven Discourses on the Zhuangzi*, edited by Scott Cook. Albany: State University of New York Press, 2003.

Ziporyn, Brook. *Ironies of Oneness and Difference: Coherence in Early Chinese Thought: Prolegomena to the Study of Li*. Albany: State University of New York Press, 2012.

Ziporyn, Brook. *Zhuangzi: The Complete Writings*. Indianapolis: Hackett, 2020.

Ziporyn, Brook. *Zhuangzi: The Essential Writings with Selections from Traditional Commentaries*. Indianapolis: Hackett, 2009.

Zhuangzi and A. C. Graham. *Chuang-Tzŭ: The Inner Chapters*. Indianapolis: Hackett, 2001.

Index

abstraction, 50, 72–73, 75–76, 83–84, 89
  desires and, 39–40
  intelligibility and, 43
  knowledge and, 33
  language and, 37–38, 64–65
  valuation and, 40, 111, 116
aesthetics, 58, 65
  Dewey on, 30, 72–74, 186n12, 187n22
  virtue and, 54–55
affect, 29, 65, 82, 123
agape, 60
agency, 123, 157–158
Alexander, Thomas M., 72
alienation, 10, 12, 156, 157, 172–174, 180–181
  attunement and, 142, 155
  capitalist, 67
  forgetting and, 36
  knowledge and, 69
  from nature, 11, 19, 110–111, 142–143, 145–146, 149–150, 152, 154
  perceptual, 13, 19, 49, 62, 122, 143, 145–146, 175
ambiguity, 1, 116, 125
American exceptionalism, 137–138, 177
Ames, Roger T., 37, 49, 195n20, 198n15

amorality, 3, 11, 15, 141, 146–147, 171–172
analytic philosophy, 25, 74, 186n10
Andersen, Poul, 90–91
animal, 29
  fitness, 84–89
  needs, 82, 88–89, 96, 145
anti-Black racism, 124, 139
antilanguage, 31–32, 187n31
antirealism, 74–75
antirepresentational, 21, 23–26, 31, 83, 110, 146, 193n9, 196n20
Anti-Semite and Jew (Sartre), 131
anti-Semitism, 102, 124, 130–134, 139, 200n45
antiwar, 106, 110, 124–125, 136–137
"any-means-necessary," 106, 110, 124, 136
Aristotle, 184n15, 191n22
Art as Experience (Dewey), 72–73
attunement, 10–11, 16, 184n16, 201n5
  alienation and, 142, 155
  to interdependence, 143, 150, 174
  to nature, 19, 59, 142–143, 150, 153
autonomous self, 160, 173
autonomy, 9–10

bad faith, 122, 131–134
Baldwin, James, 176–178
beauty, the beautiful and, 4, 112

216 | Index

Behuniak, James, 192n1, 199n31
benevolence (*ren*, 仁), 5, 51–54, 147–148
Bernstein, Richard, 10, 184n15
Beyond Objectivism and Relativism (Bernstein), 10, 184n15
Beyond the Troubled Waters of Shi/Fei (Ma, Braak), 9
biological needs, 82, 84, 98–99
blame, 159, 164
Brakel, Jaap Van, 9, 23n26, 183n12, 201n5, 202n17
Buddhism, 2, 8, 75, 178, 185n7
buyu (not desiring, 不欲), 22–23, 37, 95

capitalism, 67
care, 168–170, 173
  motherly, 3, 159, 171–172
"carving up" nature, 96–98, 146–148, 150–151, 154
causality, 13–14, 126–129, 134–135, 159
  desire and, 65
  "simply located" realities and, 69
center (*zhong*, 中), 5, 84–85
  central meridian (緣督), 87
  empty, 6, 80, 86–88, 92–93, 101–102, 170, 179
Chai, David, 203n27
Chong, Kim-chong, 195n29, 196n39
Christianity, 60
classes, social, 65–66, 96, 102, 163–168
cocreative processes, 53, 112, 114
  knowledge as, 139
  meaning as a, 32
  values emerging as, 120–121, 138, 198n21
coercive conduct, 37, 49–52, 65–68, 75, 95–97, 153
cognitive, 16–17, 35–36, 61, 74, 77, 138, 187n22, 189n3
  Dewey on, 43

coherence (*li*, 理), 114
  attunement and, 10, 181
  Zhuangzi on, 43
  Ziporyn on, 50, 189n1, 195n21, 201n5, 203n26
colonialism, 176
color, 82–83, 109–110
comfort (*shi*, 適), 153–154
compassion, 19, 159, 200n42
  amorality and, 171–172
  criminals and, 162
conceptualization, habits of, 16, 36
concrete valuing, 120–121, 138
conditioned, 7, 130, 157–158, 164
conduct. *See also* non-egoistic action
  coercive, 37, 49–52, 65–68, 75, 95–97, 153
  human, 5, 13–14, 60, 66, 80–82, 99, 120, 138, 158
  moral, 52, 60, 68, 171
  right, 51, 53–54, 68, 151, 201n4
Confucianism, 2, 5, 141, 143, 162, 170–171, 185nn6–7, 201n3
  criminals and, 165–167
  the *Daodejing* on, 148
  on endowed circumstances, 152
  Hansen on, 24
  morality, 49, 86, 100–101
  as self-undermining, 53
  in the *Zhuangzi*, 57–59
consciousness, 4, 11, 14–15, 107–108, 146, 188n47, 189n3
  Dewey on, 41, 43
  meaning and, 30
  racism and, 132
  reflective, 62
  responsibility, 133
  value and, 120–121
Contingency, Irony, Solidarity (Rorty), 64, 69–70
corruption, 57, 97, 102, 158, 167
cosmology, 33–34, 144, 197n2
Coutinho, Steve, 81, 194n13

creation of desires (*yu zuo*, 欲作), 23, 79, 84, 95, 97, 99
criminal society, 163, 165–167, 173
criminality, criminals and, 146–147, 158
  the *Zhuangzi* on, 141–143, 161–168
cruelty, 9–10, 74
cultivation practices, Daoist, 13, 16, 23, 35–36, 44, 59, 61, 75–76
cultural forms, 54, 68, 84, 151, 203n31

D'Ambrosio, P., 191n23
Dao (the "way," 道), 3, 80, 90–91, 166–167
  ignorance and, 63
  as nameless, 22, 95, 97–98
  virtue and, 53–54
the *Daodejing*, 4, 12, 175, 185n3, 185n7, 189n6, 199n30
  antiwar position of, 136–137
  on being without desire, 23, 39, 94–98
  on being without heart/mind, 19, 100
  on being without self-interest, 99–100
  on Confucianism, 148
  on Daoist sages, 5–6, 19, 81–84, 99–100, 142, 157–162, 171–172
  on desire, 21–22, 145
  Hansen on, 31–32, 194n15
  on knowledge, 39
  on naming, 21–22
  non-egoistic conduct in, 13–14, 47, 50–55, 97–98, 142
  on spontaneity, 16
  on valuing, 111–113
  the *Zhuangzi* and, 2–3, 7, 83–85, 112–113, 171, 195n19
Daoism. *See specific topics*
A Daoist Theory of Chinese Thought (Hansen), 23, 194n15

de (德). *See* virtue
death, 54–55, 136–137, 141, 190n6, 203n25
  murder and, 133, 164–165, 167–168
deontology, 160, 178
desire (*yu*, 欲), 9–11, 16, 36, 185n2, 191n22, 193n22. *See also* eye, desires of the; without desire, being
  absence of, 3, 22, 37, 93
  abstraction and, 39–40
  causality and, 65
  Coutinho on, 194n13
  creation of, 23, 79, 84, 95, 97, 99
  the *Daodejing* on, 21–22, 145
  Dewey on, 29, 35, 71
  "end-in-itself" and, 128
  Hansen on, 24, 37–39
  interdependence and, 18–19
  knowledge and, 21, 79–80, 82, 86, 88, 95–96, 131
  Liu, X., on, 193n8
  morality and, 65
  naming and, 21–23, 83
  non-egoistic action inhibited by, 79–80
  ontology and, 26
  selfish, 65–66, 94, 150, 179
  spontaneity impacted by, 81–83, 86
  of the stomach, 39, 44, 79, 82, 84, 145, 194n12
  values and, 27, 37–39
  Virág on, 193n6
  Ziporyn on, 39, 194n12
determinate (*you*, 有), 33–34, 43, 51
  mutual generation of the indeterminate and, 4–5, 37, 112
Dewey, John, 15, 75, 184n15, 188n42, 188n49, 192n1. *See also specific works*
  on aesthetics, 30, 72–74, 186n12, 187n22
  on consciousness, 41, 43

Dewey, John *(continued)*
  on desire, 29, 35, 71
  on embodied experience, 40–43
  on ineffability, 34–35
  on meaning, 27–31
  naturalism of, 35, 40, 43, 76
  on noncognitive meaning, 29–30, 72–73
  ontological relativism and, 26–27, 40, 43
  philosophical fallacy of, 38–39, 106–110, 197n5
  Rorty and, 18, 25
  on valuation, 111, 120, 125–127, 135
difference, 36, 89, 131–132, 155
dignity, 128–129
disciplinary decadence, 8, 178–179
dualism, 4, 18, 25, 75, 136
  Alexander on, 72
  determinate/indeterminate, 22
  metaphysical, 41
  mind/body, 42
  Wong on, 9
  the *Zhuangzi* on, 91

egalitarian society, 94–99, 166
egoism, 6, 49, 142–143, 150, 155, 168, 180. *See also* non-egoistic action
  knowledge and, 80
  virtue and, 53, 55
  the *Zhuangzi* on, 94
embodied
  account of meaning, 31–32
  experience, 2–3, 7, 16–18, 21–24, 40–44, 74, 77
The Emotions in Early Chinese Philosophy (Virág), 193n6
emotivism, 72, 74
empirical, 107
  experience, 15, 27, 67, 87, 132–133, 189n3

  reality, 40, 65, 105–106, 132–133, 178
emptiness, 56, 58
empty center, 6, 80, 86–88, 92–93, 101–102, 170, 179
"end-in-itself," 125–129, 134–138
endowed circumstances (*xingming*, 性命), 141–143, 147, 150–155
epistemological frameworks, 1–2, 10–11, 13–16, 162, 175, 179–180
  alienation from nature and, 110
  desire and, 79–80
  egoism and, 142–143
  of qualities, 105
  of substance metaphysics, 43–44
erasure, 176
ethics, 57–58, 123–124, 161
  metaphysics and, 7, 17–18, 44, 143–144, 177
  naturalism and, 15, 107, 180
  nonnaturalism and, 108–109, 175
  perception and, 71
existence, quality of, 11, 43, 73
Experience and Nature (Dewey), 27–28, 38, 40–42, 76, 107, 186n12
external relationships, 7–8, 24n7, 180, 183n9
eye, desires of the, 82, 84, 123, 138, 145, 153, 155, 194n12
  as distinct from stomach-desires, 44
  knowledge and, 79
  Ziporyn on, 39

facts, moral, 1–2, 8, 18, 24–25, 62, 69, 176, 178–180
fallacy
  nonnaturalistic, 19, 105–111, 113, 122, 136, 139
  philosophical, 38–39, 106–110, 197n5
Fanon, Franz, 176
fasting of the mind (*xin zhai*, 心齋), 44, 58–59, 76

Index | 219

final vocabularies, 14–15, 64, 67, 71–72, 194n18
   Rorty on, 70, 74, 131, 189n3
The Fire Next Time (Baldwin), 176–177
Flanagan, Owen J., 158–159
forgetting (*wang*, 忘), 49, 55, 91, 93, 117, 139, 149
   abstraction and, 40
   alienation and, 36
   being without self-interest and, 98
   sitting and (*zuowang*, 坐忘), 44, 59, 76
   in the *Zhuangzi*, 59–60
free will, free choice and, 158–159, 164–165, 199n38
fundamentalism, moral, 11–18, 64, 69, 193n2

Gadamer, Hans Georg, 189n3
genuine-humans (*zhenren*, 真人), 16, 143, 168, 196n39
   spontaneity and, 155–156
   the *Zhuangzi* on, 86, 89–94, 195n29
Goh, Irving, 194n11
good (*shan*, 善), 4–5, 102, 108–109, 112, 172
"good-in-itself," 19, 110, 119, 124
Gordon, Lewis, 122, 132–133, 178, 180, 183n10
greed, 3, 6, 65–66, 81, 166
Grondin, Jean, 17
Groundwork (Kant), 160
guan (observation, 觀), 21–22, 79, 81
Guo Xiang, 85, 144, 152, 164

Hall, David L., 37, 49, 73, 195n20, 198n15
Hamrick, W. S., 188n47
Hansen, Chad, 185nn6–7, 186n9, 186n10, 193n9, 202n13
   on the *Daodejing*, 31–32, 194n15
   on desire, 24, 37–39

   on language, 24–32, 37–38
   on the *Zhuangzi*, 24–30, 39, 194n15
"having desire" (*youyu*, 有欲), 38, 79, 81
Heaven (*tian*, 天), 5–6, 86, 88–90, 101, 112–113, 149
Heidegger, Martin, 75, 186n10, 188n43, 188n47, 192n41
heteronomous selves, 172–173
hierarchies, 19, 23, 66–67, 159–160, 163
   desires and, 96
horizon of relevance, 14–15, 51, 64, 71–72, 131, 171
Huizi, 114, 189n6
human, 18, 39–40, 151. *See also* genuine-humans; suffering, human
   conduct, 5, 13–14, 60, 66, 80–82, 99, 120, 138, 158
   perception, 12–13, 14–17, 23, 56, 71, 75–76, 80–84, 109
   rights, 71
human nature, 8, 66, 68, 151–152, 188n48, 201n3, 202n8
humanism, 176–177
"Hundred Schools of Thought" (*zhuzi baijia*, 諸子百家), 2
hundun ("muddy confusion," 渾沌), 143–146
Hung, Jenny, 193n6

Idhe, Don, 30
ignorance, 63, 123, 144, 157, 159, 180
   alienation as, 154–156
   of interdependence, 36, 41
   nonnaturalistic fallacy and, 105
imperialism, 137
inborn natures (*xing*, 性), 141–142
independent
   self, 8, 59–61, 63, 94–95, 150
   sense of self, 19, 52, 61–62, 80, 91, 93–94, 119, 159, 172

indeterminate (*wu*, 無), 40, 171–172
  interdependence and, 154, 156
  knowledge, 144–145
  mutual generation of the determinate and, 4–5, 37, 112
  nature as, 4, 33, 83, 86, 94, 100–102, 146–147, 149–150, 153, 179
  as not reducible to propositional forms, 34
individualism, 7, 134, 143, 169, 177
individuation, 7, 48, 79, 83–85, 90, 102
  as and aspect of experience, 36–37
  knowledge and, 62
  value and, 29
ineffability, 34–35
inequality, 66, 96–97
instrumental value, 124–127, 130, 134, 136, 196n1
intelligibility, 25, 27, 30–32, 34–43
intercommunication, 42, 121
interdependence, 7, 100, 158–162, 179–180, 204n10
  attunement to nature and, 143, 150, 174
  desire and, 18–19
  ignorance of, 36, 51
  indeterminacy and, 154, 156
  spontaneity and, 12
interdependent self, 158–162, 204n10
internal relationships, 4, 7–8, 108, 120, 180, 183n9
intrinsic value, 106, 119–139, 160, 177, 196n1
irony, 18, 50–51, 69–75, 102, 168, 180, 189n1, 194n18
  morality and, 60–63
irrationalism, 32–35, 42

James, William, 71
jing (tranquility, 靜), 22–23, 44, 95, 142

Johnson, Mark, 10, 15, 69, 73, 109, 184n15
  on Dewey, 30
  on language, 27

Kant, Immanuel, 125, 160, 191n22, 197n2, 200n42
  metaphysical framework of, 127–134, 138–139
knowledge (*zhi*, 知), 10–11, 14–17, 19, 184n15, 193n5, 195n29. *See also* without knowledge, being
  abstraction and, 33
  alienation and, 69
  being without heart/mind and, 19–20, 157
  being without self-interest and, 61
  as cocreative, 139
  conduct inhibited by, 51
  in a criminal society, 163
  cultural, 80, 150
  the *Daodejing* on, 39
  desire and, 21, 79–80, 82, 86, 88, 95–96, 131
  egoism and, 80
  heteronomous selves and, 173
  indeterminacy and, 144–145
  individuation and, 62
  miseducation and, 96–97
  morality and, 108, 124
  naming and, 57, 68–69, 101
  nature and, 106–107, 146–147, 180–181
  oppression and, 105–106
  propositional, 74, 107, 118, 139
  reality and, 180
  representation and, 25–26
  right-wrong distinction and, 93–94
  spontaneity impacted by, 80, 89
  suffering and, 66–67
Kui, Wong Kwok, 193n5

Lai, Karyn, 11–12, 198n23, 201n7
  on interdependence, 204n10
Lakoff, George, 27, 41–42, 184
language, 9, 12, 50, 83, 86, 106, 153, 180
  abstraction and, 37–38, 64–65
  difference and, 36
  final vocabularies and, 74
  Hansen on, 24–32, 37–38
  Johnson on, 27
  limits of, 87, 195n27
  meaning and, 24, 32
Lao-Zhuang Daoism. *See specific topics*
LaPolla, Randy, 185n3
Lee, Jung, 85–86
li (理). *See* coherence
libertarianism, 158–159, 204n1
Liu, Jeeloo, 197n2
Liu, Xiaogan, 193n8
love, 60, 152

Ma, Lin, 9, 183n12, 201n5, 202n17, 203n26
McCumber, John, 123, 130–131, 191n22
meaning, 187n32
  as a cocreative processes, 32
  cognitive, 29–30, 72
  consciousness and, 30
  Dewey on, 27–31
  embodied, 31–32
  as emergent, 33–34
  intelligibility and, 35–43
  language and, 24, 32
  noncognitive, 18, 25, 28–33, 72–73
  perceptual, 28–29
  propositional, 31, 36, 43, 84
  truth and, 74
  value and, 40
means/end relationships
  "any-means-necessary," 106, 110, 124, 136

"end-in-itself," 125–129, 134–138
"good-in-itself," 19, 110, 119, 124
"quality-in-itself," 114–115
Mencius, 187n31, 199n21
merit, 123, 159, 161, 169–170
Merleau-Ponty, Maurice, 186n10, 188n47
metaphysics, metaphysical frameworks
  and, 12, 14, 49, 175, 178–179, 184n24, 185n2, 191n21, 200n53, 202n9
  Chinese, 123, 196n1, 199n38
  dualism, 41
  ethics and, 7, 17–18, 44, 143–144, 177
  Greek, 124, 177
  of interdependence, 179
  Kantian, 127–134, 138–139
  moral, 70, 130–131, 137, 139
  nonnaturalist, 2, 10–11, 44, 61, 70, 102, 123–125, 133, 159
  oppression and, 130–134, 137–138
  processual, 3–4, 6–7, 15, 17, 98, 134
  question-begging, 1–2, 35, 102, 192n2
  as self-undermining, 64–69
  substance, 11, 17, 19, 43–44, 64, 81, 102, 123, 156, 183n10
  Western, 6, 35, 41, 80–81, 188n48
Metaphysics and Oppression (McCumber), 130
mind fasting (*xin zhai*, 心齋), 44, 58–59, 76
mind/body dualisms, 42
mirrors, 56
miseducation, 13, 67–68, 97, 158
misperception, 34, 44, 79–84
Moeller, Hans-Georg, 5, 183n1, 191n23, 201n58, 202n16, 203n21, 204n13
Mohists, 141, 162, 165, 170–171, 196n39
  morality, 49, 86, 100–101

Moore, G. E., 108–110
moral
  bigotry, 156, 164–165
  conduct, 52, 60, 68, 171
  facts, 1–2, 8, 18, 24–25, 62, 69, 176, 178–180
  fundamentalism, 11–18, 64, 69, 193n2
  law, 129
  metaphysics, 70, 130–131, 137, 139
  narcissism, 53–54, 62, 94, 168
  objectivism, 9, 11, 177–178, 192n2, 198n21
  obtuseness, 54, 124, 166
  subjectivism, 7–9, 192n2, 198n21
Moral Fool (Moeller), 201n58, 203n21, 204n13
Moral Manicheanism, 19, 64, 69, 156, 157, 165–167, 170
morality, moral order and, 1–3, 17–19, 56–57, 147–148, 177–181
  Confucian, 49, 86, 100–101
  criminality and, 162–168
  desire and, 65
  human conduct and, 60
  individualism and, 7
  institutionalized, 50, 64–69
  irony and, 60–63
  knowledge and, 108, 124
  narcissism and, 94
  self-undermining, 68
  Slote on, 60
Morality for Humans (Johnson), 10, 15, 69, 184n15, 197n2
motherly care, 3, 159, 171–172
"muddy confusion" (*hundun*, 渾沌), 143–146
murder, 133, 164–165, 167–168
mutual generation (*xiang sheng*, 相生), 4–5, 37, 112

named (*youming*, 有名), 35–36, 185n2

nameless (*wuming*, 無名), 23, 31, 83, 185n2
  aspects of experience, 35–36
  Dao as, 22, 95, 97–98
naming (*ming*, 名), 16–17, 31, 55–56, 112, 185n2, 197n2
  desires and, 21–23, 83
  knowledge and, 57, 68–69, 101
narcissism, 155, 179–180, 183n10
  moral, 53–54, 62, 94, 168
Natural Moralities (Wong), 9–10
naturalism, 2, 7, 43–44, 98, 111, 122, 197n2, 199n31
  of Dewey, 35, 40, 43, 76
  ethical, 15, 107, 180
  noncognitive meanings of experience and, 74
  Quine on, 25
  valuing and, 119
naturalness, 2, 16, 68–69, 89, 91, 97, 155, 194n13
nature, 3, 5, 10, 15–18, 75–76
  alienation from, 11, 19, 110–111, 142–143, 145–146, 149–150, 152, 154
  attunement to, 19, 59, 142–143, 150, 153
  "carving up," 96–98, 146–148, 150–151, 154
  color and, 110
  of experience, 26–27, 30–35, 41, 75, 89, 188n48, 197n3
  human, 8, 66, 68, 151–152, 188n48, 201n3, 202n8
  inborn, 141–142
  as indeterminate, 83, 86, 93–94, 146–147, 149–150, 153, 179
  knowledge and, 106–107, 146–147, 180–181
  as nameless, 23
  spontaneity of, 85–86

as an uncarved block of wood, 40, 80, 83–84, 97–99
values and, 14–16, 19, 168–169
Nature and Experience (Dewey), 75
needs
  animal, 82, 88–89, 96, 145
  biological, 82, 84, 98–99
  human, 39–40
Nietzsche, Friedrich, 69–70, 188n47, 191n21, 204n12
No Name in the Street (Baldwin), 176–177
nonanthropocentric, 50, 85, 194n11
noncoercive action, 47, 49, 138, 143, 150, 154
noncognitive, 34–35, 58–59, 187n22, 189n3
  features of experience, 32–33, 36, 40, 77, 107
  meaning, 18, 25, 28–33, 72–73
non-Daoist sages, 19, 56, 143, 155, 161, 168, 173
non-egoistic action/without action (*wuwei*, 無為), 18–20, 48–49, 179, 181, 185n3, 193n8, 201n5
  in the *Daodejing*, 13–14, 47, 50–55, 97–98, 142
  desire inhibiting, 79–80
  knowledge and, 75
  spontaneity and, 55–60, 70, 100–101, 142
  in the *Zhuangzi*, 47, 55–60
nonintrinsic value, 125, 127
nonnatural reality, 92, 122, 124, 138, 159
nonnaturalism, 15, 106, 173
  ethical, 108–109, 175
  valuing and, 120–123
nonnaturalistic fallacy, 19, 105–111, 113, 122, 136, 139
nonpropositional, 31–32, 36, 90

not desiring (*buyu*, 不欲), 22–23, 37, 95
not good (*bushan*, 不善), 4, 112, 172
nurturing behavior, 19, 157–158

objecthood, 26, 147
objectivism, 2, 7–10, 41–42, 180, 183n12, 184n15
  moral, 9, 11, 177–178, 192n2, 198n21
observation (*guan*, 觀), 21–22, 79, 81
obtuseness, moral, 54, 124, 166
Olberding, Amy, 189n6
oneness of all things, 93–94, 102–103, 154–155 92, 168–173
ontological relativism, 26–27, 43, 84–89, 142–146
Ontological Relativity (Quine), 27
ontology, 22, 26–27, 128, 184n25
  substance, 6–7, 44, 64, 118, 131, 175
oppression, 1, 19, 152, 154, 162, 177–178, 180
  "end-in-itself" and, 14, 134–138
  knowledge and, 67, 105–106
  metaphysics of, 130–134
  racial, 124, 130–134, 139
  structural, 44, 134–135
  suffering and, 44, 68, 102
ousia, 130–131
overexploitation, 67, 96–97, 164
Özbey, Sonya, 160

Pappas, Gregory Fernando, 107–108
patriarchy, 196n1
perception
  ethics and, 71
  human, 12–13, 14–17, 23, 56, 71, 75–76, 80–84, 109
  misperception and, 34, 44, 79–84
  of situations, 13–14, 23, 36, 40, 44, 56, 117–118, 122, 180

perceptual alienation, 13, 19, 49, 62, 122, 143, 145–146, 175
Perkins, Franklin, 7, 18, 202n9
perspectivism, 85, 195n22, 204n2
phenomenology, 36, 76, 188n48, 199n32
philosophical fallacy, 38–39, 106–110, 197n5
philosophy. *See specific topics*
phronesis, 184n15
Plato, 24, 108, 186n9, 191n22
play, 29
pluralism, 25, 160, 197n2
political
  authority, 146, 185n6
  power, 84, 123, 167
poverty, 96–97
prereflective, 35
private self, 114, 119
process, processual framework and, 9–11, 75, 124, 194n14, 196n1
  desire and, 79
  metaphysics, 3–4, 6–7, 15, 17, 98, 134
propositional, 27, 30–31, 73–75, 84, 121–122
  knowledge, 74, 107, 118, 139
provincialism, 17, 178–179
pu (樸). *See* uncarved block of wood
Putnam, Hilary, 9, 24, 108–109

qi ("vital energy"), 33, 58, 197n2
"quality-in-itself," 114–115
Quine, Willard, 18, 24–25, 27–28, 69, 193n9, 202n13

racism, 102, 130–134, 196n1
rationality, rational beings and, 106, 125–130, 138–139, 160, 188n43, 192n41
Rawls, John, 160–161

The Real Is Not the Rational (Stambaugh), 188n43
reality, 74–75, 194n14
  empirical, 40, 65, 105–106, 132–133, 178
  nonnatural, 92, 122, 124, 138, 159
  representations of, 76, 83
  "simply located," 64, 69, 100, 110–113, 116, 122, 135, 159, 180, 199n27
  subjective, 40–41, 114, 121
reason, 12–13, 17
relativism, 2, 7–11, 42, 183n12, 184n15, 198n21
  moral, 1, 3, 112, 175, 177–178, 192n2
  ontological, 4, 26–27, 32, 43, 84–89, 142–146, 202n13
religion, 2, 22, 25, 60, 66, 199n29
ren (benevolence, 仁), 5, 51–54
responsibility/right conduct (*yi*, 義), 51, 53–54, 68, 151–152, 163, 169–170, 201n4
  in the Zhuangzi, 59, 146–147
rightness, 33, 112–114, 201n5, 203n26
rights, 9–10, 71, 74
right-wrong (*shi-fei*, 是-非), 90–94, 101, 113
robbers. *See* criminality, criminals and
Rorty, Richard, 18, 25, 64, 69–72, 74
  on final vocabularies, 70, 74, 131, 189n3
rouruo (柔弱), 12, 190n6
ruling class, 66–67, 101, 137, 163–164, 166–168

sages, Daoist, 1, 12, 18, 102, 162–163, 179–181
  as being without desire, 37, 95–96
  as being without heart/mind, 80–81, 99–100, 157–158

Index | 225

as being without knowledge, 21
compassion and, 155, 171–172
the *Daodejing* on, 5–6, 19, 81–84, 99–100, 142, 157–162, 171–172
non-Daoist, 19, 56, 143, 155, 161, 168, 173
the *Zhuangzi* on, 11, 19, 55–60, 112–113, 141–143, 146–149, 150–156
sameness, 89, 145–146, 155, 173
Sandel, M. K., 160–161
Sartre, Jean Paul, 122–123, 131–132
self. *See also* without self-interest
autonomous, 160, 173
heteronomous, 172–173
independent, 8, 59–61, 63, 94–95, 150
independent sense of, 19, 52, 61–62, 80, 91, 93–94, 119, 159, 172
interdependent, 158–162, 204n10
private, 114, 119
true, 91–93
self-determining (*ziding*, 自定), 22–23, 95
self-interest (私), 5–6, 181. *See also* without self-interest, being
self-seeing (自見), 143, 146, 150–154
"self-so." *See* spontaneity
self-undermining, 6, 14–15, 50, 102, 124, 161, 176
Confucianism as, 53
metaphysics as, 64–69
morality, 68
sentient beings, 29–30
the "serious man," 122, 180
settler-colonialism, 176
shan (good, 善), 4–5, 102, 108–109, 112, 172
shi (comfort, 適), 153–154
shi-fei (right-wrong, 是-非), 90–94, 101, 113

Shusterman, Richard, 71–72
"simply located" realities, 100, 110–113, 135, 159, 199n27
causality and, 69
consciousness and, 116
the nonnaturalistic fallacy and, 122
subsatnce ontology and, 64
values and, 180
sitting and forgetting (*zuowang*, 坐忘), 44, 59, 76
skepticism, 1–2, 26, 70, 113–114, 197n3
Slote, Michael, 60, 191n14
social
classes, 65–66, 96, 102, 163–168
hierarchy, 55, 97
Socrates, 191n22
sound, 30
spontaneity ("self-so," *ziran*, 自然), 2, 168, 181, 195n20, 203n19
attunement and, 10–11
the *Daodejing* on, 16
desire impacting, 81–83, 86
genuine people and, 155–156
interdependence and, 12
knowledge impacting, 80, 89
of nature, 85–86
non-egoistic action and, 55–60, 70, 100–101, 142
Stambaugh, Joan, 75, 188n43, 192n41
stomach, desires of the, 39, 44, 79, 82, 84, 145, 194n12
subjectivism, 42, 184n15
moral, 7–9, 11, 192n2, 198n21
reality and, 40–41, 114, 121
substance
metaphysics, 11, 17, 19, 43–44, 64, 81, 102, 123, 156, 183n10
ontology, 6–7, 44, 64, 118, 131, 175

suffering, human, 17–18, 105–106, 144–145, 175, 178
  alienation from nature and, 110–111
  knowledge and, 66–67
  misperception and, 44
  oppression and, 68, 102
  recognition of, 71–72

Tan, Christine, 199n38
Theory of Valuation (Dewey), 125–126, 135
thieves. *See* criminality, criminals and
tian (Heaven, 天), 5–6, 86, 88–90, 101, 112–113, 149
totalitarianism, 103, 124, 177, 180
tranquility (*jing*, 靜), 22–23, 44, 95, 142
true persons. *See* genuine-humans
true self, 91–93
truth claim, 74

uncarved block of wood (*pu*, 樸), 16, 142, 144–145, 148–149, 153–154
  desire and, 82
  genuine humans as, 91
  nature as an, 40, 80, 83–84, 97–99
unconditioned, 8, 126, 128–129, 159
uncut, 57, 90, 148–149
universalism, 9, 17, 149–150, 176
uselessness, 168–170, 173

Valmisa, Mercedes, 85
valuing, valuation and, 4, 105, 110, 112–115, 117–118, 132, 180
  abstract, 40, 111, 116
  as a cocreative process, 120–121, 138, 198n21
  concrete, 120–121, 138
  desires and, 27, 37–39
  experience of, 29–30
  instrumental, 124–127, 130, 134, 136, 196n1

  intrinsic, 106, 119–139, 160, 177, 196n1
  miseducation and, 67–68
  moral subjectivism and, 8
  nature and, 14–16, 19, 168–169
  nonintrinsic, 125, 127
  positive moral, 106, 136
  reified, 58, 94, 123
  Western, 9–10
Van der Veken, J., 188n47
Van Norden, B. W., 64, 191n23, 194n18
violence, 106, 120, 136–138, 165, 167, 176
Virág, Curie, 193n6
virtue (*de*, 德), 27, 51–52, 145–146, 178, 189n1
  aesthetic appeal and, 54–55
  egoism and, 53, 55
vital energy (*qi*), 33, 58, 197n2

wang (忘). *See* forgetting
Wang, Robin, 16, 23, 27
Wang, Youru, 87, 187n50, 197n3
Wang Bi, 6, 81, 185n2
wealth, 6, 65–66, 96
webbed toes, cutting of, 146–150, 152, 154–155, 169, 173
Western
  culture, 73, 76, 175–178
  values, 9, 176–177
"What Is a Thing (wu 物)?" (Perkins), 7, 202n9
white people, whiteness and, 132–133, 176–177
without action. *See* non-egoistic action/without action
without desire, being (*wuyu*, 無欲), 47–49, 80–81, 86–87, 93–101, 179, 193n5
  the *Daodejing* on, 23, 39
without heart/mind, being (*wuxin*, 無心), 19–20, 92, 100, 102, 157–158, 168, 171

without knowledge, being (*wuzhi*, 無
知), 21, 47–51, 74, 80, 86–87,
100, 102, 179
   the *Daodejing* on, 39
without self-interest, being (*wusi*, 無
私), 6, 19, 80, 94–95, 98–102,
168–170
   forgetting and, 98
   knowledge and, 61
Wittgenstein, Ludwig, 9, 24, 186n10
Wong, David, 9–10
wu (無). *See* indeterminate
wusi (無私). *See* without self-interest,
being
wuwei (無為). *See* non-egoistic action
wuxin (being without heart/mind, 無
心), 19–20, 92, 100, 102, 157–
158, 168, 171
wuyu (無欲). *See* without desire, being
wuzhi (無知). *See* without knowledge,
being

Xiang, Shuchen, 196n1, 200n45,
200n53, 203n31
xiang sheng (mutual generation, 相生),
4–5, 37, 112
xin zhai (fasting of the mind, 心齋),
44, 58–59, 76
xing (inborn natures, 性), 141–142
xingming (endowed circumstances, 性
命), 141–143, 147, 150–155
the *Xunzi*, 143, 151–152, 202n8

"Yan He's problem" (*Zhuangzi*),
164–167
yi (義). *See* responsibility/right
conduct
yin/yang, 33, 37
yu (欲). *See* desire
yu zuo (creation of desires, 欲作), 23,
79, 84, 95, 97, 99

zhenren (真人). *See* genuine-humans

zhi (知). *See* knowledge
zhong. *See* center
Zhuangzi, 113, 183n12, 187n34,
192n1
   Hansen on, 25
   Huizi and, 114
   Lai on, 198n23
   Wang on, 197n3
   Ziporyn on, 204n11
the *Zhuangzi*, 159–160, 185n7,
186n11, 192n44, 193n6, 201n3,
205n19
   on cosmology, 33–34
   on criminals, 143, 146–147, 162–
168
   the *Daodejing* and, 2–3, 7, 83–85,
101–102, 112–113, 171, 195n19
   on death, 189n6
   on egoism, 94
   forgetting in, 59–60
   on genuine-humans, 86, 89–94,
195n29
   Hansen on, 24–30, 39, 194n15
   interdependence in, 204n10
   non-egoistic action in, 47, 55–59
   ontological relativism and, 143–
146
   as perspectivism, 204n2
   on sages, 11, 19, 55–60, 112–113,
141–143, 146–149, 150–156
   on self-seeing (*zijian*, 自見), 150–
154
   on valuing, 113–114
   Van Norden on, 64
zhuzi baijia ("Hundred Schools of
Thought," 諸子百家), 2
ziding (self-determining, 自定), 22–23,
95
Ziporyn, Brook, 82, 186n9
   on coherence, 50, 189n1, 195n21,
201n5, 203n26
   on the *Zhuangzi*, 39, 43, 204n11
ziran (自然). *See* spontaneity

www.ingramcontent.com/pod-product-compliance
Lightning Source LLC
Chambersburg PA
CBHW032042020325
22763CB00016B/324